Sociology in the Balance

Johan Goudsblom

Sociology
in the Balance
A Critical Essay

Columbia University Press
New York   1977

For Norbert Elias

Published in 1977 in Great Britain by
Basil Blackwell and in the United States of
America by Columbia University Press

Printed in the United States of America

Library of Congress Cataloging in Publication Data

Goudsblom, Johan.
  Sociology in the balance.

  Revised translation of the author's Balans van
de sociologie, published in 1974.
  Bibliography: p.
  Includes indexes.
  1. Sociology.   I. Title.
HM61.G713   1977   301   77-4368
ISBN 0-231-04290-6

Contents

Acknowledgements

In addition to those who contributed to the original Dutch edition of my book *Balans van de sociologie* (Utrecht: Uitgeverij Het Spectrum, 1974), I wish to thank several people who have helped me in preparing this new English version. At an early stage, Derek Phillips and James Feather gave valuable comments on a draft of the first part. Later, Rod Aya, Stephen Mennell, and Bryan Wilson read the entire manuscript; besides amending my English they offered constructive criticism from very different angles. Norbert Elias generously spent many hours discussing the book with me; anyone familiar with his work will notice how much I owe to him.

J.G.   *Amsterdam, December 1975*

1

Introduction: The Aims and Claims of Sociology

The present confusion

What can we reasonably expect from sociology? We live today in a social world which has become so vast and complicated, and in many ways so terrifying, that we may well despair of gaining more than an emotionally tainted and fragmentary insight into it. Can sociology be of any help at all in comprehending our social world, or does it merely add to our confusion and perplexity?

Thousands of people all over the world are nowadays engaged in sociological work: doing research, teaching, or applying their knowledge as advisers or policy-makers. Yet while the researchers, aided by increasingly sophisticated equipment and techniques, produce an immense wealth of data, it becomes more and more difficult to see how their findings cohere. The overall result appears to be a mass of unconnectable fragments. There is a proliferation of specialisms in empirical research and of 'new directions' and neo-isms in theories, but a synthesis which can commend a measure of consensus is nowhere to be found.

In order to see that sociology today does not suffer from a lack of data we need only, to look at one of its many specialisms, the sociology of the family. Over the years, enormous amounts of material have been collected bearing on numerous apsects of family life in all sorts of settings.

1

There can be no doubt that family sociology forms a specialism in its own right, with special conferences, journals, and textbooks. Anyone entering the field will have to master a body of substantive knowledge about family life and, in addition, a set of methodological skills that have been acquired through the accumulated experience of many researchers.

There are at present dozens of comparable specialisms in sociology, focused on areas such as industry, bureaucracy, leisure, migration, race relations, and so on. Many of these areas clearly overlap; but the sociological specialisms stand apart. One of the reasons for specialization is the sheer bulk of available knowledge. As an example we can take the study of suicide, a firmly-established branch of sociology. In order to become an expert in this field one has to keep up with a continuous stream of specialized literature relating to newly-discovered facts, to current theoretical disputes, and to developments in the techniques of data collection and analysis. For those who have acquired the necessary competence, the sociological study of suicide can be a fascinating subject, capable of fully absorbing their intellectual interests. But they may not have enough time and energy left to follow critically what is going on in other areas of sociology.

As well as empirical, there are theoretical specialisms. From the outset, sociologists have been drawn not only to investigations of specific subjects like family budgets or suicide rates, but also to the systematic ordering of facts and concepts. There is a steady tradition of theoreticians and system builders, ranging from Auguste Comte to Talcott Parsons and Nicolas Luhmann, who have excelled in the art of drawing up classificatory schemes and explanatory models. In the study of society, these theoreticians argue, facts are not enough; it is even doubtful whether we can speak of facts at all as long as we do not have a general scheme of co-ordinates within which the facts will fit. Sometimes, attempts at systematic theory-building are directly connected with problems arising in empirical research. More often than not, however, theorists set themselves to the task of furnishing general schemes of analysis for sociology as a whole. Continuing various philosophical traditions they devote themselves to elaborate scholarly constructions under such headings as theory of action, functionalism, structuralism, exchange theory, systems theory, marxism or neo-marxism, phenomenology, etc. As in the empirical branches of sociology, competence in any of these branches can only be acquired through sustained effort. The initiated find genuine excitement in their discussions about theoretical systems—often to the outsider's amazement.

If a wealth of accurate and reliable facts on the one hand, and a choice of systematic theories on the other, were all that one had to ask of sociology, one might well call it a flourishing discipline. It displays, if anything, abundance, not want, in both respects. An assessment based on merely these two criteria, however, would be too meagre. It would leave out two quite important aspects which may be summarized as, first, the range or scope of sociological knowledge, and, second, its relevance.

The problem of range or scope is of vital significance to sociology. Detailed empirical studies can bring to light many interesting facts, for example about changes in family life. However, since families form part of larger social figurations, it will be very difficult to explain the observed changes in terms of family life alone. A wider perspective, in both a spatial and a temporal sense, is needed: the family must be seen in the context of other groups, and the changes occurring here and now must be recognized as episodes in much further reaching long-term developments. What seemed erratic and inexplicable at first may thus be better understood.

Specialists in social sciences often regard as 'external' whatever lies beyond their immediate problem area as they have learnt to define it. Thus, many economists treat as external such factors as the motives for economic action, the legal and political setting, and the state of technical knowledge. While granting that these factors are immensely important to an understanding of economic production and distribution, they do not incorporate them into their own theories. To do so would interfere with the elegance, the mathematical neatness of the theories; a broadening of scope would require a sacrifice of systematic rigour. As it is, a great deal of economic theory can be characterized as formal and analytic rather than realistic. The lack of realism seems to a large extent due to a lack of scope.

As I shall show later in this book, in sociology too there are some quite sophisticated theoretical models (most of them inspired by examples from economics) which, while meeting high standards of systematic elegance, turn out to be disappointingly narrow in scope. If they do attain a certain internal consistency, this is all too often at the cost of a loss of substantive significance. This is not to say, of course, that 'systematics' and 'scope' are always at odds. On the contrary: no general perspective in sociology could be of any value if its concepts were a mess. A measure of systematic ordering of facts and concepts is indispensable; but one has to guard against the tendency to indulge in ordering for its own sake, and to make sociology primarily an exercise in 'systematics'.

Central to the sociologist's task is a quest for connected-ness–for finding and demonstrating the connections between events that are seemingly separate, either because they are not altogether synchronous, or because they are usually categorized under different labels such as 'political', 'cultural', 'economic', 'psychological'. In empirical studies, the danger of a certain myopia is always present. While concentrating on details one tends to neglect the wider structures in which they are embedded. In this respect, Durkheim's famous study of suicide (1897) can serve as a good counter-example. Durkheim proceeded from the notion that although to end one's own life is perhaps the most individual decision a person can take, the total rate of suicides within a society can be regarded as a 'social fact', reflecting certain overall tendencies within that society. His book is written, as it were, on two levels at once: from the analysis of suicide figures a general interpretation of contemporary social trends is derived; and this interpretation is used in turn to explain the suicide rates. Although controversial in most of its substantive conclusions (cf. Douglas 1967), *Suicide* continues to be an inspiring example of a sociological study combining in fairly high degree factual precision, systematic reasoning, and a broad scope.

While today studies of empirical details and theoretical

systems abound, there is comparatively little literature on problems of the scope of sociological knowledge. To many sociologists this is a somewhat embarrassing subject, a reminder of their professional limitations which, on the whole, they are ready to acknowledge but reluctant to discuss. A similar attitude is often taken with regard to the issue of relevance. The very word relevance, with the slightly hysterical overtones that the student movement of the late 1960s gave to it, tends to be discredited as naïve and political. However, the issue of the social functions of sociology, to call it by another name, is not to be so easily dismissed. The very existence of sociology depends on expectations that it can somehow be useful, that the costs of tolerating and even rewarding it will somehow 'pay off'. It is perhaps illustrative of the high degree of ignorance about our social world, how little we know about the actual effects of sociology. All sorts of fantasies circulate. According to some, sociology is a breeding-ground of revolutionary ideas, a threat to any established order. According to others, it serves mainly as a means of legitimation and manipulation for those in power. How various sorts of sociology actually affect different social groups is largely unknown.

Yet the problem remains: what functions does sociology have for which groups? And, directly connected, what functions *can* it have? Most of the problems with which human beings have to cope today are clearly 'sociogenetic': they are the outgrowth of social developments, of social structures. A great many people enjoying a relatively high degree of physical safety and material prosperity still suffer from severe anxieties; most of these anxieties spring from their social experiences with parents, spouses, children, colleagues, neighbours, friends, competitors. The great catastrophes of the twentieth century—wars, deportations, concentration camps, unemployment, large-scale starvation, destruction of vital physical resources—are all similarly the outcomes of the interlocking actions of huge groups of interdependent human beings. Is there any hope of gaining a better understanding of the blind social forces that have brought men to their present predicament?

Raising questions of such magnitude may have a paralyzing

effect. How are individual researchers, doing their modest best, going to fare if they know that their work will be judged on such a global scale? Is not the order far too tall even for our discipline as a whole?

Points of departure for a re-assessment

Since I intend in this book to appraise critically the works of other sociologists, it seems advisable to state at the beginning as explicitly as possible the point of view from which I shall do so. This point of view is informed by a few basic ideas about human societies—ideas derived to a large extent from the writings of Norbert Elias. Formulated as general principles, these ideas sound deceptively simple and self-evident; yet their importance is frequently overlooked. The failure to keep them in mind consistently is responsible for some characteristic fallacies in sociology.

The following principles, then, will serve as points of departure: (1) Human beings are interdependent, in a variety of ways; their lives evolve in, and are significantly shaped by, the social figurations they form with each other. (2) These figurations are continually in flux, undergoing changes of different orders–some quick and ephemeral, others slower but perhaps more lasting. (3) The long-term developments taking place in human social figurations have been and continue to be largely unplanned and unforeseen. (4) The development of human knowledge takes place within human figurations, and forms one important aspect of their over-all development; the development of sociology should be seen in this context: as an aspect of the largely unplanned and unforeseen development of industrial state societies.

Unfortunately it is not superflous to remind ourselves that in sociology we are dealing with people. All too often sociologists, especially when they are theorizing at a general level, start out with an abstract conception of 'social action' or 'social system'. Moreover, in some types of sociological research the reality of living human beings also tends to disappear in the statistical analysis of quantified data. It makes sense, therefore, to state quite explicitly that we are

concerned with *people*, bonded together in dynamic constellations which, because of their specific nature, may best
be designated by a specific generic name: figurations.

Living together in mutual dependencies is a basic condition
for all human beings. From the moment it is born a child is
dependent upon others who will feed, protect, fondle, and
instruct it. The child may not always like the constraints
exerted by its strong social dependencies, but it has no
choice. By its own wants it is tied to other human beings–to
its parents in the first place, and through its parents to many
others, most of whom may remain unknown to the child for
a long time, and perhaps forever. All of the child's learning,
its learning to speak, to think, to feel, to act, takes place in a
setting of social dependencies. As a result, to the very core of
their personalities men are bonded to each other. They can
be understood only in terms of the various figurations to
which they have belonged in the past and which they
continue to form in the present.

The first fallacy to avoid, then, is that of treating man in
the singular–a fallacy that is very often committed, as I shall
demonstrate in Chapter 4. A second fallacy, which we
encounter no less frequently, is that of treating man and
society as static givens. Time and again we are confronted
with an incapacity or an unwillingness to acknowledge that
human figurations are continuously changing and developing.
Our whole conceptual apparatus is attuned to permanence
rather than change. We all seem to be afflicted by an aversion
to see the present in which we live as transient, as if by
ignoring change we could magically avert our own ageing and
death. In all of us is a deeply-rooted tendency towards
'hodiecentrism' or today-centred thinking, towards taking as
immutable the world as it is now. Of course, some changes
occurring in and around us are so obvious that they cannot
be denied. Other changes, however, especially those which
take place over long periods, are easily overlooked. Thus, for
example, the emergence of certain new words or idioms in
our language may be recognized as changes; the fact,
however, that our whole language is the result of long-term
developmental processes which continue to go on during our
own life time may remain un-noticed. A certain detachment

from the routine of everyday occurrences is required to become aware of long-term developments affecting these daily occurrences, especially since most of these developments, like the structural development of a language, are by and large unplanned and unforeseen.

Only to a limited extent are individuals capable of knowing or controlling the figurations which they form together. Within a figuration, there may be enormous differences in power and insight. Even those people, however, who have a great deal of power over others *within* a certain figuration may be almost powerless when it comes to controlling the figuration as a whole. Thus, as Marx has shown, capitalists are themselves caught in the webs of capitalism; they are unable to steer or stop the development of the figurations within which they hold such privileged and powerful positions. In our own century, marxist rulers of socialist states, while clearly possessing more power than any other group, have similarly found themselves entangled in processes beyond their control.

The development of sociology is one aspect of the continuing attempts of men to orientate themselves within the social figurations they form together. Sociologists, like all other men, are involved in these figurations, sharing the pleasures as well as the frustrations of social existence. Without such involvement they would be neither motivated nor able to understand. At the same time, however, by being committed to certain groups and to the immediate hopes and fears of these groups they may fail adequately to grasp larger figurational structures and long-term developments. They may thus be led to rely upon images based more on fantasy than on careful investigation.

The standard repertory of sociology

It is a reflection on the traditional lack of interest among sociologists both in language (and their own use of language in particular) and in history, that there is no comprehensive history of the word 'sociology'. For a long time, the only study promising in its title to deal with this topic was a paper presented to the first meeting of the British Sociological Society (Branford, 1905). Far from being a scholarly survey, however, this was a persuasive treatise intended to demonstrate that the word sociology had been used often enough by respectable writers to be acceptable in academic circles. Only recently, Anthony Oberschal (1972, pp. 209 ff.) has documented the uses of the word sociology in the United States at the turn of the century. We still lack, however, an overall survey of its fortunes.

This is a pity, for such a word-history could bring out several important aspects of the development of sociology, relating to its intellectual content as well as its institutional position. As far as we know, the first public use of the term occurred in the fourth volume of Comte's *Course of Positive Philosophy* (1838, p. 185), a volume entitled not 'Sociology', but 'Social Physics'. This inconsistency is still a matter for dispute. According to some (e.g. Hayek, 1952), Comte launched the new word merely because he wished to dissociate himself from the Belgian statistician Adolphe Quetelet, who had appropriated the term 'social physics' for his own work. Others (e.g. König, 1949) hold (in my view correctly) that, apart from any personal motives on Comte's part, the introduction of the word sociology was a deliberate intellectual improvement on 'social physics'. It had the great advantage of not implying that the study of society should necessarily be an offshoot of physical science with essentially similar methods and theories.

Like other neologisms of the nineteenth century, the word sociology slowly made its way into the vocabulary of the reading public. While it was vehemently rejected by some, often on no other grounds than the 'barbarous' mixture of Greek and Latin stems, it caught the imagination of others. Apologists for slavery in the *ante bellum* South of the United States seized upon the term to publish books and pamphlets under such imposing titles as *A Treatise on Sociology* (Hughes, 1854) and *Sociology for the South* (Fitzhugh, 1854). John Stuart Mill (1865) discussed at great length Comte's programme of a general science of society called sociology, and reformulated it in more subtle terms. At one time, Leo Tolstoy played with the idea that sociology could become the 'science of human happiness'; unfortunately he never returned to it. Among the advocates of sociology in the last decades of the nineteenth century was Thomas Masaryk, later to become president of Czechoslovakia. Sociology's most famous proponent in this period was Herbert Spencer, who became as it were the personification of sociology, as Comte had been previously. At the same time, throughout the century, quite a number of writers whom we now rank highly as contributors to sociology never applied the term to their own work at all; this group includes such diverse figures as Alexis de Tocqueville, Karl Marx and Charles Booth.

Only after sociology had become established as an academic discipline at several major universities (such as Chicago in 1893, London in 1907, the Sorbonne in 1913) was some agreement reached about which kinds of work should be called sociological, and which scholars sociologists. Emile Durkheim was probably the most determined, among his generation of academic pioneers, to be a sociologist and nothing else; he had to struggle hard to gain the title. Others, like Max Weber, gradually moved in their writings towards a position which came to be clearly defined as sociological. In this same generation there were also men like Georg Simmel who wrote widely-respected books about sociology without identifying with it.

Today, now that sociology has been part of the academic curriculum for several decades, there are clearly distinguishable core-groups of practitioners whose professional status as sociologists is generally recognized, and a corpus of writings that is known, if only by reputation, as the standard repertory of the field. Still, even today the position of sociology among the sciences and humanities remains somewhat insecure, and its boundaries remain disputed. The relationships of sociology both with allegedly non-scientific notions about society and with other 'social sciences' are uncertain and beset with problems of demarcation that touch upon each of the various claims which can be made for sociology: its supposedly superior precision of fact finding, the internal consistency of its theories, its scope, and its relevance.

However, under the pressures of academic specialization,

sociology has developed into a more or less distinct field with a number of undisputed landmarks. Its standard repertory, which was shaped in the twentieth century mainly by American writers, is now familiar in many parts of the world. We find it, to give a few examples, in a number of well-known books approaching sociology from apparently quite divergent angles—*The Structure of Social Action* by Talcott Parsons (1937); *Theories of Society*, edited by Parsons and others (1961); *The Sociological Imagination* by C. Wright Mills (1959); *The Origins of Scientific Sociology* by John Madge (1962); *The Sociological Tradition* by Robert Nisbet (1966); *The Coming Crisis of Western Sociology* by Alvin Gouldner (1970); and *Main Trends in Sociology* by Paul Lazarsfeld (1970). Although these books differ widely in viewpoint, level and scope, together they contain a common core of problems, ideas, concepts and names.

This common core will also be the subject of this book. Of course, sociology can have no fixed boundaries, either in time, or in relation to other fields like history, psychology, economics, philosophy, political theory, journalism or literature. One may well sympathize with Pitirim Sorokin (1956 and 1966) who included among the major contributions to sociology the ideas of great sages of all times and places, from Buddha and Lao-Tse to Albert Schweitzer and Jean-Paul Sartre. In assembling such a broad list Sorokin deliberately went against the tendency of textbook writers to begin sociology with Auguste Comte and to limit its present range to the works of a narrow group of academic specialists working almost without exception at American universities. It seems, however, that he pressed his case a little too far: just as not all sociologists are wise men, neither are all wise men sociologists.

The spectrum of sociological inquiry

There are various ways of studying human figurations. One way is to sit down and think, reflecting upon one's own experiences as a member of society, upon what one has lived through, witnessed, heard and read. No matter how unscientific such a procedure may seem, it is hard to imagine how sociology could have developed without it. A great deal of 'pre-sociological' theorizing, from Plato to Hegel, was done in just this manner, and several twentieth-century writers who have greatly influenced sociology clearly stand in the same tradition: George Herbert Mead, Ludwig Wittgenstein, Alfred Schutz. Most of the writings of Talcott Parsons, one of the central figures in modern sociology, belong to the genre of theoretical reflection, as do the recent contributions of such prominent sociologists as Jürgen Habermas and Alvin Gouldner.

While theoretical reflection may be the easiest kind of sociology to do (one need not go out and leave one's study), it is probably the most difficult to do well. With no clearly established standards of quality, and hardly any restraints exerted by empirical facts, a practitioner of this genre may easily ramble off in speculative and wishful fantasies. At best a writer who derives his ideas mainly from theoretical reflection provides valuable original insights; at worst, he becomes stuck in parlour superficialities or in epistemological profundities. How well one succeeds depends strongly on one's personal capacity to notice unlikely resemblances and differences, to detect connections, to think of explanations, to formulate and to compose. Partly owing to the great success of a few gifted writers, the genre continues to attract too many with only minor talents.

An obvious way of avoiding the pitfalls of speculative discourse, inherent in reflection as a style of sociological work, is to buttress one's arguments with documents. Often the two styles blend into one another almost imperceptibly: theoretical reflection may raise problems which can be investigated only by consulting documentary evidence, while documentary findings in turn may lead to interpretations based upon reflection. Although the study of documents is today not always recognized as a major sociological work-style (it is overlooked, for example, by Ritzer, 1975), some of the most outstanding works in sociology belong to this genre, among them the bulk of the writings of Karl Marx, Emile Durkheim and Max Weber. In the twentieth century, sociologists have tended to turn away from the study of documents, and to rely instead upon original evidence collected by themselves. Nevertheless, C. Wright Mills, Norbert Elias, Barrington Moore, Jr., and other modern sociologists who have not lost sight of long-term developments have made ample use of documentary material. Some of the best products of contemporary sociology, therefore, belong to this genre.

The possibilities of documentary studies are obviously limited, to the extent that many aspects of social life are not sufficiently documented. Moreover, many documentary materials which are indeed available have been collected originally for certain practical purposes which may have occasioned incorrigible systematic distortions; one may well doubt the reliability and the validity of such sources. These considerations have prompted researchers to go out and collect their own evidence. Frédéric LePlay was one of the first sociologists to do so; his strictures that a theorist like Comte shrank away from the hard work of data gathering will still meet with approval among many empirically-inclined contemporary sociologists.

Whereas LePlay in his empirical studies of European workers' families combined questionnaire surveys with a certain amount of field work, in the twentieth century the two methods have grown distinctly apart, and the questionnaire survey has become the almost exclusive source of findings for many researchers. At an early stage in this development, serious warnings were raised against a one-sided reliance upon questionnaires (LaPiere, 1934); yet, although these warnings continued to crop up in textbooks for a long time, they did not change the direction sociology was taking. Samuel Stouffer and Paul Lazarsfeld, and in the next generation James Coleman and Otis Duncan, became the leading virtuosi of the questionnaire method, great experts in the techniques of collecting and analyzing survey data.

There is a clear continuation from theoretical reflection, through the study of documents, to questionnaire research. If one does not trust one's own erudition and intuition, one may turn to documents. If the documents are found to be inconclusive or unreliable, one may conduct a questionnaire survey to provide the necessary data. Continuing along these lines, one may decide that for certain purposes questionnaires do not yield sufficiently accurate and trustworthy evidence. The next step, then, is to go out and see for oneself, to engage in 'direct empirical investigation of the social world' (Blumer, 1969). The method thus employed is known as fieldwork or participant observation. In one sense, sociologists engaged in partipant observation come near to closing a methodological circle: for, as any reader of the methodological appendix to William Foote Whyte's *Street Corner Society* (1955) knows, it is only a short step from participant observation to intelligent reflection on one's own social experiences. Fieldwork reports also touch upon the area of autobiography and journalism—where such writers as Simone Weil, George Orwell, and Frantz Fanon, who were not professional sociologists, have made impressive contributions to our understanding of the social world.

Curiously lacking in the arsenal of standard methods in sociology is the method without which the natural sciences could never have developed to their present richness: experimentation. Many sociologists have solemnly repeated Pareto's stern statement that the only hope for sociology ever to become a science lies in its being 'logico-experimental'; but in spite of their solicitations there have been hardly any sociological experiments even faintly echoing the importance of crucial experiments in physics, chemistry or biology. The reason is not that experiments with human figurations are forbidden or impossible; the neighbouring field of social psychology, embedded in the laboratory culture of psychology in general, abounds with experiments. Nor is the reason that sociologists have too acute an awareness of the importance of larger structures and longer-term developments than can be manipulated within a laboratory setting; a lot of sociological research is too short-sighted to justify such a noble-sounding explanation. In all likelihood the lack of experiments in sociology is due to the firmly-established division of labour between sociologists and psychologists. As it is, a good number of experiments carried out in psychological laboratories would lend themselves very well to a sociological interpretation, and could fruitfully be incorporated in the corpus of sociological knowledge. That most of these experiments–like the research on the sociogenesis of self-control by Hudgins (1933)–have remained virtually unknown to sociologists, speaks of the large gulf that has grown between the different specialisms in the study of men. Psychologists are supposed to deal with 'the individual', sociologists with 'society'.

On the development of the concept of society

How intricately the development of sociology is connected with other social processes becomes quite clear when we take a closer, more sociological look at the concept of society than is customary today. Textbook writers nowadays tend to neglect the polemical functions that the term originally served, and often still serves in common parlance. In introducing this central concept, they usually mention only logical problems of definition. But the word 'society' is more than a topic for serene logical discourses; when we look at its development over the past centuries, and regard its changing social functions for various groups, a much livelier picture emerges. It is worthwhile, therefore, to make a foray into historical semantics, to find out something of the 'socio-genesis' of the concept of society.

The first thing to be noted, is that it is a fairly recently formed concept. In ancient Greek and Latin there were cognates like *polis, societas*, and *civitas*; but they did not have quite the same meanings. One difference pertains to membership: on the whole, the *polis* was conceived as including only free citizens; slaves did not belong to it. In the later development of the Roman Empire and during the Middle Ages, the words *societas* and *civitas* came to have a wider meaning in this respect, encompassing all Christians. But even in these later periods, Latin did not provide a word to express clearly the contrast between 'society' and 'state'. In the vocabularies of the modern European languages, this contrast has become sharply marked.

There are striking similarities in the development of *society* in English, *société* in French, *Gesellschaft* in German, and *maatschappij* in Dutch–the words that are used in contemporary sociological literature as the generic name for the largest social unit to which men belong. All these vernacular words were used initially to refer to various sorts of 'companionship' in which people in close proximity encountered each other as comrades or associates, as *Gesellen* or *maten.* In the seventeenth and eighteenth centuries, new meanings gradually accrued, corresponding to new social formations, among both the aristocracy and the bourgeoisie.

For the aristocracy in the age of absolutism, the concept of society came to have the function of referring to the leading social circles centred on the principal courts of Europe: *la haute société, die gute Gesellschaft*, 'high society' (or Society with a capital S). In the Dutch language alone, there emerged no equivalent, for the simple reason that the United Netherlands had no royal court. In the other countries of Western Europe, Society consisted of a small élite, mostly of noble birth and breeding, which set itself off from other, less privileged, strata: not only by its titles and material possessions, but also by a cultivation of *savoir-faire* and gallantry. The codes by which they judged their own and each other's performances on this field of honour were not issued as official decrees. Nevertheless, in the status struggles with other groups and in the internal rivalries for favours and reputations the need for polished self-possession was so strong that courtiers often felt themselves to be the servants rather than the masters of etiquette. Living under continuous pressure to exhibit good taste and good manners, they did not experience 'society' as a neutral concept; loaded with connotations of prestige and envy, of pride and humiliation, of boredom and anxiety, it stood for that omnipresent and inescapable force that sociologists would later call 'social control' (cf. Elias, 1969b).

The concept of society underwent a quite different but no less dramatic shift of meaning among the urban bourgeoisie who initiated various new forms of organization alongside, and often in competition with, the older institutions of church, estate, and guild. They founded, first of all, commercial enterprises, but also non-commercial associations devoted to the advancement of learning, to charity, to popular enlightenment. The names given to these organizations still reveal something of their first beginnings: they were called company, society, *société, Gesellschaft, maatschappij*, names deriving without exception from the sphere of small associations.

In bourgeois circles as in court circles, the word society came to have strong emotional connotations. It played an important part in the political polemics of the seventeenth and eighteenth centuries, directed against the domains of, first of all, the 'state', represented by the powers of the king and his servants, and, secondly, the old feudal estates, nobility and clergy. As John Locke (1690) argued, in many spheres of life neither the state nor the estates had any influence—and if they had, they *ought* not to have; these spheres constituted the 'civil society'. Initially 'society' may, in this sense, have been regarded as a sphere existing side by side with the older institutions; but by the time of Locke's polemic against the absolutist state the word had gained wider implications. Society, so the argument ran, preceded the state; the state essentially functioned in and for society—which, translated into more personal terms, meant: the people do not exist for the sake of the king, but the king for the sake of the people. The French Enlightenment philosophers reasoned in the same vein, with even more radical conclusions. As intellectuals, they conceived of themselves as living in a free society of letters, independent of either state or estates. And, broadening this idea, they spoke of the society of mankind, in which all men are free and equal, not bound to any specific class or nation. As Holbach put it: 'Laws in order to be just must have as their unchangeable end the general interest of society, that is to say, they must guarantee to the largest possible number of citizens the advantages for which these have associated themselves. These advantages are freedom, property, and safety' (Holbach, 1770, quoted by Schulz, 1969, p. 61). Thus, the word society played a significant part in the ideology of the French Revolution. And, again, in the German revolutions of 1848, *Gesellschaft* served as a rallying-cry against state and estates (cf. Schulz, 1969, pp. 13-111).

As theoreticians of 'society', the political philosophers of the bourgeoisie may be said to have provided the matrix from which sociology as a distinct intellectual enterprise could emerge. In the ideology of absolutism and mercantilism, the largest social units had been described as kingdoms or realms, identifiable by the person of the ruling sovereign: it was he who determined the boundaries of the realm and who possessed its riches; the history of the realm was, accordingly, written as the history of successive monarchs. The Enlightenment philosophers discarded this ideology, and replaced the highly personified notion of 'realm' by the more anonymous and egalitarian concept of 'society'. When in their historical writings they tried to pay more attention to the ordinary people, this was in line with their general programme of reducing the importance of kings. Moreover, by viewing society as not just a realm, ruled by a king, but as a collective entity, subject to fundamental laws of its own, they prepared the way for sociology. The thrust of their ideas was summed up some hundred years later by Herbert Spencer, with remarkable clarity:

> As in past ages the king was everything and the people nothing; so, in past histories the doings of the king fill the entire picture, to which the national life forms but an obscure background . . . That which it really concerns us to know, is the natural history of society [Spencer, 1854-59, p. 67].

First claims for a science of society

It is customary to write the history of sociology in terms of individual contributors. Some books begin with Montesquieu (Aron, 1965), others with Ferguson (Raisin, 1969), others again with Saint-Simon and Comte (Coser, 1971). No matter which name is chosen, there is something arbitrary and misleading about the choice. For although the emerging science of sociology was the product of the endeavours of individual men, these men did not stand alone. Their work represented, in its most articulate form, a general shift in the way that the broader strata of European societies conceived of the social world. As suggested in the previous section, this shift in thinking—which in turn reflected changes in the distribution of power in society—involved a tendency to regard society as a field of impersonal forces.

When we ask ourselves what it is that made such men as Montesquieu, Ferguson, and Comte 'great sociologists', a reasonable answer is that they succeeded, more than any of their contemporaries, in attaining a synthesis of scattered notions and facts. Previous centuries had witnessed wars and upheavals; but never before had people been aware of changes as rapid, continuous, and ubiquitous as in the late eighteenth and nineteenth centuries. Industrialization, democratization, urbanization, secularization—these were just a few of the prolific terms coined to capture the manifold transformations that society was undergoing. The major feat of the first great sociologists was their design of a perspective from which these various changes no longer appeared random and inexplicable. They attempted, as Raymond Aron (1965, p. 18) puts it, to find 'intelligible order' in the seemingly 'meaningless diversity of history'. Their primary concern, and their most important achievements, were to cast sociological theories of a large *scope.*

To characterize their work merely in terms of scope, however, would be to neglect other crucial aspects. In contrast to the philosophers of earlier ages who had also designed all-embracing social theories, the first sociologists prided themselves on being scientific: their theories, they claimed, were not just constructions of the intellect, but were based on solid *facts.* To be sure, the facts they sought were not the conventional facts of history like the dates of battles and the names of commanders. Just as they tried to break away from a social philosophy suspended in abstract reasoning, so they also wished to move beyond the confines of traditional historiography. They aimed instead at revealing the regularities or 'laws' underlying the seemingly chaotic sequences of events in the world of men. There was, then, among the early sociologists also an urge to lend an abstract rigour to their perspectives, to build them into coherent intellectual *systems.* Finally, but no less crucially, they all intended their theories to be *relevant,* supplying answers to vitally important problems, providing a means of orientation with the aid of which people would be able to take a more enlightened and better-informed stand on the moral and political questions of their time. In this respect they adhered to a primary aim of the Enlightenment: 'to substitute reliable information and rational theory for guessing and meta-physics, and to use the newly-won knowledge in behalf of man' (Gay, 1969, p. 323).

For a long time, the inspiring model for all sciences was physics. Physics embodied the ideal of theoretical synthesis founded on detailed observation of facts. The work of Galileo, besides constituting an admirable feat of meticulous observation, also demonstrated how the observed 'empirical' regularities could be expressed in law-like 'theoretical' for-mulae. Even more impressively, Newton's *Principia* proved that systematic reasoning and reflection were capable of ordering and explaining a tremendous range of observable processes in the physical universe. The emerging social sciences should similarly attain increasing sophistication in theoretical synthesis—theory serving to explain observed regularities and leading, in turn, to new observations. The model of physics was clearly emulated by Montesquieu when he wrote in the preface to *The Spirit of the Laws*:

> I have laid down the first principles, and have found that the particular cases follow naturally from them; that the histories of all nations are only consequences of them; and that every particular law is connected with another law, or depends on some other of a more general extent [Montesquieu, 1748, p. 1].

The early development of sociology was by no means a concerted endeavour. There were no institutional ties between the pioneers. They belonged to an intelligentsia which was not attached to any professional organization. Even though most of them acted, whether intentionally or not, as spokesmen for a specific social class, they were accountable to no-one. Consequently each writer could pursue his own train of thought for a good distance without ever even referring to the work of his colleagues. The internal logic of his system, as he himself saw it, could take on paramount importance to him, overruling all other considerations. Moreover, the desire to be 'relevant', to provide fully worked-out solutions for all the problems of the age, sometimes impaired the critical faculties.

As a result, some of the early self-styled 'scientific' theories were filled with naïve fantasy. Charles Fourier, for example, staked a wholly unconvincing claim to have discovered the general laws of social attraction, the equivalent of Newton's laws of gravity in physics. As a critic of modern civilization, Fourier displayed many imaginative, and still noteworthy, insights; but his theoretical system had a very weak empirical basis, and rested mainly on a genuine longing for utopia and a strong penchant for classification. Karl Marx was one of the first to dismiss the writings of Fourier as unscientific. When later on sociology became an academic discipline, its practitioners did not care to include such a visionary as Fourier among their intellectual ancestors. Yet, between the works of Fourier and Comte, the differences are only a matter of degree. There are also basic resemblances, both in their claims to have founded a science of society and in the mixture of scholarship and idiosyncracy with which they bolstered those claims (cf. Manuel, 1962).

Claims for sociology's coming of age

Sociology's progress in twentieth century universities has had considerable substantive consequences. In the academic setting, sociologists became more sensitive to methodological problems regarding the reliability and validity of their facts and theories. At the same time, they tried to normalize their relations with neighbouring disciplines like economics and psychology by limiting the scope of sociology to the study of only certain aspects of the social world. Grandiose schemes *à la* Comte, with an enormous range of perspective, wherein sociology appeared as the supreme science crowning all other sciences, were rejected as unrealistic. Ambitions with regard to the relevance of sociology were also lowered; instead of offering far-reaching suggestions for the reorganization of society as a whole, sociologists now preferred to give advice on short-term issues.

As their field became more respectable and 'objective', the concept of society lost its sharp polemical function for sociologists. The word has retained clear emotional overtones in non-academic language; it is nowadays often used to mean an anonymous bogeyman, a collective object of blame for all kinds of social wrongs. But whereas this meaning has been nicely caught, for example, in the line 'society's played him a terrible trick' in one of the songs of the musical *West Side Story* (Laurents, Bernstein and Sondheim, 1958, p. 105), sociologists have incorporated the word society into a solemn 'value-free' vocabulary in which it has been given such thorough definitional treatment as this:

> A society is defined as a system of social action: (1) that involves a plurality of interacting individuals whose actions are in terms of the system concerned and who are recruited at least in part by their own sexual reproduction [sic], (2) that constitutes a set of social structures such that action in terms of them is at least in theory capable of self-sufficiency for the maintenance of the plurality of individuals involved, and (3) that is capable of existing long enough for the production of stable adult members of the system of action from the infants of the members [Levy, 1966, pp. 20-21; the awkward formulation in (1) has been corrected in the 1969 edition].

The tenor of this elaborate statement is now subscribed to by most sociologists; they see society generally as a 'self-sufficient social system' (Etzioni, 1968, p. 59). One may well wonder where on earth nowadays such a 'self-sufficient system' is still to be found, unless all of humanity is regarded as one global society. When pressed for an answer, some sociologists will probably reply that they do not care whether societies in the sense of their definition really exist; with the candour of avowed nominalists they will state that a concept like society is merely an analytic device, to be used for heuristic purposes—one should not be so naïve as to look for any 'real' society. But, as Marion Levy has reassuringly added for the baffled reader of his definition, 'one will not be misled seriously if he considers societies to refer roughly to the systems of action ordinarily called nations, countries, or societies' (Levy, 1966, p. 21). Indeed, if we scrutinize the abstract formulations a little more closely, and consider them in their wider context, in most cases we are soon led to guess that at the back of the theoreticians' minds when they defined society as a self-sufficient social system was an image of a 'real' enough social figuration, namely the nation-state to which they themselves belong. Since most definitions of society have been made by American sociologists, it is an image of the American nation-state in particular that lurks behind the prevailing notion of society in contemporary sociology.

Since the early 1930s, the most important institutional centres of sociology have been located almost without exception in the United States. Whatever contributions individual European sociologists made in the period between 1930 and 1960 were completely overshadowed by the prestigious, well-organized and well-financed projects of their American counterparts (cf. Shils, 1970). When, in 1962, the Englishman John Madge published a book under the promising title *The Origins of Scientific Sociology*, it was not surprising that of the twelve studies he chose as milestones in the development of empirical sociology, only the first one, Durkheim's study on suicide, was of European origin—just as dialectical materialism was predominantly Russian, so sociology seemed to have become a largely American affair.

A strong optimism and self-confidence characterized the generation of American sociologists who started their academic careers from the early 1930s onward. Before the century was even half over, in 1945, a collection of essays was proudly presented as *Twentieth Century Sociology* (Gurvitch and Moore, 1945). In spite of the international format of this book, the majority of the contributors were Americans. In one article Talcott Parsons stated firmly 'that sociology is just in the process of emerging into the status of a mature science', a statement that can be read as either factual or programmatic, as can the following: ' . . . we stand on the threshold of a definitively new era in sociology and the neighbouring social science fields'. Parsons saw the crucial breakthrough in the achievement of a theoretical system composed of 'a body of logically interdependent generalized concepts of empirical reference' (Parsons, 1954, p. 212), a formulation that was taken over almost literally by his best-known and most influential student, Robert Merton. While Merton was somewhat more cautious than Parsons– instead of 'general theory' he advocated 'theories of the middle range'–his overall evaluation of the status of sociology was no less favourable:

> For in building the mansion of sociology during the past decades, theorist and empiricist have learned to work together . . . Specialization and integration have developed hand in hand. All this has led not only to the realization that theory and empirical research *should* interact but to the result that they *do* interact [Merton, 1967, p. 156].

Many pages could be filled with quotations, from numerous American sociologists, that all bear witness to the same mood. Sociology appeared to have reached the state of what Thomas Kuhn (1970) would later call 'normal science': a state in which individual researchers need no longer bother about a variety of fundamental problems, but could concentrate, with the aid of tested methods and theories, on filling in the gaps on the map of knowledge (cf. Friedrichs, 1970, pp. 11-56). In introducing a collection of essays by Samuel Stouffer, Paul Lazarsfeld epitomized the prevailing confidence with the remark: 'The present set of papers is, therefore, not only the record of a man's work: it symbolizes the growth of a science' (Stouffer, 1962, p. xv).

In Europe, general academic recognition came to sociology soon after the Second World War. As many new chairs were established, and the number of students greatly increased, most European sociologists, especially the younger generation, turned eagerly toward the recent accomplishments of their American colleagues. How both the intellectual content and the mood of American sociology were taken up in Europe, is clearly demonstrated in *Moderne Sociologie. Systematiek en analyse* (Modern Sociology. Systematics and Analysis) by J.A.A. van Doorn and C.J. Lammers (1959), which for many years was by far the most widely-used and most frequently-quoted sociological textbook in the Dutch language. In words strongly reminiscent of Parsons and

Merton, the authors stated in their introduction that 'a convergence in sociological thought and research is observable, which is beginning to result in an integrated scientific system'. The time has come, they claimed, 'for modern sociology to be understood as the dynamic and balanced interplay of theorizing and research, for the purpose of developing an increasingly sophisticated analytic system of knowledge' (1959, pp. 11-12). The word 'analytic' received special emphasis from Van Doorn and Lammers. It was, they held, the analytic approach that distinguished modern sociologists from earlier generations, whose style of sociology had been either too speculative and insufficiently grounded in empirical work, or too encyclopaedic and lacking in theoretical substance. By applying systematically conceived analytic categories, the modern sociologist should be able to wed research and theory: to examine those selected aspects of the social world that are relevant for testing and further developing scientific theories.

A staunch upholder of the belief in the combination of research and theory was the Swedish-American sociologist Hans Zetterberg, according to whom 'as a science, sociology has already bridged the gulf between theory and research; this is true both in principle and in the work of several gifted scholars' (1965a, p. viii). In *On Theory and Verification in Sociology* (1965a), Zetterberg tried to show how sociologists can develop and test scientific theories; in *Social Theory and Social Practice* (1965b), he set out to explain how the theories thus arrived at can be applied. His point of departure in the second book is well-chosen. Sociologists, he points out, usually answer requests for advice with offers to do research. Do they not then have a reservoir of knowledge at their disposal? Zetterberg claims they do: 'There is a body of seasoned sociological knowledge, summarized as principles of theoretical sociology, which is superior to our common-sense notions about society' (1965b, p. 22).

This knowledge is twofold. In the first place we have our scientific terminology, a taxonomy, which enables us to classify social phenomena in a clear and coherent conceptual framework. As proof, Zetterberg sets forth an impressive scheme of concepts and definitions. Unfortunately, however,

this scheme is no more than Zetterberg's personal codifi-
cation of a rather loose set of current terms and phrases;
while reflecting the strong influence of Parsons, it by no
means represents a systematic conceptual apparatus shared
by all sociologists.

Besides having a taxonomy, Zetterberg asserts, we know
laws. The first law he mentions is: 'the number of actions per
person is limited'. But why should this statement be called a
'law'? What specific regularity does it express? According to
Zetterberg's eighth law, 'persons who come into contact with
a great diversity of opinions tend to exhibit less stability in
their own opinions'. Again, what kind of a 'law' is this, which
can only be stated in the vaguest terms of 'great', 'tend to'
and 'less'? Most of the other 'laws' Zetterberg enumerates
also turn out to be vacuous generalities.

A similar discrepancy between claim and accomplishment
can be noted in many publications of the 1950s and 1960s.
To take one other example, in the well-known textbook
Sociology. A Systematic Introduction by Harry Johnson
(1960), the reader is informed with modest pride in the
opening paragraph that

> . . . sociology to some extent has the following charac-
> teristics of science:
> (1) it is *empirical*; that is, it is based on observation and
> reasoning, not on supernatural revelation, and its results
> are not speculative . . .
> (2) it is *theoretical*; that is, it attempts to summarise
> complex observations in abstract, logically related propo-
> sitions which purport to explain causal relationships in the
> subject matter
> (3) it is *cumulative*; that is, sociological theories build
> upon one another, new theories correcting, extending, and
> refining the older ones
> (4) it is *nonethical*; that is, sociologists do not ask whether
> particular social actions are good or bad; they seek merely
> to explain them [Johnson, 1960, p. 2].

At the time this passage was written, most sociologists would
readily have agreed to it. In Johnson's four points the
emphasis is on the reliability of facts and the consistency of

theories, rather than on scope or relevance. Although some of his colleagues might have given more emphasis to research, and others to theory, there would have been little argument against the cumulative effects of combined empirical and theoretical efforts or against the idea of ethical neutrality.

After reading Johnson's textbook, however, one can hardly fail to be disappointed. It contains relatively little empirical information, the author's prime orientation being theoretical. Even on the theoretical level, however, the book is very uneven. Some chapters have a highly systematic design, strictly adhering to the theoretical schemes of Parsons; others, dealing with subjects on which Parsons had not yet shed light by 1960, are written from various *ad hoc* perspectives, without the faintest reference to a possible Parsonian interpretation. The suggestion of theoretical rigour fostered by, among other things, an ample use of definitions, vanishes when one reflects on statements like: 'a norm is an abstract pattern, held in the mind, that sets certain limits for behaviour' (Johnson, 1960, p. 8: are there non-abstract patterns?, what does 'held in the mind' mean?), or a curious expression of misguided pedantry: 'culture consists of abstract patterns of and for living and dying' (ibid., p. 82).

While they are not the most outstandingly original sociologists of their generation, Zetterberg and Johnson are in a way more representative of sociology in the 1950s and 1960s than such a towering figure as Talcott Parsons. In writings like theirs, which echoed the ideas of more eminent authors, a set of standard notions about sociology was widely promulgated. I shall take a closer look at some of the work of other, more prominent representatives of the discipline in later chapters. What concerns me here is, first, to note the prevailing climate of self-confidence that inspired American sociologists as well as those of their colleagues elsewhere who emulated them, and, second, to point out that the quality of the performances scarcely warranted complacency.

Sociological self-critiques

If, during the postwar era, the ideas of Parsons, Merton, and

Lazarsfeld were dominant in American sociology, they were never altogether uncontested. Throughout the whole period, a few stubborn, though small and scattered, centres of opposition remained. Of these, the University of Chicago was the most visible as an institution. While it was increasingly overshadowed by the East Coast departments of Harvard and Columbia, in Chicago the idea still lingered that it offered an alternative to the dominant styles in sociology. Herbert Blumer, in particular, acted as a critical spokesman of this alternative which, in the long run, came to be known by his term 'symbolic interactionism'. Meanwhile, at Harvard, Pitirim Sorokin engaged in a long and lonely polemic against the dominant trends in sociology which he branded as superficial, pretentious, and lacking in originality. Others, like Barrington Moore, Jr., wrote similar, though less lengthy and less embittered critiques. By far the most influential attack, however, was made by C. Wright Mills; his *The Sociological Imagination* (1959) became the manifesto for the next generation of radical sociologists.

In his strictures against 'grand theory' and 'abstracted empiricism', Mills attacked the a-historic, analytical stance of mainstream sociology. Sociologists should not aim at developing concepts and theories about social action and the social system in the abstract; such an approach, Mills argued, can only generate hollow formulae. What is needed is to give people insight into their present historical situation: in what kind of social structures their lives are embedded, and which groups control those structures. This challenge is neglected in the theories of Parsons as well as in the empirical studies of Lazarsfeld and his students, who are too preoccupied with technical methodological questions. Using the natural sciences as a model, the latter try to isolate those aspects of society which are observable and measurable by standardized procedures. Not only do they thus miss the most important problems of social structure and social development, they also forget their own involvement in the very society which they study.

This last statement goes against the notion that sociology is 'non-ethical'. In stressing the moral and political implications of sociological methods and theories, Mills shows affinity to the Marxist-oriented group of German writers who had worked at the Institute for Social Research in Frankfurt in the 1920s, and most of whom had fled to America from the Nazi regime: Max Horkheimer, Theodor Adorno, and a few others. While they remained on the periphery of academic sociology for a long time, they never tired of criticizing the majority of their colleagues for neglecting the political and moral implications of sociological work. In the last ten years, interest in their writings has increased steadily (cf. Jay, 1973), as part of a general movement towards a 'radical sociology' (Colfax and Roach, 1971), or a 'critical sociology' (Birnbaum, 1971). In this movement, one of the central concerns of the founders of sociology has survived: to arrive at a comprehensive critique of modern society.

There is a growing disaffection with sociology as it has been practised over the last decades. Some of the most vociferous statements of doubt regarding the credibility of methods and theories have been made by Derek Phillips (1971 and 1973). In the first chapter of *Knowledge From What?*, Phillips relates how, after years of diligent testing of hypotheses, he came to the conclusion that 'sociology in no way represents some codified, cumulative body of knowledge', and that 'individuals acquainted with certain sociological theories are unlikely to know any more about the real world than people who are unfamiliar with these theories'. The declared purpose of *Knowledge From What?* is to make the reader understand 'how little sociology has to say about the social world we live in' (Phillips, 1971, pp. xi-xx).

Of the many recent critiques of 'textbook sociology', the most eloquent and widely-read is *The Coming Crisis of Western Sociology* in which Alvin Gouldner (1970) deals with Talcott Parsons in particular as the main author of the theoretical orthodoxies of American sociology. Contrary to Parsons's own avowal that his prime aim has always been 'to further the development of scientific theory in the field of human behaviour' (Parsons, 1961, p. 311), Gouldner states that Parsons is really continuing a long tradition of social philosophy in which the object is to map and explain the social world so that it appears intellectually understandable and morally justified. If today Parson's ideas are becoming less popular, this is not, as methodological texts would suggest, because they have been tested and proved wrong in empirical investigations, but because they fail to supply satisfactory answers to questions which many, especially the young, are asking. The lament 'how little sociology has to say about the world we live in' does not only say something about sociology, but about our world as well. This world has become 'unbearable' (J. Berger, 1972, p. 51) for many, and a sociology that does not speak to this basic experience loses its impact.

At the same time that mainstream sociology is being attacked for being too academic and insufficiently 'relevant', it is also criticized for a lack of scientific rigour (cf. Lachenmeyer, 1971 and 1973). The methods of fact-finding and theorizing are scrutinized and exposed as not meeting professed standards of reliability and precision. To overcome these deficiencies, all sorts of remedies are proposed. Thus, we find those sociologists engaged in the quest for greater certainty turning to mathematics, to formal logic, to general systems theory, to phenomenology, to linguistic structuralism, to behaviouristic psychology, to computer techniques. Looking at these manifold currents, one gets the impression of utter confusion. Not only is sociology split up into an enormous variety of empirical specialisms; it is also rapidly developing into a Babylon of competing schools, each cultivating its own terminology, methodology, and epistemology. If sociology is to help us in clarifying the social world we live in, some clarification of sociology is needed first.

2

Attempts at Fact-Finding
in Sociology

Antecedents to Sociology

It is impossible, in the continuous development of human societies, to pinpoint a moment where sociology 'began'. Looking back into the history of mankind, we cannot conceive of a time when men had no knowledge at all of the figurations they formed with each other. No matter how vague and fragmentary and fantastic this knowledge may have been when measured by our present standards, men could not have lived without it.

As long as people remained illiterate, their knowledge was handed down by oral tradition. It consisted of pieces of 'collective memory' relating to events in a remote and undated past, combined with the remembered experiences of the living. In the parlance of contemporary sociology we may say that the 'social facts' available to people in these circumstances were based upon direct 'participant observation' and some measure of 'theoretical reflection' (see above, pp. 11-15). With the advent of literacy, a new source of social knowledge was added: documents. In most cases, this brought about drastic changes: first, it became much easier to preserve and accumulate the knowledge of consecutive generations, and, second, the increasing fund of knowledge came to be distributed more unevenly than before, as it was largely monopolized by priests or mandarins who had access to the documents and the ability to read them.

For an assessment of present-day sociology it may be useful to bear in mind a broad picture of this overall development. To aid the developmental imagination, one may call up an image of a small community where all members know each other personally, and everyone is likely to be acquainted with the major events occurring within the community: births, weddings, initiations, accidents, scandals, deaths. Since it will be relatively difficult for any individual to hide important information about himself, the members of such small and isolated communities may be said to live in a state of 'knowledge by all about all'.

As societies grow larger, all members can no longer know each other personally. In so far as people are not directly aware of ties of interdependence by which they are linked to other, more distant members of their society, they need not feel bothered by a lack of clear information. They may have vague notions, filled perhaps with fear, awe or contempt, about the inhabitants of surrounding towns and villages; but they will usually consider it beyond their own power and interest to find out more exactly who these strangers are and how they live.

The first groups, so it seems, to become interested in detailed information about what goes on in larger societies are the ruling groups. They require such information for quite practical reasons, like estimating the annual tax revenues and the number of potential soldiers. The oldest written documents that we have from Mesopotamia and other ancient kingdoms, were drawn up mainly for such purposes. Likewise, in medieval Europe, the administrators of large feudal and church estates were the first specialists in gathering precise social data: to them we owe such sources as the *Domesday Book*. With the increasing power of central governments in European state societies the demand for administrative data describing 'the state of the kingdom' grew correspondingly. Mercantilistic state policies required annual surveys of imports and exports. A strong new impetus toward governmental social research came when conscription was re-instituted after the French Revolution. In one European country after another, the state took over the parish registers from the church; national censuses were set up to check and enlarge upon the data of local administrators. Even in the era of liberalism, governments took sufficient interest in commerce and industry to produce 'economic statistics'; centralization of jurisdiction made it possible to draw up 'moral statistics'; uniform educational systems gave rise to 'educational statistics', and so on (cf. Wrigley, 1972).

In addition to the anonymous information compiled in statistics, rulers needed other kinds of intelligence as well. In particular, they wished to be informed about the loyalty of their subjects, especially those within their own inner circle who were direct rivals for power. This sort of intelligence was less easy to come by through administrative channels and less well-suited to tabulation; here rulers had to rely primarily on espionage, on direct observation by trusted agents. Thus, Louis XIV had at his service both a corps of tax officials and a small personal staff of spies reporting directly to him (cf. Elias, 1969a, II, p. 273).

The two functions, administrator and spy, were never wholly separated, and very often they were combined in one and the same person. Yet the corresponding methods of collecting precise information about what is going on in large and complex societies are clearly distinct. We can still recognize them today in the two techniques most commonly applied by sociologists in empirical social research: the questionnaire survey and participant observation. As professional techniques, both forms of data-gathering were first developed mainly to meet the specific practical demands of rulers. Early social research, therefore, did not aim at formulating or testing sociological theories. Most of its findings were kept secret (cf. Oberschall, 1972, pp. 1-4). It was only after the beginning of the nineteenth century that the governments of advanced industrial state societies started to publish regularly their major statistics, thus making them available for scholarly analysis.

Early statistical approaches

The results of social research are registered in words and

gures; other symbolic representations, such as diagrams and formulae, are only derivatives. Administrative research is, on the whole, most suited to the production of quantitative data, while the most significant results of participant obser- vation techniques can usually be expressed better in words than in figures. Although, in the social sciences, words are at least as important as figures, the techniques for handling figures are far more developed than those for handling words.

To realize how high our contemporary standards of quantitative precision are in comparison with those of previous periods, we need only recollect how, in the Old Testament, it is said of Methuselah that he lived to the age of 969, and of Gideon that with a band of 300 soldiers he killed an army of 120,000. The message conveyed by this rhetoric of numbers is clear enough: Methuselah reached a very old age, Gideon and his men bravely defeated a great many enemies. Yet today only small children could handle figures so lightly.

Various groups have contributed to the gradual rise of more precise attitudes towards figures: rulers and adminis- trators of large realms and estates, military leaders, bankers, merchants, navigators, engineers, scientists (cf. Clark 1948). By the seventeenth century, a general spirit of book-keeping had emerged among the classes of capitalistic entrepreneurs, both large and small; this spirit manifested itself in a wide interest in figures and calculations. Thus, in social research a movement of 'political arithmetic' began, which produced such impressive documents as Gregory King's description of 'the state and condition of England (1696). Drawing upon manifold sources, King produced detailed estimates of the population of England, its occupational structure, and the distribution of income. While his numerical data are con- sidered by modern historians as 'surprisingly accurate' (Laslett, 1965, p. 245), the verbal scheme in which he presented his figures sounds very much outdated. He classi- fied 37 per cent of the English population as 'increasing the wealth of the kingdom', and 63 per cent as 'decreasing the wealth of the kingdom'. Within the first category, he counted those whom he considered financially 'independent': noble- men, gentry, merchants, farmers, artisans, and shopkeepers;

in the second category, he placed the 'dependent': common seamen and soldiers, labouring people, servants, cottagers, paupers, and vagrants. Obviously, his categories belong to a mercantilistic era; to a twentieth-century reader they may convey an instructive 'shock of non-recognition'.

Besides King, quite a few other scholars in the seventeenth and eighteenth centuries, using the official data available in local registers, assembled large amounts of facts on births and deaths, and tried to develop general 'scientific' conclusions on this empirical basis. Although most of them had outspoken political ideas and interests, they did not carry out their work in direct service to rulers; in this sense, their contributions were theoretical rather than practical. The most famous theorem to emerge from this early demographic tradition was Thomas Malthus's (1798) 'law' that population growth, when unchecked, tends to outrun any increase in the means of subsistence—one of the first examples of a lawlike formulation with the 'other things being equal' clause that was to become very popular among social scientists in the twentieth century.

The establishment of national statistics greatly widened the opportunities for theorizing on the basis of population data. The first investigator fully to use the new wealth of information was the Belgian astronomer, Adolphe Quetelet. In many respects, Quetelet was the counterpart of Auguste Comte; even today it is a matter for discussion which of the two men is most entitled to the name 'founder of sociology' (Landau and Lazarsfeld, 1968, p. 255). Like Comte, Quetelet claimed to have laid the foundations for a science of society, but his approach was far less encyclopedic, and much more 'analytic'; by studying one type of data, statistics, he hoped to find general principles of human behaviour in large aggregates. He considered it his great discovery to have found an inexorable regularity, not only in the involuntary events of birth and death, but also in the voluntary, 'moral' acts of marriage, crime and suicide. He concluded on this ground that social phenomena are just as much subject to general laws as physical phenomena—laws which reveal themselves if we study the phenomena in sufficiently large numbers to efface the disturbing effect of single deviating cases. It can be shown that for every human attribute, be it physical height or proneness to crime, there is an average that can be established for any nation, and a regular distribution around this average that is determined by probability or 'the law of accidental causes'. Working from this theorem Quetelet managed to discover, for example, the rate of draft evasion in the French army in 1844:

> By noting the discrepancy between the distribution of height of 100,000 French conscripts and his prediction [i.e., the theoretical distribution calculated by assuming a probable error of 49 millimetres], he came to the conclusion that some 2,000 men had escaped service by somehow shortening themselves to just below the minimum height. Thus, quite by accident, Quetelet emerged with the first practical, although perhaps somewhat trivial, application of his statistical techniques [Landau and Lazarsfeld, 1968, p. 251].

Quetelet symbolizes the hope, widely cherished in the nineteenth century, that it would be possible to arrive at a science of society, based upon 'hard' quantitative data, that would reveal the 'laws' regulating social life. An astronomer by training, he could apply his mathematical skills to the enormous amounts of statistical data collected by European governments. Since his day, the stock of material has increased manifold, and the techniques of analysis have become far more refined. The original hope, however, that a proper handling of the available figures would eventually reveal the fundamental 'laws' of the social universe has not come true. This may have led some people to the conclusion that, as there are no fixed laws to be found, no real science of society is possible. Such disillusioned scepticism is almost inevitable for those who have first pinned their hopes on the ideal of a 'social physics' as envisioned by Quetelet. The ideal as such has never fully disappeared from sociology; nowadays, however, most sociologists have learnt to conceive of societies as more than mere statistical aggregates.

While official statistics continue to be a valuable source of information, especially in such fields as the study of 'social indicators' (cf. Bauer, 1966), it is now generally recognized that the gamut of potential data for sociology ranges far more widely. Moreover, sociologists have become increasingly aware of the limitations of official statistics (cf. Hindess, 1973). Instead, they have come to rely more and more on other sources, particularly on data collected by themselves for the sole purpose of sociological research.

Early middle-class inquiries into working-class conditions

In modern European societies, collecting social data has never been entirely a state monopoly. Wherever a commerical bourgeoisie came into its own, some of its members developed into specialists in social knowledge, experts on the ways of foreign peoples or on the state of affairs at home. Some, like Ludovico Guicciardini, the Florentine author of a *Description of all the Low Countries* (1567) were writers and publishers by profession; others engaged in social research as amateurs, prompted by intellectual curiosity or the desire to give well-founded advice to statesmen. As private researchers, these men drew freely upon all documents within their reach, supplying what they read with their own observations and personal communications.

Alexis de Tocqueville's *Democracy in America* (1835-40) is one of the best-known examples of this tradition as it still flourished in the nineteenth century. It contained some of the features of a travelogue, presenting the French reader with interesting notes and comments on life in the new world. It combined these features, however, with general sociological observations on democracy and on the trends at work in modern societies at large, including France. Thus Tocqueville sought to enlighten his readers on at least two levels: he provided them with facts about an unfamiliar and intriguing world, and, apparently on the basis of these facts, he suggested insights to them with which they would better be able to understand their own society.

This twofold intent is characteristic of most travelogues. They form a continuum ranging from evocations of entirely fictitious exotic worlds, constructed by the author for no other purpose than to instruct his readers about themselves, to minute ethnographic reports pretending to portray a strange society 'as it really is'. Throughout the nineteenth century the output of travelogues and ethnographic reports steadily increased and, on the whole, the standards of accuracy and completeness became higher. It was on the basis of the wealth of scattered sources that Herbert Spencer could start the ambitious undertaking of his *Descriptive Sociology*, intended as an ordered compilation of all that was known about human societies.

At the same time there was a growing interest in empirical reports on European societies—particularly on those aspects that came to be known as 'the social question'. It is probably no exaggeration to say that this issue dominated the field of social research throughout the century, and that most empirical studies of the period were directly inspired by it. The literate bourgeoisie saw, to its dismay, that industrial progress and colonial power did not bring general prosperity and peace within their own nations. As factories expanded, so did the cities, and in the cities burgeoned the multitudes of the poor, who to the orderly bourgeois formed a mysterious and menacing presence. Intellectuals of different political persuasions set themselves to study the lives of this large and unknown section of the population. Just like Tocqueville studying the Americans, they hoped through their enquiries to gain more accurate information about 'the others' and a better understanding of the society of which these others and they themselves formed parts.

To arrive at general conclusions regarding the nature of society and the social changes of their own time, nineteenth-century social investigators frequently employed what one might call the rhetoric of induction, a mode of argument which rests on the assumption that 'the facts speak for themselves'. Thus, in his monumentous research on the lives of workers' families in different parts of Europe, Frédéric LePlay, through painstaking field investigations, collected accurately-itemized family budgets, revealing in minute detail sources of income and patterns of expenditure, which he then interpreted as clues to the whole mode of life of the people studied. To describe his method, LePlay used a figure of speech that was very characteristic of his time: he sought, as he put it, a 'photographic representation' of social reality. Far from actually confining himself to a mere 'representation', however, he designated an ambitious typology of family structures, passed strong moral verdicts on the instability of the modern family, and made sweeping proposals for better social arrangements—always urging his readers to accept that this was what the facts demonstrated. So strongly did LePlay rely on the inductive evidence of his facts that, setting himself off against the deductive arguments of the Enlightenment philosophers, he could proclaim: 'thus, by analysing the facts and processing the figures, social science furnishes, *au fond*, the same conclusions as morality' (LePlay, 1855, p. 294).

The facts obviously told a different story to LePlay than to Friedrich Engels who, during a stay of almost two years in England, had studied the situation of the working class there 'through personal observation and authentic sources'. Both men saw great poverty and misery, which they could document in telling figures. But while LePlay interpreted his findings as indicating an increasing moral degradation, caused by 'unbelief and revolution', Engels (1845) attributed the suffering of the workers to their exploitation under the capitalist system, and for him the inevitable conclusion pointed to the imminent class struggle between bourgeoisie and proletariat.

Engels's book was not the only contemporary account of social conditions in early Victorian England. Several other books, by both Englishmen and foreigners, were published in the same period. That today Engels's report is by far the best-known is due primarily to the fame Engels acquired through his part in the socialist movement. In the second half of the century, more and more surveys documenting the miserable health and housing of the poor were undertaken, not only in England but in all industrializing nations. Increasingly, the investigations were instigated by parliamentary commissions and carried out by governmental agencies. One of the last, and most impressive, products of private initiative in this sector was Charles Booth's monumental *Life and Labour of the People in London* (1902-3). Although Booth avowedly set out to contribute to a better general understanding of 'the problems of human life', he became so immersed in fact-finding that he eventually produced a body of work which, while still standing as a magnificent source of detailed factual information, also signifies that social research may pass a point of diminishing returns, beyond which its results tend to be merely repetitive. In this respect, Booth's seventeen volumes foreshadowed something of the barrenness that was to characterize a great deal of social research in the twentieth century.

Fact and theory in Durkheim's study of suicide rates

Over the years, enormous amounts of facts about the social world have become available, to governments, to corporations, to various groups of specialists, and to the public at large. In most countries nowadays statistical yearbooks or almanacs are published, comprising in the form of a digest only a fraction of all known information. No matter how useful or interesting we may find this material, it is, on the whole, mainly descriptive and has little explanatory value. Statistical yearbooks are, in this respect, comparable to telephone directories, railway timetables, stock exchange indices, or lists of tax brackets. All these sources of information usually meet high standards of accuracy and reliability, and are indispensable for specific practical purposes. Taken together, however, they do not form a coherent and meaningful pattern. They contain only isolated fragments of knowledge.

The original ambitions of sociologists went considerably further than the mere compilation of useful social data. Sociological facts, as they hoped, would not only be accurate and reliable but would also contribute to our general understanding of the social world. This was clearly what Emile Durkheim had in mind when, in the first chapter of *The Rules of Sociological Method* (1895), he raised the question: 'What is a social fact?' The social world, Durkheim argued, presents us with facts of a very special kind. For example, that people in France speak French; that theft is generally condemned and punished; that more men than women commit suicide; that the relative amount of civil versus penal lawsuits is increasing—these are facts of the social world, which can be established by empirical evidence and are in need of explanation.

How then do we account for such facts? In our daily lives we hardly stop to think about the reasons; we are inclined to believe that we already know them. Such a belief, however, is quite erroneous. The first requisite for a sociologist is that he realises how little he knows: 'When he penetrates the social world, he must be aware that he is penetrating the unknown' (1895, p. xlv). We must, in other words, rid ourselves of the naïve opinions of common sense. We must forget our cherished notions about the meaning of social customs and institutions; these notions should be the object of our studies, not the basis on which our studies are conducted. Rather than relying on their seemingly trustworthy capacities for emotional identification and introspection, sociologists must adopt the attitude of natural scientists, treating social facts as unfamiliar things—*comme des choses.*

The problem, then, was to find social facts that were sufficiently accurate and reliable to sustain theoretical analysis. Durkheim's major charge against his predecessors Comte and Spencer was that they had too light-heartedly built theories in the air, without grounding them on observable facts. In his own great study of suicide (1897) Durkheim intended to show that it was possible to work on a firm empirical basis. Joining the tradition of Quetelet, he took official statistics as his material. These were the facts which he tried to analyze without moral or emotional bias. As was well known in his time, the annual suicide rates for different nations and for certain groups within each nation showed remarkable regularities; thus, for the Danes the suicide rate was ten times higher than for the Irish, and for men it was almost everywhere between three and four times higher than for women. The available data thus strongly suggested that even the most individual decision a person might take—to end his own life—appeared subject to impersonal tendencies. As Quetelet had advised, one should take the figures as indicators, or 'effects', of the tendencies, or 'causes', operative in society. Following this lead, Durkheim tried to trace 'suicidogenic tendencies' which, in turn, would reflect even more fundamental social forces.

In many ways, Durkheim's study is still a paradigmatic example of sociological research based on officially-documented facts. It has been objected that his data are not as 'hard' as he himself thought: fluctuations in suicide rates might reflect nothing but changing habits in the registration of deaths. These objections—which so far have been brought forward mostly as surmises rather than substantive findings—are certainly worth empirical examination. They lose much of their plausibility, however, if we inspect the detailed figures relating to such categories as sex, age, marital state, or occupation. One would have to press the case against the surface validity of the official statistics to a rather absurd point, for example, if one were to account for the suicide rates of different age groups. One would then actually have to assume as an almost universal rule that the older a deceased person, the greater the propensity on the part of the officials to record a death as a suicide (see also Hindess, 1973, for a critique of Durkheim's critics).

If we do accept the general trends suggested by the official figures, we are still left with the intriguing problem raised by Durkheim: how to explain these 'social facts'. A quick glance at the crude national figures as they are available today is enough to reject several plausible hypotheses. The rate of suicide is not, as one might expect, a direct index of the degree of industrialization; for this, one need only compare the rates for England with those for France or Denmark, which are consistently higher. Nor is poverty an explanation: the lowest suicide rates of Europe belong to Ireland and Spain, relatively poor countries. Whether a national economy is predominantly capitalist or socialist also appears to have little bearing on the problem: in Hungary and Finland the suicide rates are high, in Norway and Poland they are comparatively low.

Other correlations, however, look more solid. Almost without exception, suicide rates are higher among men than among women. Could this be because men are genetically more prone to melancholy and depression? This proposition would be hard to prove; in any case, it does not explain the remarkable fact that in most industrial nations the ratio between the sexes is changing. Nearly everywhere the relative number of women compared with men registered as suicides is higher than a hundred years ago—as if the suicide rate were a morbid index of emancipation. With regard to the obvious age differentials, there is much to be said for an explanation in terms of increasing physical infirmities and weariness of life. There are, however, distinct deviations from the linear curve of correlation between age and suicide rates. Especially in the so-called welfare states one notices a high incidence of suicides among adolescents, and an interrupted increase around the 65th year of life, at which age the majority of the population begins to receive old-age pensions (Kruijt, 1975). With regard to marital status, which, unlike sex and age, is a purely social variable, the regularities observed by Durkheim still hold: there is a steady increase in suicide rates between, respectively, married people with children, married people without children, the unmarried, the widowed and the divorced.

It is hard to deny, then, that suicide rates have a sociological significance, that they do tell us something about the social world. Their significance is not, however, self-evident. It seems unlikely that by studying suicide rates alone their significance can be made clear. Close factual scrutiny is not enough; it needs to be informed by a general awareness of social structures and developments. As Durkheim knew well, there is no single 'indicator' to be found which can serve as the key to understanding the social world. For the analysis of any particular series of facts to be fruitful, it will have to be linked to other aspects of society.

The rhetoric of induction in early American sociology

Durkheim wrote his study of suicide in a strongly persuasive style. In the first part, he dissected a number of competing theories which had been proposed to explain the different suicide rates. Through an ingenious analysis of tables Durkheim succeeded in eliminating these theories one by one, thus clearing the way for his own, sociological, interpretation. This he put forward as if it were indeed the only interpretation which the facts allowed for, as if it followed of necessity from the empirical evidence.

The rhetoric of induction continued to pervade sociology during the first decades of the twentieth century. It became particularly popular in American sociology, where it found an influential manifestation in *The Polish Peasant in Europe and America* (1918-20) by William Thomas and Florian Znaniecki. The research for *The Polish Peasant* was instigated by Thomas while he was a professor of sociology at the University of Chicago; as such, it was one of the first large-scale sociological investigations carried out from within an academic department. In their introduction, the two authors stated that their study 'was not undertaken exclusively, or even primarily, as an expression of interest in the Polish peasant', but rather to try out certain methodological ideas. Like Emile Durkheim in *Suicide* (1897), they were concerned, first of all, to lay the foundations for an empirical science of sociology, and they considered the actual topic of their investigations, while certainly not devoid of significance, as of secondary importance. By studying 'a limited social group at a certain period of its evolution', they hoped to stimulate further research on other groups, thus 'preparing the ground for the determination of really exact general laws of human behaviour' (II, pp. 1822-3).

Thomas and Znaniecki did not hesitate to assert that they used 'the inductive method in a form which gives the least possible place for arbitrary statements' (I, p. 76). A large part of their book consisted of a verbatim presentation of 'human documents': letters, newspaper accounts, court records, reports of welfare agencies, and one full autobiography of a Polish immigrant. By concentrating on personal life-histories, Thomas and Znaniecki brought out the importance of 'subjective' factors; and in order to give adequate weight to these factors, they introduced the concepts of 'value', 'attitude', and, only casually at first, 'definition of the situation' into the technical vocabulary of sociology. They formulated the problems of adjustment of Polish immigrants as arising out of their encounter with strange values, requiring a revision of attitudes which would enable them to cope better with their new life situations. Further elaborating on these notions, Thomas and Znaniecki developed a widely-ranging set of 'laws' about social organization, social change and personality.

The Polish Peasant made a lasting impression on American sociology. In 1938, a symposium was held to appraise its contribution. Here, in an incisive critique, Herbert Blumer (1939) made short shrift of the inductive design of the study. While expressing his admiration for the authors' pioneering research efforts and for their profound insights into human social life, he demonstrated quite convincingly that the theories propounded in *The Polish Peasant* did not follow with any logical necessity from the empirical materials, which were inconclusive with regard to all the major generalizations. A great deal of wisdom and 'intimate familiarity' with the lives of Polish Americans had gone into the study, and herein lay the rudiments of the authors' theoretical schemes—not, as they themselves claimed, in the procedures of data gathering and inductive reasoning.

In their replies to Blumer at the symposium, Thomas and Znaniecki acknowledged this: the link between the documentary and the theoretical parts of *The Polish Peasant* was indeed tenuous. This admission seemed to settle matters. It appeared that sociological facts could only be established and interpreted within a previously-conceived theoretical scheme; any pretence at the reverse, suggesting not only that facts could be found independently of preconceived theoretical notions, but even that facts could point the way to theory, seemed to be false. Since the time of Blumer's critique, empiricism and inductionism in sociology have come under increasingly heavy fire. Talcott Parsons and George Homans have led the movement to give priority to the formation of theoretical concepts and propositions, a movement that has received even more radical support from philosophical methodologists, most prominent among whom have been Carl Hempel in the United States and Karl Popper in England.

Along with the virtual rejection of inductive argumentation, the study of documents as a sociological research technique has also suffered a severe setback. While not being altogether discredited, it has come to be regarded as lacking in scientific rigour; attempts to remedy this and to develop standardized procedures of 'content analysis' on a statistical basis have never struck firm roots in sociology. Only occasionally has the case for a more inductive stance been restated, among others by Howard Becker in *Outsiders* (1963), by Barney Glaser and Anselm Strauss in *The Discovery of Grounded Theory* (1967), and lately even by Blumer himself in a plea for 'direct examination of the empirical social world' (1969, pp. 1-60). These are, however, minority voices in a field that has come to be predominated by hypothetical-deductive reasoning as the typical style in which research is designed and reported.

The rhetoric of experimentation: the Chicago school

If the pretence of merely inductive reasoning is a very vulnerable means of interpreting observed facts, by contrast the most powerful method of linking facts and theories is the controlled experiment. Over the centuries, scientists have developed experimental techniques which have enabled them to elicit empirical answers to a host of precisely-formulated questions. By way of physiology the controlled experiment has entered one of the social sciences, psychology, where it has been a favourite method for almost a hundred years now. To sociologists, too, it has often been held up as the ideal model of scientific procedure (cf. Stouffer, 1962, pp. 290-9).

In a controlled experiment scientists seek to establish the effects of one single factor, the 'independent variable', by creating a situation in which they can introduce this variable while holding all other relevant factors constant. In order to check whether the observed effects are not due to any unforeseen interfering event, they duplicate the entire experimental situation without, however, reintroducing the independent variable. If the effects observed in the actual experimental situation fail to occur in the control situation, one can ascribe them with reasonable certainty to the independent variable. This, in brief, is the ideal setup of the controlled experiment. No other method of empirical research appears to be capable of yielding such strongly conclusive evidence.

In the social sciences one encounters, apart from theoretical problems, many practical difficulties which limit the feasibility of controlled experiments. It has been argued that these difficulties are not, in principle, insurmountable; that, in fact, people are conducting social experiments all the time: whether it is a shopkeeper opening a new shop, or statesmen declaring war, we find people who consciously enter upon a new course, the result of which they do not yet know (cf. Popper, 1957). If the word is taken in such a wide sense, literally any conscious social act may be called an experiment; but then obviously the conditions of a *controlled* experiment are seldom met. If social scientists, on the other hand, try to set up truly controlled experiments, they may have to devise situations that are so artificial as to make the results entirely unfit for generalization to 'real-life settings'.

As a plausible substitute for creating experimental situations, sociologists have tried to come upon them by simply finding them. Human societies, they have argued, offer a wide variety of situations which can readily be studied as the settings of 'natural experiments'. Such was the gist of Durkheim's (1895) plea for the comparative method as a fit alternative to experimentation. The same idea was promulgated in the methodological manifestos of the first identifiable American school of sociology, the Chicago school.

Robert Park and his junior colleague Ernest Burgess were generally recognized as the two most influential leaders of this school. Their jointly-written *Introduction to the Science of Sociology* (1921) contained the general intellectual framework within which a whole group of sociologists worked during the 1920s and 1930s. As the title indicated, the book presented sociology as a science, the science of collective behaviour. Sociologists were advised to study the principal forms of human interaction: competition, conflict, accommodation and assimilation, in their diverse historical manifestations. They were urged to do so in the spirit of natural scientists, not letting their investigations be guided by moralistic concerns or by the need for practical reforms. If these recommendations were followed, Park and Burgess promised, sociology would soon become 'an experimental science' (p. 45).

As a natural setting for quasi-experimental research, Park and Burgess drew their students' attention to their own city, which seemed to present itself as a laboratory for studying human behaviour under many varied conditions. Chicago in the early twentieth century was one of the most rapidly growing cities in the world, with a very heterogeneous population, increasing at a rate of more than half a million per decade. Although the spatial arrangements of the city were almost wholly unplanned, they showed a clear pattern of richer and poorer zones, some expanding, some shrinking, and each marked by distinct social characteristics. Different areas tended to attract or select different types of inhabitants; and once people had moved into a particular area they tended to become even more clearly marked by it. Noticing these unplanned tendencies, the Chicago sociologists spoke of 'natural areas', and set themselves the task of mapping the city's socio-spatial structure and explaining it in terms of a 'human ecology' that drew strongly on biological notions.

To study the socio-spatial development of a city was not an entirely novel idea. Friedrich Engels's (1845) report on Manchester, for example, was an admirable anticipation of an 'ecological' approach. What was new in Chicago was that for more than two decades a whole group of researchers undertook studies in a scientific spirit, originally inspired by the notion of the city as a 'laboratory'. Nevertheless, the promise of an experimental science was not fulfilled. The ecological model proved to be most fertile as a grid for mustering large amounts of facts. Over the years the Chicago sociologists succeeded in reporting virtually every conceivable facet of life in their city. Often the focus was on a certain area, like the 'ghetto' or the 'black belt'. Other studies were concerned with the spatial distribution of almost anything that could be documented, including suicide, mental illness, prostitution, and crime. In addition, certain social types were singled out for monographic treatment, preferably such 'marginal' types as hobos, juvenile delinquents, and thieves.

In all these investigations, liberal use was made both of administrative sources and of interviews and personal observations; the style of reporting was documentary, at times quite lively, and always relying heavily on figures, maps, and diagrams.

Some of these studies, like Harvey Zorbaugh's *The Gold Coast and the Slum* (1929), about two neighbouring districts with extreme contrasts in wealth and life styles, still make fascinating reading. After a while, however, the ecological model lost its inspiring freshness. Diminishing returns set in, the investigations evolved more and more into a routine, and the outcomes became roughly predictable. There can be no doubt that the original ideas about human communities, as outlined in Park's and Burgess's seminal work, contain much that is sound and illuminating. Their notions of interdependence, process, and conflict have received too little attention in more recent sociology. The trouble was, however, that, in spite of the authors' scientific ethos, these notions remained at too high a level of abstraction and generality: the empirical investigations in Chicago could refer to the ecological model, but never really test or modify it. In this sense, the rhetoric of experimentation suggested too much.

The rhetoric of experimentation: Hawthorne

At the same time that Chicago sociologists were trying their hand at interpreting the city as a 'laboratory', other American sociologists were entering the field of industrial relations, where they joined a tradition of experimentation initiated around the turn of the century by Frederick Taylor and other proponents of 'scientific management'. The result was one of the most celebrated 'experiments' in sociology, the Hawthorne studies.

The Hawthorne studies, conducted at a plant of the Bell Telephone Company, are usually taken to mark the beginnings of industrial sociology (cf. Blumberg, 1968, p. 14). Here, for the first time, so we are told, during a period stretching from 1927 to 1932, in a series of painstaking experiments, interviews, and observations, the great importance of social factors in industry was empirically established. The results were published in several weighty volumes, the most famous of which was *Management and the Worker* by F.J. Roethlisberger and William Dickson (1939), a 'pioneering work' that has been hailed as constituting 'one of the major developments in social science in the twentieth century' (Levy, 1966, pp. 170 and 364). Few studies have been so abundantly discussed (cf. Landsberger, 1958). The findings were 'lifted' from the special field of industrial relations by general sociologists such as George Homans, who used one section of *Management and the Worker* as a major source for his theory of 'the human group' (1950). Hardly any sociology textbook of the 1950s and 1960s failed to contain a summary of the Hawthorne studies.

The investigations first began in the early 1920s, following the regular methods of Taylorist research. By manipulating physical and physiological conditions, engineers tried to establish the relationship between such factors as the intensity of light in a workshop and labour productivity. They worked in a genuinely experimental fashion, with experimental groups and control groups. Regardless of the well-controlled study design, however, no clear correlations emerged. No matter whether light intensity was increased or decreased, the experimental group consistently raised its productivity; and to confound the engineers even more, the same occurred in the control group where lighting conditions were held constant. The only conclusion could be that there was something wrong with the whole manner in which the problem had been conceived. Apparently, other factors were at play, and this realization inaugurated what today might be called a shift of paradigms: a new group of investigators were called in who turned, from the investigation of physical variables, to the study of 'social conditions'.

The story of what happened then belongs to the standard lore of sociologists. A special Relay Assembly Test Room was set up in which five girls performing routine assembly tasks were put under minute and continuous observation. During the first phase of the investigations, lasting more than two years, various changes in work conditions were introduced at irregular intervals: longer and shorter work hours, longer and shorter breaks, group rates, free lunches, and so on. The investigators hoped in this way to determine the effect of each of these conditions on productivity. In *Management and the Worker* Roethlisberger and Dickson gave a detailed description of what happened in each consecutive period. Comparing the earlier and later stages of the study, they noted an unmistakable rise in productivity. As an explanation, they suggested that the close personal attention given to the girls in the Test Room had stimulated them to work harder. They warned their readers, however, that this was no more than an hypothesis. In spite of the positive tenor of their report they had to conclude that, because of the looseness of the experimental design, 'the results from a research point of view were negative' (p. 184).

This candid statement has not saved the Hawthorne studies from becoming a bone of contention for industrial consultants and labour leaders. They clearly illustrate how the results of social research, once they are published, can lead to interpretations never intended by the original investigators. The Relay Assembly Test Room studies have evoked long and vehement debates about the priority of either 'social rewards' or 'economic incentives' in workers' productivity. According to one authoritative version, the investigations proved the paramount importance of 'human relations'. Thus the leader of the project, Elton Mayo, summarized the episode in the Relay Assembly Test Room in the following jubilant words:

> What actually happened was that six individuals became a team and the team gave itself wholeheartedly and spontaneously to co-operation in the experiment. The consequence was that they felt themselves to be participating freely and without afterthought, and were happy in the knowledge that they were working without coercion from above or limitation from below [Mayo, 1945, p. 64].

While Mayo and many others took the Hawthorne studies as evidence of the beneficial effects, for both workers and management, of the 'human relations' approach, others, suspicious of management's intentions in sponsoring the research, regarded the whole project as lending scientific support to the manipulation and exploitation of the workers. In opposing the alleged applications of the findings, however, they never questioned their validity. On the contrary, a complete willingness to accept the results runs through even the most biting cricitisms:

> For nine years about every kind of experiment a very bright Harvard professor could think of was tried on the women. Everything you do to white mice was done to them, except their spines and skulls were not split so the fluid could be analysed . . . What did make them produce and produce and produce with ever-increasing speed was the expression of interest in their personal problems by the supervisor; interviews by psychiatrically-trained social workers and (later on) the way they were paired off with friendly or unfriendly co-workers. Now obviously this is the greatest discovery since J.P. Morgan learned that you can increase profits by organizing a monopoly, suppressing competition, raising prices and reducing production [from a trade union journal, 1949, quoted by Baritz, 1960, p. 115].

Numerous other comments could be quoted, pointing to either favourable or sinister implications of the Hawthorne studies. One recent participant in the discussion claimed to have discovered as 'the forgotten lesson of the Hawthorne experiments' that they supported his own ideas about the benefits of industrial democracy (Blumberg, 1968). Of the many commentators, hardly any have doubted the actual validity of the research results; the findings, presented with the rhetoric of experimentation, may have invited dissent, but not disbelief. Only recently has the Australian sociologist, Alex Carey, broken the spell by stating unequivocally that the research design in the Relay Assembly Test Room was so shaky as to allow no conclusions at all: 'The limitations of the Hawthorne studies clearly render them incapable of yielding serious support for any sort of generalization whatever' (Carey, 1967, p. 416).

In no way did the Relay Assembly Test Room meet the standards of a proper experimental setting. Not only were the changes in work conditions introduced in an unsystematic, haphazard manner; not only was no attempt made to form a control group; worst of all, at a crucial moment in the study two girls were expelled from the Test Room for 'gross insubordination', to be replaced by two others, one of whom was strongly motivated by great financial stress in her family to push up wage rates. By far the most impressive rise in productivity took place immediately after she had joined the group. Soon afterwards (in 'period 10'), work conditions were made identical again to 'period 7', when the two un-cooperative girls were dismissed; productivity remained at a high level. Although the entire incident was reported in detail by Roethlisberger and Dickson, neither they nor any of the later commentators have taken it up as seriously invalidating the entire research design.

   Carey's critique was devastating and convincing. It ended in a question: why were the obvious flaws in the research design overlooked or smoothed out in practically all interpretations and textbook summaries? Why were these studies received so eagerly and uncritically? This is indeed an intriguing question, and it has not yet received the attention it deserves (cf. Deutscher, 1968). One of the reasons probably lies in the closed circuit of criticism within the field of industrial sociology. This, however, does not explain the ready acceptance of the Hawthorne studies by so many general theoreticians and textbook writers. The answer must probably be sought in a combination of, on the one hand, a widely-felt need for real sociological facts, which the many figures and tables in the Hawthorne reports apparently supplied, and, on the other hand, the nature of the alleged results which, irrespective of their practical implications, looked inherently plausible to anyone with a feeling for the importance of social relations.

Emergence and growth of survey research

The great sociologists of the nineteenth and early twentieth centuries were individual scholars, relying largely on the study of books and documents. The generation of sociologists flourishing in America between the two World Wars was highly eclectic in its techniques of data-gathering; often working not individually but in small teams, they drew their facts from such varied sources as documents, interviews, observations, and attempts at experimentation. After the Second World War the questionnaire survey, which required for its successful handling at least a modest organizational basis, emerged as the most popular sociological method.

The major breakthrough of the survey method appears to have occurred during the Second World War, when the American armed forces were subjected to a battery of penetrating researches by questionnaires. At the time of the war, interest in these studies was primarily practical: it was hoped that they would yield clues on how to raise morale. In the years following the war the results were analyzed for more theoretical purposes, and subsequently published in four volumes (Stouffer et al., 1949-50). The whole project is known as *The American Soldier*, a name that bears witness to the widespread tendency to refer to men in the singular.

American sociologists received *The American Soldier* with great admiration. The sheer size of the work, based on more than 600,000 questionnaires, and the sophisticated use of statistical techniques to handle this huge mass of material, were widely regarded as evidence that sociology had at last become a real science. Just as the writings of Talcott Parsons attested to the mature theoretical status of the discipline, so *The American Soldier* demonstrated the high level of mastery in practical research procedures. Hailing the publication in a long and laudatory review, Paul Lazarsfeld jubilated: 'Never before have so many aspects of human life been studied so systematically and comprehensively' (1949, p. 378).

Lazarsfeld began his review by enumerating some of the limitations inherent in survey methods: no use of experimental techniques; a primary reliance on what people say and hardly any 'objective observations'; an emphasis on individuals rather than groups; and, obviously, a restriction to contemporary topics, for the dead cannot be consulted by questionnaires. Nevertheless, Lazarsfeld continued, survey methods are capable of yielding very valuable sociological data. As an example, he quoted six findings from *The*

American Soldier:

(1) Better-educated men showed more psycho-neurotic symptoms than those with less education.
(2) Men from rural backgrounds were usually in better spirits during their Army life than soldiers from city backgrounds.
(3) Southern soldiers were better able to stand the climate in the hot South Sea Islands than Northern soldiers.
(4) White privates were more eager to become non-coms than Negroes.
(5) Southern Negroes preferred Southern to Northern white officers.
(6) As long as the fighting continued, men were more eager to be returned to the States than they were after the German surrender.

After underlining how perfectly plausible and obvious these conclusions were, Lazarsfeld made his rhetorical point: '*Every one of these statements is the direct opposite of what actually was found*' (1949, p. 380, italics in the original). Clearly the evidence of *The American Soldier* confirmed the lesson taught by Durkheim in *The Rules of Sociological Method* (1895), and repeated by Park and Burgess in their *Introduction to the Science of Sociology* (1921): that the impressions of common sense are vague and unreliable, and that we can come to know the social world only through painstaking research. As Lazarsfeld put it: 'Since every kind of human reaction is conceivable, it is of great importance to know which reactions actually occur most frequently and under what conditions; only then will a more advanced social science develop' (1949, p. 380).

One may well concur with this general conclusion without being impressed by the particular findings quoted by Lazarsfeld. For some of them at least, the evidence is hardly conclusive; it is also questionable, for that matter, whether they all run counter to common sense—even this would have to be established by research rather than by conjecture. What makes it most difficult to share Lazarfeld's enthusiasm, however, is that the items he quotes are not connected by a systematic theory or a general perspective. They are presented as fragmentary pieces of information which, viewed against the background of the Second World War, and considering the enormous costs invested in the research, appear rather trivial.

Quite literally, the army studies showed how frequently and under what conditions certain reactions occurred among American troops during and immediately after the Second World War. Thanks to these investigations we now know, for example, that during the entire war no more than 27 per cent of all military personnel had been in combat; on no previous war do we possess such accurate factual information. Stouffer and his co-workers aimed at more, however, than a mere documentation of facts. For them, as for most commentators, the major accomplishments of *The American Soldier* lay in its contribution to the integration of empirical and theoretical work. Interestingly, in linking research and theory they tended to jump directly from the data relating specifically to American soldiers in the Second World War to general propositions about human social behaviour. Thus, one of the favourite general notions usually cited as having arisen from the analysis was the concept of relative deprivation. Empirically, this concept was linked to such indicators as the way men appraised their own chances of promotion; theoretically, it was linked to general psychological and sociological ideas like 'frame of reference' and 'definition of the situation'. It was shown, among other things, that soldiers' assessments of their career chances depended not only on the actual opportunities within their units, but also on rank, longevity of service, and level of education. Each of these factors appeared to operate more or less independently to raise or to lower career expectations. The workings of each 'factor' could be made intelligible by introducing the concept of relative deprivation as an 'interpretative intervening variable' (Merton, 1957, pp. 92-93), referring to the supposedly universal propensity among men to judge their own fates not by absolute standards, but in comparison with the fates of (relevant) others.

This type of 'factor analysis' appeared to open the way for the use of the questionnaire method, not only for descriptive surveys, but for explanatory investigations as well. The challenge became, as in experimental work, to find those 'factors' or 'variables' which could be fitted into a theoretical framework and 'operationalized' in research. In the years following publication of *The American Soldier*, sociological research moved strongly in this direction. A whole new 'language of social research' (Lazarsfeld and Rosenberg, 1955) was developed, suited to the tasks of isolating, measuring, scaling, and further processing 'sociological variables'.

In many ways a typical example of factor analysis based on survey data is the study *Sociale determinanten van het vrijetijdsgedrag* ('Social Determinants of Leisure Behaviour') by the Dutch sociologist R. Wippler (1968). The author shows hardly any interest in the descriptive issue: what do certain people do in their non-working hours? His concern is far more general: is it possible to discover and explain regularly-occurring patterns or clusters of leisure activities? As the title of his book indicates, Wippler does not attach his problem to any specific time or place; he intends to examine 'which social factors determine *the* nature of leisure activities' (p. 3). Echoing the rhetoric of induction, he refuses to affiliate himself with any theoretical stance; as his starting-point he takes the least compromising definition: 'by "leisure activities" we mean all activities taking place in leisure time' (p. 7). In his conclusions he does not go beyond the correlations found in his own data. These data consist of completed questionnaire forms. Through a statistical analysis Wippler tries to discover 'dimensions' in leisure behaviour and to explain the distribution of these 'dimensions' among various groups. He arrives at five different dimensions which he calls vital-expansive, cultural-participatory, practical-useful, latent-exciting, and relaxing-intellectual. His explanation of the variances is couched in such technical terms as:

Inspection of the basis correlation matrix shows that 29 out of 50 independent variables correlate significantly with vital-expansive leisure behaviour. Altogether these 29 variables explain 47.4% of the variance in the variables to be explained. Only 6 predicators, however, contribute independently to the explanation of variance; together they explain 44.8% of the differences in vital-expansive leisure behaviour, which means that the contribution to the explanation of the remaining 23 independent variables is only 2.6% [Wippler, 1968, p. 81].

Translated in terms of groups or social categories this same conclusion reads as follows:

Vital-expansive leisure behaviour occurs frequently among young people with a high level of education who have high career expectations, who are unmarried and not members of one of the protestant churches and who perform intellectually demanding work [ibid., p. 82].

It is remarkable how much of the variance remains actually 'unexplained' in these conclusions, which, therefore, in the second, 'ordinary language', version sound disappointingly vague. About their further implications nothing can be said with any certainty. Although the conclusions are formulated in terms of generally valid words and figures, they are based on no more than one particular survey, conducted in the year 1965 in the Dutch province of Groningen. In an even more drastic manner than the authors of *The American Soldier*, Wippler has moved directly from specifics to universals, thus completely bypassing all problems of scope. It might be argued in his defence that since the design of his study is explanatory and not descriptive, it need not meet high standards of representativeness (cf. Zetterberg, 1965a, pp. 128-30). This, however, would raise the ticklish problem: what are words like 'explain' and 'determine' supposed to mean in this context? How are we to conceive of the process of 'determination' of 'dimensions' of 'behaviour'? Wippler's analysis does not address itself at all to these questions. It represents no doubt a high level of quantitative exactitude; but the underlying paradigm leaves a number of fundamental problems untouched and unsolved.

If we apply the general principles mentioned in Chapter 1 of this book to Wippler's survey analysis, we are forced to quite negative conclusions. The first point, the interdependence of human beings, is hardly taken into account: each respondent is treated as a single and separate unit. The second point, the developmental nature of the social world, is altogether neglected, and so are, as a consequence, the two further points relating to the blindness of social developments and to the developmental nature of sociological knowledge. It is to be feared that a similarly cursory appraisal of other specimens of survey analysis will, in the majority of cases, yield a similar outcome.

Critiques of survey research

While survey research was still in an early phase, the sociologist Richard LaPiere (1934) reported on a rather disturbing experience. He had travelled all over the United States with a Chinese couple. About six months later he had sent a questionnaire to the proprietors of the hotels and restaurants he and his friends had visited, and by whom they had been welcomed as guests. The questionnaire contained the apparently unambiguous question: 'Would you accept members of the Chinese race in your establishment?' The result was shocking, from both a moral and a methodological point of view: almost without exception, the respondents stated that they would not accept Chinese guests. Just to make sure that the results were not influenced by the behaviour of his own companions, LaPiere sent the same questionnaire to a control group of other hotel and restaurant owners; their reactions were the same. Thus the questionnaire method produced results that were at odds with LaPiere's own experience. He therefore concluded:

> Only a verbal reaction to an entirely symbolic situation can be secured by the questionnaire. It may indicate what the responder would actually do when confronted with the situation symbolized in the question, but there is no assurance that it will. . . . The questionnaire is cheap, easy, and mechanical. The study of human behaviour is time-consuming, intellectually fatiguing, and depends for its success upon the ability of the investigator. The former

method gives quantitative results, the latter mainly qualitative. Quantitative measurements are quantitatively
accurate; qualitative evaluations are always subject to the
errors of human judgment. Yet it would seem far more
worthwhile to make a shrewd guess regarding that which is
essential than to accurately measure that which is likely to
prove quite irrelevant [LaPiere, 1934, p. 237].

These words may sound unduly harsh. Perhaps the fault lay
not in the questionnaire method as such, but rather in too
crude a way of handling it. If LaPiere had explicated various
conditions, such as: would you accept a middle-class Chinese
couple, accompanied by a white American professor?, the
replies might well have been different. His study was too
small in scope to justify his wholesale indictment of survey
research. But if allowance is made for some exaggeration on
his part, his warning still stands that there may be profound
discrepancies between the intentions of a sociologist who
phrases a question, and the reasons for which a respondent
decides to answer it in a certain way. In most cases it will be
very difficult to detect, let alone to correct, such discrepancies without having recourse to methods other than
the questionnaire (for a graphic example, see Blau and
Duncan, 1967, pp. 457-62).
    It is sometimes argued that the questionnaire method is
inherently at fault because it only probes 'verbal behaviour':
it registers words instead of deeds—what men say, and not
what they do (cf. Deutscher, 1973). This critique omits to
acknowledge, however, that most social behaviour is verbal.
Even the most decisive acts and events, like proposing
marriage or declaring war, are effected through words—
through what the philosopher J.L. Austin (1962) has called
'performative language'. Since most social acts have strong
verbal components, all sociological research, no matter by
which technique, is bound to rely heavily on verbal information. The interpretation of verbal information raises many
ticklish problems; however, these are not unique to the
questionnaire method.
    Other criticisms of survey research are more pertinent to
the weaknesses of this particular technique. One such

criticism, brought forward on numerous occasions by Herbert Blumer (1969), points to the great social distance between a survey researcher and the people whom he studies. In most cases, the researcher never even sees these people personally; they are visited by paid interviewers who are not expected to take a lively interest in either their personalities or the aims of the investigation. As a result, the researchers lack 'intimate familiarity' with the actual field of their study; they are too remote from 'what is going on' to be able to judge the questionnaire results on any but purely technical grounds. In this respect, survey research compares unfavourably with participant observation as a method of 'direct examination of the empirical social world'.

In addition, Blumer raises some serious objections to the usual practice of random sampling in survey research. This practice is based on the assumption that society is only an aggregate of disparate individuals. Polling a random cross-section of individuals within this aggregate should therefore give a representative picture of the distribution of opinions in the society as a whole. Now this assumption is in line with the democratic ideal that the opinions of each individual are of equal social significance; but it is, none the less, unrealistic. What it fails to take into account is the fact that societies are structured, and that the opinions of people who are located in strategically important positions are far more consequential than those of the majority of the population. Survey research, in short, is insufficiently attuned to the social structure of opinion formation.

Blumer's criticisms are well-chosen. The results of a great deal of survey research suffer from a lack of familiarity with the people under study, and, correspondingly, from too easy a reliance on probability sampling. The lack of familiarity can become particularly striking in cases of secondary analysis, where the results from previous surveys are taken up by investigators who had nothing to do with the original study. Lacking the insight and caution of a Quetelet, these investigators are capable of interpretations that reveal a total lack of acquaintance with the social field from which the original data derive. Thus a Dutch reader may find to his surprise that in a secondary analysis of survey data relating to 'religion, economic development, and lethal aggression' (Witt *et al.*, 1972), his own country, with a Roman Catholic population of less than 40 per cent, and a strongly Protestant tradition, is classified for purposes of analysis as 'Roman Catholic'. Such mistakes occur frequently; they arise from the attempt to deal with large amounts of quantitative data without intimate knowledge of the situations to which these data pertain.

The crucial test of survey analysis does not lie, however, in its weakest, most mechanical applications–even if these are in a great majority. The principal problem is whether a method that consists in gauging individual opinions as separate and distinct data can adequately grasp wider social structures and developments. Such advocates of survey analysis as Lazarsfeld have repeatedly reassured us that it can, that the technique does not suffer from an inherently individualistic or atomistic bias. In spite of these protestations, survey research, even when executed in the most thoughtful manner, remains focused on separate individuals. They provide the basic data; and while their responses are subsequently boxed together into all sorts of social categories, the actual figurations formed by the respondents never come into the foreground. Even if an investigator starts out well aware of sociological problems of a wide scope, the very requirements of a competently executed analysis may force him against his original intentions to 'trivialize', to reduce the range of his investigations from 'macro' to 'micro', from 'dynamic' to 'static', and from 'objective' to 'subjective' factors (cf. Baldamus, 1971; cf. below, p. 192). He may thus necessarily end up with results in which, so to speak, sociological significance has been sacrificed to statistical significance (cf. Elias and Scotson, 1965, p. 11).

Field and case studies

If one of the obvious limitations of survey analysis lies in the lack of personal contact with the people under study, what is a more likely alternative than participant observation? As a deliberate technique for finding out the secrets of other people's lives, participant observation is as old as spying. It has been used as a source of information by travellers since times immemorial. Only by the end of the nineteenth century did ethnologists, or social anthropologists, try to develop it into an academically respectable, 'scientific' research method (cf. Wax, 1971, pp. 21-40). By temporarily joining a native tribe, partaking in its activities, and in the meantime noting down in detail what was going on, such men as W.H.R. Rivers, Franz Boas, and, somewhat later, Bronislaw Malinowski, sought to combine the roles of on-the-spot participant and neutral observer. Their reports, full of inside information and at the same time written with an outsider's detachment and apparent objectivity, did not fail to make an impression on students of Western societies. In the words of Robert Lynd, one of the first sociologists to emulate the anthropologists in studying an American town: 'nothing can be more enlightening than to gain precisely that degree of objectivity and perspective with which we view "savage" peoples' (1929, p. 5).

Lynd himself, in collaboration with his wife, Helen Lynd, was the author of two of the most famous American community studies, *Middletown* (1929) and *Middletown in Transition* (1937). Both books are written from an anthropological orientation, as if the site of the study, Muncie, Indiana, were an entirely strange and exotic community. From the first page onward, the reader is confronted with lively and telling details about life in Middletown. A stranger arriving in Middletown at 10 AM, we are told, would find the streets deserted; at this time of the day, out of every 100 inhabitants, 43 are engaged in 'getting a living', 23 in 'making a home', 19 in 'receiving training'; the remaining 15 are 'the very old' and 'the very young'. As these figures suggest, 'getting a living' is the most important activity in the community, the axis around which virtually everything else revolves. It is crucial whether in getting a living one works 'with people' or 'with things'; in the former case, one belongs to the business class, in the latter case, to the working class—the most pervasive distinction in Middletown. In their basic economic activities the Middletowners are almost entirely dependent on trade with the outside world: 'Only to a negligible extent does Middletown make the food it eats and the clothing it wears' (p. 39). Thus the description proceeds, drawing upon the authors' own observations, supplemented by interviews and a variety of documents.

Even though the authors avowedly abstain from judgements, the overall picture that emerges from their book is on the whole critical, reminiscent of the atmosphere depicted by Sinclair Lewis in his novels *Babbit* and *Main Street*. To a question like: 'Why do they work so hard?', they respond that the Middletowners are caught up in forces which they themselves can neither control nor understand. For an explanation, the Lynds rely primarily on a 'cultural lag' theory: 'the emergence of "social problems" would seem to no small extent traceable to the ragged, unsynchronized movement of social institutions' (p. 499). In *Middletown in Transition*, they continue to subscribe to the notion of cultural lag; in addition, however, they put greater emphasis on the strong power position of a one-family ruling class in Middletown. Although devoid of even the faintest allusion to Marxism, the two volumes together can be read as a well-documented critique of the capitalist economy and class structure.

Also inspired by the example of anthropology were a series of studies in Newburyport, Massachusetts, or 'Yankee City', by W. Lloyd Warner, who had previously done fieldwork among Australian aborigines. Aided by a team of assistants, and using every available instrument, from genealogical tables to aerial photography, Warner tried to lay bare the whole web of social relations in Yankee City. As his major discovery, he claimed to have found that the population consisted of six social classes, ranging from the upper-upper to the lower-lower, and characterized not so much by their economic position as by their status or prestige. Never before, to paraphrase Lazarsfeld's remark on *The American Soldier*, had so many aspects of life in a medium-sized town been recorded so meticulously. Warner could put forward with great certainty such conclusions as: 'The person most likely to be arrested in Yankee City is a Polish lower-lower-class male aged around thirty years of age. . . . The person least likely to be arrested is an upper-class or upper-middle class female Yankee below twenty years of age' (Warner and Lunt, 1941, p. 373). The six volumes of the Yankee City series abound with such details, minor feats of careful documentation and classification. The result is so overwhelmingly descriptive that it might perhaps better be called 'sociography' than 'sociology'. As C. Wright Mills (1963, pp. 39-52) has remarked in a review of the first volume: while the topics are often fascinating, the report seldom rises above the level of 'flat, tallying busy-work with a minimum of sociological imagination'.

Almost the opposite of Warner's figure-packed reports is William Foote Whyte's *Street Corner Society* (1955), with the curiously Americo-centric subtitle *The Social Structure of an Italian Slum* pointing to a slum not, as a European reader might guess, in Rome or Genoa, but in Boston, Mass. In contrast to Warner, Whyte is by no means concerned with giving a full documentary picture of Cornerville, the site of his study. His book contains hardly any sociographic data, not even the total number of inhabitants of Cornerville. Whyte's main interest is in the power structure among Cornerville's male population: Why is it that some men are 'big shots', and others 'little guys', and how do the 'big shots' succeed in dominating the 'little guys'? After having lived for more than two years in Cornerville, Whyte was trusted and respected by many people there, and he had learned to see how they themselves saw their own situation. By virtue of his 'intimate familiarity' he was able to write a report full of striking details, chosen and presented in such a manner as to be suggestive of more far-reaching theoretical interpretations (as by Homans, 1950; Cohen, 1955; Stein, 1960).

Whyte's most important informant in Cornerville was a young unemployed worker named Doc. We can safely assume that practically everything that Whyte had to say about life in Cornerville was known to Doc; in fact, he had probably learned most of it *from* Doc. Yet it is difficult to imagine that Doc would have written a book like *Street Corner Society*. When we ask ourselves: what then did Whyte know that Doc did not know?, we can only conclude that it was something more than facts, more than 'intimate familiarity'. What enabled Whyte to write his account of life in

Cornerville was a combination of theoretical interests, stimulated by sociological reading, and the thorough inside knowledge acquired through living in Cornerville.

An obvious limitation of participant observation studies is that they have to be confined to comparatively small units, like a town, a neighbourhood, a factory, an office, a hospital. As the Middletown studies as well as *Street Corner Society* show, however, it is possible for a sensitive observer to see how the groups under study are embedded in larger figurations. Living in Middletown or Cornerville has given the Lynds and Whyte a keen sense of the interdependencies from which at the time there was almost no escape for the inhabitants of a Midwestern town or an immigrant quarter. Thanks to a prolonged stay and, in both cases, a repeat visit after a number of years, the investigators were able to discern several important ongoing developments—developments on which neither the Middletowners nor the Cornervillers could exert any significant influence. The economic depression of the 1930s was, of course, the most notable of these uncontrollable developments; such smaller-scale processes as the regular rise and fall of gangs in Cornerville, however, went on in a hardly less compelling manner. In the light of such developments the Lynds and Whyte were able to perceive structural regularities behind what the people involved tended to experience as single events, often of a catastrophic nature.

Participant observers always have to face the problem of bias. How greatly personal impressions can diverge, and how deeply preconceptions can influence the details that one actually sees, is highlighted in one of the rare cases of replication in community research, the studies of the Mexican village Tepoztlán by, respectively, Robert Redfield (1930) and Oscar Lewis (1951). The two investigators returned from the same village with almost diametrically opposed reports: whereas Redfield emphasized the inner harmony of life in Tepoztlán, Lewis came forth with a picture of 'fear, envy and distrust' (p. 429). Commenting on these pervasive discrepancies, Redfield concluded

that we are all better off with two descriptions of Tepoztlán than we would be with only one of them . . . I think we must recognize that the personal interests and the personal and cultural values of the investigator influence the content of the description of the community . . . There are hidden questions behind the two books that have been written about Tepotzlán. The hidden question behind my book is, 'What do these people enjoy?' The hidden question behind Dr. Lewis' book is, 'What do these people suffer from?' [Redfield, 1955, p. 136] .

It may be argued against Redfield's generous view that in participant observation as in any other method of research the investigator is always well-advised to formulate his questions as explicitly as possible. Instead of merely following his personal predilections, he should consider whether the particular points that interest him may not be subsumed under a wider sociological perspective. Thus, the two questions: What do these people enjoy?, and: What makes them suffer? need not be treated as isolated and ultimate problems, to be selected on no other basis than the investigator's personal interests. Both questions can be formulated in more general terms, without loss of empirical substance. Which are the major problems of social existence in this particular community? How, in coping with these problems, are the men, women, and children in the community dependent upon each other? An investigation of the community in these terms is more firmly grounded on sociological foundations; and it may equally well touch upon the problems brought to the fore by Redfield: the social sources of human pleasure and pain.

The question of what people enjoy and what makes them suffer does indeed run through many community studies. As a theme, it is clearly present in the two Middletown volumes. Addressing themselves to such problems as why the Middletowners strained themselves to work so hard, and how they coped with the ordeal of the depression, the Lynds have demonstrated the close links between 'personal troubles' and 'public issues' (Mills, 1959, p. 8). Many other studies could be mentioned, ranging from the literary and journalistic writings of such authors as George Orwell and Simone Weil to professional sociological reports like *Small Town in Mass*

Society by Arthur Vidich and Joseph Bensman (1968) and *Soulside* by Ulf Hannerz (1969). While a number of these books deal with the problems of social existence as experienced by the modern middle classes, in a great majority they have continued the tradition of documenting for a middle-class audience 'how the other half lives'.

One of the most penetrating recent contributions to this tradition is *The Hidden Injuries of Class* by Richard Sennett and Jonathan Cobb (1973). The book contains a collage of extensive conversations with manual workers in the Boston area. As the authors make plain, they have taken great liberties in arranging their materials in order to make their account telling; in contrast to the virtuosi of survey analysis they have, as it were, attempted to maximize sociological significance, thereby completely neglecting statistical signifi- cance and other codes of orthodox social science metho- dology. Although their report is marred by a tendency to moralize, and rashly to contrast 'individual freedom' and 'society', the authors succeed very well in showing how 'class as a problem of day-to-day existence' (p. 148) enters into the deepest pores of the personalities of American workers, and how crossing the line 'from a life of scarcity and constant economic insecurity to a life of some affluence' (p. 178) need not alleviate their feelings of humiliation and failure.

The Hidden Injuries of Class manifests a trend to inform sociological reportage with techniques and viewpoints borrowed from psycho-analytic practice and theory. The trend is not new, but it is increasing as a reaction against the superficiality of mechanically-applied survey analysis. The welding of participant observation and psychoanalysis has led to such studies as *Pathways to Madness* by the anthropologist Jules Henry (1973), a probing report on American families with an emotionally disturbed child. The style of *Pathways to Madness* bears no trace of the rhetoric of induction. Rich in detailed observation and subtle commentary, it moves continuously to and fro between various levels of specificity and generality. Single incidents are described at great length, with the explicit acknowledgement that the description has been made possible by some general perspective; this per- spective, in turn, becomes clearer by its confrontation with striking details. Throughout the book the author makes it quite clear that he is dealing with living human beings who have to wrestle continuously with the problems arising out of their social interdependencies.

The most obvious limitation of fieldwork of any kind is that it is restricted to one particular community during a relatively short period. There are, however, ways of surmounting this limitation. In most cases it is possible to extend one's range of information by tapping a wide variety of resources. Thus by talking to members of different age-groups, especially the old, one may gain a broader time perspective. Oral tradition need not always be reliable; but it does reveal something about how people experience their past (cf. Vansina, 1965). Documents, both official and personal, are a welcome addition; in spite of their selectiveness they may contain information not easily accessible by any other means. The method of combining participant observation and documentation as advocated by the Lynds and the Chicago sociologists (cf. Burgess and Bogue, 1964), has recently been revived by anthropologists (cf. Blok, 1974, pp. 5-16; Pitt, 1972). It can be most rewarding as it may yield immediate knowledge of the local scene as well as insight into how the here and now fit into more encompassing figurations and long-term developments.

On the social relationships between social investigators and their subjects

Finding and relating facts about the social world is not just an academic concern, of interest to sociologists, but is a practical matter for everybody. In their daily routines people draw on an enormous stock of detailed knowledge regarding 'Who is who?' and 'What is what?' They continuously re-adapt this knowledge by exchanging gossip, by reading newspapers and watching television, and just by going about with their eyes and ears open. Any drastic change in living conditions (like another job, another house, illness, or a death, to mention only events in the directly personal sphere) is bound to reveal gaps in one's factual knowledge, and to remind one of the importance of accurate and reliable information in coping with the problems of social life.

By and large, our factual knowledge of the social world can be fragmentary and yet sufficiently precise to get by. In order to catch a train or to mail a letter we need specific information; but we do not need to know how the railways or the postal services actually operate to make the trains run and to get the mail delivered. Similarly, in conducting our daily affairs we take it as a matter of course that we are able to tell the time, by the minute, the hour, the day, the month, the year. By virtue of our learned capacities to read clocks and calendars we manage to live up to the intricate time schedules which are vital parts of our societies. Yet our general understanding of the meaning and functions of the concept of time may be very limited (cf. Elias, 1975).

During the past centuries, the amount of publicly-available facts about the social world has increased tremendously. Only three hundred years ago, it was impossible to tell with reasonable certainty the total number of inhabitants of any country. Today, we have detailed population statistics for practically every country in the world. However, whereas some areas of social life are documented abundantly, we know very little about others, even in the way of mere 'facts'. In the early nineteenth century, sufficiently precise figures about the height of army recruits were already available to enable Quetelet to make his ingenious calculations. The availability of these data can be readily explained: measuring physical height of conscripts presented few practical or theoretical difficulties; it served a clear purpose of selection for the military; and the findings were harmless enough to be treated without secrecy. To other aspects of society, however, none of these reasons apply. Take, for example, the distribution of power. No doubt this is an interesting topic, of far greater general importance than the height of recruits. Studying it, however, presents us with enormous difficulties: there are no ready means of measurement; it is hard to conceive of direct practical purposes for which such measures might be developed; and the whole area of power is loaded with feelings of anxiety and resentment, blocking unbiased investigation.

Problems of power enter into every process of social fact-finding. If certain people require certain information about other people, it is always to the point to ask why they require this information and what means they have of collecting it. The proto-typical forms of administrative and participatory social research show unmistakable power aspects. Administrative research originally served no other purpose than to strengthen the government; the people, the 'subjects', were forced to comply with the demands of the inquisitors. Contemporary sociologists cannot bring equally strong sanctions to bear in order to elicit their subjects' cooperation. Yet thriving survey research can only be understood as part of an encompassing process of bureaucratization in the course of which people have found themselves obliged to fill in forms and to provide information on more and more occasions. Participant observation is also embedded in power relations. Spying in the sense of peeping or prying into other people's affairs can, of course, be carried out socially 'upward' as well as 'downward'. In the actual practice of sociology, however, the most frequent pattern of participant observation is that young academics temporarily move 'downward', joining groups of 'corner boys' (Whyte, 1955; Liebow, 1967) or 'outsiders' (Becker, 1963). To be sure, participant observers have also studied equals like civil servants (Blau, 1955), managers (Dalton, 1961), or probation officers (Cicourel, 1968). They have only rarely, however, penetrated into ruling groups in their own societies; for the study of contemporary élites we have to rely largely, as for the study of élites in the past, on documentary evidence. As Aaron Cicourel has aptly put it: 'In order to study power you need power'.

It is sometimes overlooked that the power relations involved in social inquiry are always two-sided. A government seeking certain information from its subjects apparently needs its subjects–for paying taxes, fulfilling military service, or some other purpose. The subjects may be in a position to withhold or distort information, and thus to sabotage the government's intentions. It has been notably difficult for many years for the central planning agencies in the Soviet Union to collect reliable production figures, owing to the tremendous pressure for lower-level authorities to exaggerate the performance in their own regions (cf. Mickiewitz, 1973, p. 2). In the Netherlands, a relatively small but stubborn opposition group has succeeded in seriously impairing the 1970 census and in delaying its publication.

As early as 1753 the first proposed census in Great Britain was violently opposed in parliament by William Thornton who branded the project as a scheme designed to destroy 'the last remains of English liberty'. 'The new Bill will direct the imposition of new taxes, and, indeed, the addition of a very few words will make it the most effectual engine of rapacity and oppression ever waged against an innocent people' (quoted by Jones, 1948, p. 23; see also Glass, 1973). In those cases where their yielding of information has no other consequence than to aggravate the pressures exerted by government, people are well-advised to distrust social inquirers. However, the availability of precise information can also be turned to their benefit. A century after Thornton, Karl Marx (1867, p. 15) emphatically praised the accuracy and completeness of British statistics, which provided him with ample material for his critique of capitalism. Another hundred years later, Barrington Moore, Jr. has suggested that every honest empirical sociological investigation is bound to have some demystifying effect, disconcerting to the ruling groups, and, therefore, in the long run beneficial to the oppressed:

> In any society the dominant groups are the ones with the most to hide about the way society works. Very often theorefore truthful analyses are bound to have a critical ring, to seem like exposures rather than objective statements, as the term is conventionally used . . . For all students of human society, sympathy with the victims of historical processes and skepticism about the victors' claims provide essential safeguards against being taken in by the dominant mythology. A scholar who tries to be objective needs these feelings as part of his ordinary working equipment [Moore, 1966, pp. 522-23].

Moore raises here the crucial problem of identification: with whom are sociologists to identify in their studies? I shall return to this problem in Chapter 6, on 'relevance'. It should be clear, however, that no methodology of fact-finding in sociology can get round the problem, stated plainly in terms of concrete human beings: who are reporting to whom facts about whom? As a rephrasing of the questions 'knowledge for what?' (Lynd, 1939) and 'knowledge from what?' (Phillips, 1971), this is a question that needs to be faced again and again.

For one thing, it throws light on the 'discoveries' claimed by sociologists as the results of empirical study. The Hawthorne investigators discovered that it mattered to female workers whether they were treated with some kindness and respect by their superiors. Whyte discovered that the seemingly unordered interactions in the streets of Cornerville showed distinct patterns of hierarchy and solidarity. Not so long ago, British sociologists discovered that kinship was still very important in a workers' district in East London (Young and Wilmott, 1962, p. 12). All these 'discoveries' may be said to reflect prior ignorance on the part of the investigators: just as Columbus had been unaware of the existence of the American Indians, so these sociologists had previously not known the facts they reported as discoveries. The Hawthorne workers, the Corner boys, or the East Londoners would have found nothing novel about the discoveries made about themselves—only the technical vocabulary in which these were formulated would have been new to them. Nevertheless, the findings deserved to be called discoveries to the extent that they were new, not only to the investigators, but also to their audiences. What the sociologists did was to fill a communication gap in their own societies, to bring facts concerning certain groups to the attention of a wider public, and to make these facts available for commentary and discussion, for analysis and explanation.

As in gossip or in the courtroom, so in sociology (or any other context where facts are presented as evidence), these facts can be used both as building-blocks to construct cases and theories, and as fuses to explode them. This is not to deny that facts can be weak or strong: some building-blocks soon collapse, some fuses never go off, others are too formidable to be trifled with. Under no circumstances, however, do facts speak for themselves. It is human beings, living together, who have learnt to discern facts and to give them meaning.

3

Attempts at System-Building in Sociology

On classification and explanation

In contemporary sociology, as in most sciences, fact-finding or research on the one hand, and theoretical work on the other are fairly distinct activities. The distinction applies to a division of labour which can be traced back at least as far as the European Middle Ages and classical antiquity. Traditionally, theorizing about society has been a more prestigious activity than fact-finding. Men like Plato, Saint Augustine, and Aquinas undoubtedly belong to the class of theorists; it would be difficult to list empirical social researchers of equal fame. Something of this status difference persists to the present day. To explain it, one must consider the social functions of theorizing.

Theorizing is a typical preoccupation, and prerogative, of classes of men who specialize in it—as priests, philosophers, or scientists. To people reared in twentieth-century academic culture the distinction between 'empirical' and 'theoretical' sounds more or less self-evident; it is to be doubted, however, whether it is easily applicable to illiterate societies in which specialist groups of theorists have not yet developed. Of course in all human societies, even the most 'primitive', people possess elaborate knowledge of the world they live in. If we call this knowledge 'empirical', we mean that it refers to observable things and events, to the realm of sensory experience. If we call it also 'theoretical', we imply that it orders the observed phenomena within some sort of intellectual system. In so far as we can distinguish a 'theoretical' aspect, it seems that we have in mind primarily two functions: classification and explanation. These same two functions still constitute the main typical theoretical activities of contemporary sociologists: the construction of classificatory taxonomies, and the formulation and testing of explanatory hypotheses.

In their pioneering study on *Primitive Classification,* Emile Durkheim and Marcel Mauss (1903) argued that the basic categories by which men classify and explain are 'collective representations', derived from their social experiences. In the process of social evolution, men have learnt such general notions as time, space, cause and number. All these notions are rooted in social life: time corresponds to the rhythm of joint activities, space to a clan's territory, cause to the power men can exert upon each other. By grouping animals and trees, the directions of the wind and the seasons, etc., men incorporated aspects of the physical world into their social world. They developed general categories like 'sacred' and 'profane', 'familiar' and 'strange', 'living' and 'dead', applying to men and non-human objects alike. Classification, by providing men with fixed concepts and practical prescriptions, served as a powerful social bond, the bond of a common orientation. Without it, human beings would be lost in a perpetual flow of immediate sense impressions (see also Durkheim, 1912, pp. 431-9).

In their elementary forms, classification and explanation are directly related. Why is it that things are, and have become, the way they are? Why is it that certain people are to be trusted, and others to be avoided? One way of dealing with such questions is by means of classification: a thing has the characteristics of its class 'because' it belongs to this class, a person is good or bad 'because' the group he belongs to is good or bad. In the development of human thought, such explanations have gradually come to be regarded as tautological and specious. The standards of explanation have changed; today, in scientific circles, schemes of classification or typologies are usually regarded as 'mere taxonomies', and explanatory power is attributed only to law-like 'hypotheses' and 'propositions' (cf. Hempel, 1965).

It is important to realize that the principles of both classification and explanation are the products of social development. Contrary to the claims implied in most of them, there is no evidence that any system of classification and explanation is 'eternal' or 'transcendental'. They all have gradually developed, in a process spanning many generations, as the societies of which they formed a part developed. Today there is a widespread tendency to disregard the sociogenetic nature of human knowledge, and to treat the fundamental categories of thought as timeless givens: the notions of time and space, or the laws of logic are considered as eternal *a prioris*. Thus, in a typical manner, Steven Lukes in his otherwise excellent monograph on Emile Durkheim, dispenses with Durkheim's ideas on the development of thought as follows:

> In arguing thus, he [Durkheim] went too far, since the operations of the mind and the laws of logic are not determined by, or given in, experience, even in social experience. No account of relations between features of a society and the ideas and beliefs of its members could ever explain the faculty, or ability, of the latter to think spatially and temporally, to classify material objects and to individuate persons, to think causally and, in general, to reason; nor could it ever show that the necessity, or indispensability, of doing all these things was simply an aspect of social authority [Lukes, 1973, p. 447].

These objections are not very convincing. What is more likely: that 'man' as a single individual comes into the world endowed with all the cognitive gifts mentioned by Lukes, or that these capacities are only acquired by people in the social process of living together? The potential for developing these faculties is, of course, part of the human genetic structure; but, then, so is the potential to split atoms or to travel to the moon. Apparently, while the most spectacular recent human accomplishments are clearly recognized as 'social', those that have been acquired in a more distant past are no longer seen as such. The unwillingness of sociologists to take a more long-term developmental view, in other words, their persistence in a 'hodiecentric' attitude, prevents them from perceiving the sociogenetic nature of their own problems of theorizing. The developmental approach is certainly not a panacea which will at once solve these problems; but it can be of great help in elucidating them, in putting them into a proper, more realistic perspective. In this respect, Durkheim was on the right track. So were Auguste Comte and Karl Marx before him.

Comte's 'Law of the three stages'

An obvious feature of most attempts at classifying and explaining the social world is what is known today as ethnocentrism. From the oldest written documents, one gains the impression that the ancient Egyptians and Babylonians never doubted that it was they themselves who formed the centre of the universe. The physical world: the sun, the sky, land, water, and the social world of their own and neighbouring peoples were fitted into a cosmology that divided the phenomena into major classes, and contained clues about how the phenomena had originated and how they were related: the Pharaoh, for example, stood above the people of Egypt as the sun stood above the earth, both king and sun embodying the same divine spirit (cf. Frankfort *et al.*, 1949).

Such systems of classification and explanation belong to what Auguste Comte has called the theological stage in the development of human thought. Comte was one of the first European writers who clearly saw that the human capacities for discerning 'facts' and for classifying and explaining these facts are closely related, and that these capacities, rather than having been given to man on an immemorial day of creation, have gradually developed in a process spanning hundreds of generations. At first, men seemed to be caught in a vicious circle, caused by 'the two necessities of observing first, in order to form conceptions, and of forming theories first, in order to observe'.

Only very gradually, and never fully, have men learned to break out of this vicious circle. One of the most powerful devices they developed was their imagination, which enabled them to explain all the events they sought to comprehend in terms of forces of a kind that they seemed to understand best: human or human-like impulses and intentions. In the more advanced agricultural societies a class of men emerged, the priests or theologians, who became specialists in fathoming the divine wills which apparently determined whatever happened in the world. Although Comte was openly hostile to the theologians of his own day, he stressed how immensely important it had been that in remote times, among populations of warriors and slaves, a privileged class managed to emancipate itself from military and menial employments, and to engage primarily in intellectual activities. Within the theological classes, the human faculties for speculative reasoning were sharpened so that in the long run people were able to dispense with theological fantasies in their efforts to understand.

The classical Greek philosophers represent the first great break with theological thinking. Although employing the vocabulary of their own time, with occasional references to gods, the writings of Plato and Aristotle can be summarized without any use of theological language. The setting of Plato's *Republic* is plainly philosophical; the most important words are not the names of gods but the names of concepts, like Justice and Truth. In a neatly logical discourse the social world is classified and explained: the division of men into rulers, warriors and slaves is shown as necessarily following both from the functional prerequisites of a society as a whole and from the different innate social destinies of its members. Compared with the sociocosmologies of ancient Egypt or Mesopotamia, Plato's *Republic* is far more universalistic in its purpose as well as in its actual contents. None the less, twentieth-century readers may detect unmistakable ethnocentric tendencies: the model for the ideal republic is obviously a Greek city-state, part of a larger figuration that compels the rulers of the polis to be permanently alert against military attacks, and stratified almost as a matter of course into noblemen, commoners and slaves.

Of course, the *Republic* was not intended as a description of any 'real' polis. Plato meant to show what a society would look like if it were designed according to an ideal plan, based on an explicit notion of justice. His treatise was not purely utopian, however: it also served to provide a set of principles to be used in discussing 'real' societies. This double purpose is even clearer in the political writings of Aristotle, and it has remained typical of the whole Western tradition of political theory which, to the present day, consists in a large measure of recurrent attempts to construct coherent models of government and society—models in which typical features of 'real' states are taken up and elaborated into general principles. In the Middle Ages, discussion was couched in theological terms; during the past three or four centuries, however, references to theology have become fewer and fewer, and political theory has tended to become once more a predominantly philosophical enterprise.

In Comte's view, this type of theorizing, represented in its most eminent form by such men as Hobbes, Locke, Rousseau and Kant, signalled the metaphysical or abstract stage. Comte recognized that thinking in terms of abstract principles meant a liberation from supernatural beliefs and theological doctrines. In a way, however, the philosophers of the metaphysical stage clung too much to the conventions of the preceding stage. Thus, although they sought untheological solutions, many of their problems still bore the mark of theology. In discussing First Causes or True Essences, they were pursuing abstract versions of divine will. The next step would have to be to abandon these concepts. As long as they stuck to metaphysical issues, men would keep themselves from the far more promising task of explaining the manifold connections between events without bothering about a Prime Mover or a Final Destiny. Concentrating on this task alone would herald the age of positivism.

Comte's 'law of the three stages' is still mentioned in most textbooks of sociology. Usually, this remains an isolated passage in a historical chapter, to which no further references are made. The theory is of more than mere antiquarian interest, however. In its emphasis on the developmental nature of human thought and knowledge, it contains much that is relevant to sociology today. We may even take some of Comte's clues as literally as he intended, and inquire whether certain difficulties in contemporary attempts to classify and explain the social world may not be due to vestiges of what Comte called theological and metaphysical thinking. It is certainly worth noting that a very 'modern' critic of sociology resorts to theological categories in order to assert that our rules of procedure are 'not God-given', our knowledge is not 'guaranteed by a divine mind', our methods are not 'gifts from the gods' (Phillips, 1973, pp. 84, 150, 179).

System-building in early sociology

The distinguishing characteristic of a science is that it is an explanatory system. It rests on a small number of principles. It is capable of explaining, or predicting, many diverse phenomena of a certain sort. It accounts for them by tracing them logically (or, what is equivalent, mathematically) to the restricted group of principles or laws . . . A scientific theory, being a system cannot grow by mere accumulation, but must be produced by an act of invention. There can be no period when a science is partly in existence: someone either has or has not brought together into an orderly whole enough principles and effects to qualify as a science, however rudimentary and fallacious [Letwin, 1963, p. vi].

This quotation from William Letwin's *The Origins of Scientific Economics* indicates a conception of science as a primarily systematic enterprise. This conception was largely formed in the seventeenth century, under the impact of Cartesian philosophy and Newtonian physics. It is, as Letwin's own words witness, still current today, and for many it is the aim toward which all sociologists should aspire. Those who embrace this view, however, while admitting that every science has undergone fundamental changes in the course of its development, nevertheless maintain in their methodological discussions a concept of science that is apparently valid for all times and places. Science, they hold, is essentially a deductive theoretical system.

The fact that Letwin, who is a historian, should subscribe to such an ahistorical view of science shows how widespread this view is. In his analytical definition of science he almost automatically follows the philosophical tradition traceable to Descartes and Newton; but in his empirical investigation of the emergence of modern economic theory he proceeds as a historian who is well aware of the social and developmental nature of human thought, and whose own explanations do not conform to the strict rules of a deductive-hypothetical model. His study contributes to an understanding of the sociogenesis of the very ideal of science espoused by himself and so many others even today.

In seventeenth-century England, so Letwin's argument runs, a number of pamphleteers were engaged in polemics on such issues as free trade, rates of interest, coinage and other aspects of economic policy. In support of their views, these writers would refer to empirical examples and to authoritative opinions. In their polemics, they were highly personal. Every pamphleteer went out of his way to proclaim his own disinterestedness, and no one shrank from imputing impure, selfish motives to his adversaries. As England became less oligarchic, however, the number of participants in public debate increased, and the *ad hominem* mode of disputation became less effective. How was the author of a political tract to convince a largely unknown audience that his arguments were sincere, sound and sensible?

One recourse was quantification, the use of figures. Thus the main advocate of 'political arithmetic', William Petty, proclaimed that 'instead of using only comparative and superlative words, and intellectual arguments' he would express himself 'in terms of number, weight or measure' (quoted by Letwin, 1963, p. 139), an intention wholly in agreement with the spirit of the scientists of his day, organized in the Royal Society. Other writers resorted to a strictly logical mode of reasoning, proceeding in a Cartesian manner from first principles that were 'clear and evident' and 'indisputably true' to necessary conclusions. This latter method would leave room for only one form of valid critique: unless flaws could be detected either in the premises or in the chain of reasoning, the inferences would be binding, regardless of the character or interests of the author. Thus, Letwin concludes, 'in the search for a way of dispelling the problem of special pleading, a scientific method was hit on. The needs of rhetoric brought forth the method of economic theory' (p. 105).

Letwin has laid bare something of the sociogenesis of the rhetoric of deduction—how it fitted the requirements of impersonal public discussion among equals, with minimal appeal to authority. As a mode of argumentation it was not restricted to matters of economic policy. Philosophers from Spinoza to Rousseau used it to build general theories of society, based upon a few plain and simple premises. Spinoza attributed to his philosophical system the same certainty as to the mathematical proposition that the three angles of a triangle equal two right angles: 'What is true, proves itself'. The romantic rationalist, Rousseau, unwilling to accept the authority of any holy script, also had little patience with empirical matters; as he once blandly remarked: 'Let us begin by discarding all facts, for they have nothing at all to do with the problem' (quoted by De Valk, 1960, p. 59).

It was this cavalier attitude toward facts which aroused the wrath of Comte in his critique of philosophical reasoning. Yet it cannot be denied that in the writings of Comte himself, as of many other nineteenth-century sociologists, there is a tendency toward law-like formulations reminiscent of the Newtonian ideal. Contrary to his own programme, Comte tended more towards speculative reasoning than empirical research. His genius lay first of all in a remarkable gift for synthesis through systematic ordering. The law of the three stages is an example. The idea of intellectual progress, upon which it elaborates, was an *idée reçue* of the Enlightenment. What was new was the manner in which Comte managed to connect a grandiose systematic conception of the sciences with an equally systematic developmental scheme applicable in principle to all human knowledge and to all societies. Once his system was formulated, Comte never seemed to be at a loss when it came to classifying or explaining: the system could be made to absorb any conceivable problem.

The other great pioneers of sociology worked in a similar

fashion. The typical image of the nineteenth-century sociologist was one of an individual savant, unbound by academic specialisms, trying to muster a broad range of human knowledge into one comprehensive synthesis. If Toqueville, for example, was not ranked for a long time among the 'founding fathers of social science', this was probably due to the fact that, being rather indifferent to systematics, he did not fit this picture very well. Typically the first sociologists were those who presumably had found certain basic principles or 'laws' capable of explaining the entire course of human history. For Comte, the law of the three stages was such a principle; for Spencer, it was evolution, the universal process of increasing integration and differentiation.

There is no particular reason to assume, as Letwin does, that the deductive style of reasoning is intrinsically democratic and innovatory. The original functions of a new intellectual system derived from 'self-evident' principles may be to defy old authorities. But as the assault succeeds, and the old authorities give way, yesterday's radicalism may develop into the orthodoxy of today. This, in fact, is what happened in large parts of the world to the intellectual heritage of Marx. Although in his lifetime he spent far less effort in system-building than Comte, it was Marx whose name has become associated with one of the dominant ideological doctrines of our age. Marx himself appears to have been very ambivalent about 'marxism' and 'marxists'. Many of his followers, however, beginning with Friedrich Engels, have done their best to forge his ideas into one coherent system (cf. Lichtheim, 1964, pp. 234-58; Ollman, 1971, pp. ix-xvi; Joravski, 1970, pp. 228-70). When later generations of sociologists entered, as Albert Salomon (1945) put it, into a debate with the ghost of Marx, in most cases they addressed themselves primarily to the mighty spectre of marxism as a system.

Towards formal theories: Pareto and Weber

The generation of scholars who founded sociology as an academic discipline took a very critical stance toward all great system-builders of the nineteenth century. Durkheim (1895) pointed out that their 'laws' and 'principles' were speculative generalizations, lacking in empirical underpinning. Max Weber hardly ever mentioned either Comte or Spencer; in his methodological writings he joined the far more sophisticated debates among the leading German historians and philosophers of his time. The harshest rejection came from Pareto; measuring the work of his predecessors by his own standards of 'logico-experimental science' he concluded that it represented little more than dogmatism and metaphysics (Pareto, 1917, pp. 3, 1975).

Even Pareto was willing to grant that the nineteenth-century sociologists exhibited a vast knowledge of human societies. But, in his opinion, they too naïvely mistook their knowledge for science. They assumed too readily that the facts as they knew them fitted into a clear pattern revealing the real structure of social reality. They overlooked that every so-called fact was in itself impregnated with theory and described only selected aspects of the events to which it referred. Scientific laws, summarizing uniformities in observed facts, were no more than analytic abstractions, statements of probability, approximating but never fully covering the empirical world.

In agreement with the general philosophical climate of his time (cf. Hughes, 1958), Pareto postulated an unbridgeable gulf between the actual social world, elusive in its complexity, and the social world as depicted by sociologists. The same premise also informed the methodological writings of Max Weber. Weber was keenly aware of what A.N. Whitehead called 'the fallacy of misplaced concreteness' (cf. Parsons, 1954, p. 222): the tendency to assume that for every concept which can be formulated there must be a corresponding object existing in reality. For Weber the very' lack of congruence between 'concepts' and 'reality' was a reason to take problems of concept formation very seriously: '*sharp* distinction is often impossible in reality; clear *concepts* are therefore even more necessary' (Weber, 1922, p. 158). In his concern for conceptual clarity and consistency Weber borrowed the term 'ideal types' to indicate that his theoretical models could be no more than mental constructions, logically coherent, but 'against the concrete reality of the historical, relatively *empty* of content' (ibid., p. 4). His well-known distinction of types of authority—charismatic, traditional, and legal-rational—was determined primarily by 'the gain in systematics it yields'; one should not expect ever to find any of these types in an 'historically pure' form (ibid., p. 160).

Pareto's substantive sociological theories, about residues and derivations, and about the circulation of élites, were attempts, informed by a large erudition and a keen insight into some dark regions of human motivation, to abstract from history—to mark unchanging uniformities behind the protean stream of social events. Weber, in a supreme display of scholarship, analyzed the legal, economic, political and religious institutions of European and Asiatic societies. In the wealth of his historical material he surpassed any of his sociological predecessors. But he was, remarkably, far more cautious in his conclusions. Nowhere did he put forward sweeping generalizations about the 'laws' underlying social development. Instead, he continually emphasized the multiplicity of aspects of social life and the impossibility of ever grasping them fully. His posthumous *magnum opus, Economy and Society* (1922), was particularly dominated by severe methodological inhibitions, resulting in a host of definitions and classifications rather than bold conclusions. Representing, as one unsympathetic critic put it, 'an orgy of formalism' (Marcuse, 1968, p. 203; for a rejoinder, see Bendix and Roth, 1971, pp. 55-69), it prepared the way for an increasing concern with systematics in sociology.

The triumph of formalism: Talcott Parsons

The emergence of sociology as an academic discipline greatly enhanced the tendency toward deductive theorizing. One reason for this was that sociologists sought epistemological support for their discipline; they hoped to find this by orientating themselves to the theoretical model of Newtonian physics and its derivations in economics or psychology. The deductive spirit was further fostered by the break between

'social science' and 'history', a break that became institutionalized in the university departments. Historians were
either supposed to deal with 'the past', and social scientists
with 'the present', or, according to another dichotomy, no
less crude and untenable, historians were supposed to focus
upon 'the particular', and social scientists upon 'the general'.
A few sociologists such as Pitirim Sorokim tried to continue
the tradition of developmental or dynamic sociology. Even in
his work, however, the tendency toward general systematic
theory often dominated. Some of his contemporaries, such as
Leopold von Wiese and Georges Gurvitch, spent much effort
in building elaborate analytical systems in which the urge to
systematize ultimately overshadowed all other interests.

No-one, however, has been so prolific and so influential a
general theorist as Talcott Parsons. In his first book, *The
Structure of Social Action* (1937), Parsons set himself up as
the great systematizer who, by integrating several converging
lines, would usher in a new phase in sociological theorizing.
Against the empiricists who were rampant in the 1930s he
maintained that no scientific progress could be made without
a clear theoretical guideline. But theory would then have to
be conceived of as something quite different from the
empirical generalizations developed by such writers as Comte,
Spencer and Marx:

> The central interest here has been in the establishment of a
> highly generalized pattern in the processes of change of
> human societies as a whole, whether it be linear evolu-
> tionism, cyclical or dialectic process, etc. . . . Such systems
> have had a notorious tendency to overreach the facts and
> their own analytical underpinning and by and large have
> not, in the meanings originally meant by their authors,
> stood the test of competent criticism. On this level no
> competent modern sociologist can be a Comtean, a
> Spencerian, or even a Marxian [Parsons, 1954, pp.
> 219-220].

For too long, Parsons argued, the social sciences were under
the spell of a naïve realism which took the form either of
atheoretical collections of 'facts' or of grandiose generalizations about the 'laws' of social evolution. Both failed to

recognize the active part played by theorizing in the progress of science. Facts, according to a famous quotation inspired by Pareto, were nothing but 'statements about experience in terms of a conceptual scheme' (Parsons, 1937, p. 28). What the social sciences, and sociology in particular, needed was a conceptual apparatus that would be both logically consistent and applicable in empirical research.

In the writings of Alfred Marshall, Vilfredo Pareto, Emile Durkheim and Max Weber, four men whom he saw as his precursors, Parsons thought he had found the outlines of an emerging theoretical synthesis. He designated this synthesis as the action frame of reference, 'the indispensable logical framework in which we describe and think about the phenomena of action' (ibid., p. 733). By working out this framework to its logical conclusions, Parsons intended to arrive at a set of theoretical categories which would put sociology on a par with such sciences as economics and even physiology.

The core assumption in Parsons' action frame of reference is that men always find themselves as live 'actors' in 'situations'. Action implies more than mechanical reactions to stimuli; it involves orientation towards one or more specific ends, and a selection of means adapted toward reaching these ends. Combining the ends-means dichotomy with a second dichotomy, between internal and external functions, Parsons came to distinguish four functional prerequisites for any system of action: pattern-maintenance (internal-means), integration (internal-ends), goal-attainment (external-ends), and adaptation (external-means). This fourfold scheme has served as the ground pattern for a complex set of taxonomies comprising practically every facet of social life. As one sympathetic commentator has noted, writing at the end of Parsons' most prolific period, the 1950s:

> As everyone knows the Parsonian theoretical forest is vast and tangled, a veritable jungle of fine distinctions and intertwining classifications. Moreover it is still growing at a prodigious rate, as evidenced by the publication of no less than fourteen additional papers in the year after this paper

was originally prepared. And, like Birnam Wood, it moves:
Parsonian theory in the late 1950s differs in some
important respects from that of a decade ago [Devereux,
1961, p. 2].

Parsons' work, to change metaphors, has grown in the course
of time like a coral reef. New themes have been added and
have overgrown others which have disappeared from view;
the whole, however, has unmistakably kept its identity. Just
as King Midas changed everything he touched into gold, so
Parsons manages to make a diagram out of every problem,
and a fourfold diagram at that. Confronted with any issue, he
first arranges and classifies his subject-matter into his own
seasoned catagories and subcategories, and then, by drawing
lines and arrows in all directions, he restores the unity of the
whole.

Parsons' writings contain enough material, including ambi-
guities and inconsistencies, to keep commentators busy for a
long time. If one agrees with his basic tenet—that what
sociology needs most of all is a set of fundamental and
universal categories—one cannot but admire the persistence
and the virtuosity he has displayed in pursuing this goal. It is
doubtful, however, whether systematic theory of the
Parsonian kind is really an asset to sociology in its present
state. As early as 1958 Barrington Moore, Jr., branded his
work as 'neo-scholasticism', and indeed this label is painfully
appropriate. Parsons' emphasis is always on abstractions
rather than men. Although he writes about human beings and
human societies, his main references are to such highly
technical general categories as functional prerequisites,
pattern variables, hierarchies of control and the like. His
work continues the tradition of those classical theorists who,
inspired by Descartes and Newton, claimed to have found the
unchanging fundamental principles of society, and never tired
of reducing everything to their own system of allegedly
universal principles. In a well-chosen image Norbert Elias
(1969a, I, p. xiv) has compared Parsons' conceptual system
to a pack of cards: the combinations change, but the
elementary units remain the same. This holds true even for
Parsons' most recent formulations about social evolution; his

ultimate ambition is to map the development of human societies in the fixed dichotomic terms of his original fourfold scheme of functions.

Formalism and reductionism in exchange theories

One of Parsons' most distinguished crities has for a long time been his colleague at Harvard, George Homans. According to Homans, 'the chief difficulty with his [Parsons'] theoretical work is that he thinks in terms of categories and conceptual schemes'. In contrast, Homans has always preferred to study the actual behaviour of individual men, trying to explain this behaviour 'with variables and with propositions stating relationships between them' (Homans, in Turk and Simpson, 1971, p. 377).

Homans' first great exercise in sociological theory was *The Human Group* (1950), published almost simultaneously with Parsons' *The Social System* (1951). At the time of their publication, these books, both about 500 pages long, were welcomed as signalling the final maturity of sociological theory. Today they are hardly referred to any more, even by their own authors—and this is probably not because the ideas they contained have become assimilated into general sociological knowledge, but rather because these ideas have proved to be more or less futile.

The Human Group was a highly ambitious attempt to arrive at 'a new sociological synthesis' in terms of a set of logically coherent propositions about 'the most general social unit', the group. To start with, Homans selected three fundamental categories to serve as the central concepts in his propositions. These categories, indicating 'the elements of social behaviour' which together were supposed to form 'the social system', were activity, interaction and sentiment. Obviously great difficulties arise when we try to demarcate these concepts. The distinction between activity and inter-action only makes sense if we are ready to accept a highly unrealistic image in which 'man' is seen as regularly engaging in 'activities' that have nothing to do with other people. Similarly, the notion of 'sentiments' as referring to a third range of phenomena can only be upheld by defining them as 'internal states of the human body' (Homans, 1950, pp. 37-8)—a behaviouristic pseudo-solution that leaves out virtually all relevant social aspects.

Equipped with this somewhat shaky terminology Homans analyzed five empirical studies of different groups, including Whyte's corner boys and a workers' team at Hawthorne. For each study, he presented a descriptive summary followed by a theoretical interpretation. Some of the propositions he derived from his material have become quite well known, as for example: 'If the frequency of interaction between two or more persons increases, the degree of their liking for one another will increase, and vice versa' (ibid., p. 112). It is not difficult to think of examples confirming this proposition. Negative stereotypes, or prejudices, between groups often reflect the combined result of aversion owing to un-familiarity, and unfamiliarity owing to aversion. But if one has witnessed just once how a romantic love-affair has deteriorated, after a period during which the frequency of interaction has inescapably increased into a bad marriage, one knows that Homans' proposition does not always hold. Soldiers, after interacting with their enemies, or businessmen engaged in cut-throat competition, know likewise.

In order to allow for such necessary exceptions Homans has added to all his propositions the clause 'other things being equal'. This clause is inevitable, given the high level of generality of his propositions. Since the scope of each proposition is, in principle, indefinite, each proposition has to be narrowed down by an equally indefinite proviso. The result is a far cry from the precision which Homans has set out to attain. His second great theoretical monograph, *Social Behaviour: Its Elementary Forms* (1961), is hardly an advance. In this book Homans has moved to an even more emphatically behaviouristic and reductionist stance. Again, he has sought for universal verities; and again he has ended up with propositions so heavily loaded with empirical ambi-guities that they can only float on the same cork labelled 'other things being equal'.

My rejection of Homans' theoretical work is not meant to detract from the value of his earlier studies in the history of

English society. Nor does it imply that all attempts at building general explanatory theories in sociology are bound to be futile. Such attempts are, however, ill-directed if they take the form of constructing deductive-hypothetical systems. Theorists choosing this model cannot but lose sight of the developmental nature of human societies. By singling out a few allegedly unchanging elements, they necessarily restrict the scope of their theories. This process of unavoidable reduction of scope comes to light very clearly in another well-known endeavour to construct a general sociological theory on the apparently simple and universal principle of exchange, Peter Blau's *Exchange and Power in Social Life* (1964). In his introduction Blau writes:

> Social exchange, broadly defined, can be considered to underlie relations between groups as well as those between individuals; both differentiation of power and peer group ties; conflicts between opposing forces as well as co-operation; both intimate attachments and connections between distant members of a community without direct social contacts [Blau, 1964, p. 4].

These words suggest that a theory of exchange will have a very wide scope. Unfortunately, it does not become immediately clear what the concept of social exchange means; one is even left in doubt whether there might be something to be called 'non-social exchange'. Every attempt at clarification Blau makes also implies a restriction. Thus on the very next page he states that 'behaviour resulting from the irrational push of emotional forces without being goal-oriented' is excluded from consideration, and in the chapter that follows we read:

> Reference here is to social relations into which men enter of their own free will rather than to either those into which they are born (such as kinship groups) or those imposed on them by forces beyond their control (such as the combat teams to which soldiers are assigned) [ibid., p. 20].

Of how many social relations can it be said with any certainty at all that they contain no 'irrational push of emotional forces' and that they are based upon wholly voluntary decisions? The answer is bound to detract seriously from Blau's claimed generality. His theory can at best be read as a consistently elaborated metaphor: social life may be viewed as exchange, just as a state may be compared to a ship, or a city to an ant-hill. The image may often be enlightening. It may be appropriate in some cases, and inappropriate in others. For a general sociological theory, however, this is a very weak basis.

Other varieties of formalism in sociology

The works of Parsons, Homans and Blau far from cover the whole gamut of sociological theory. Indeed, so many different sorts of theories can be distinguished that their systematical classification has virtually developed into a sociological specialism of its own (cf. Sorokin, 1928; Martindale, 1960; Wagner, 1963; Wallace, 1971; Mullins, 1974; Ritzer, 1975). Among all the elaborate and pompous classifications, one keeps recurring, though in different formulations. This is the division into what may conveniently be called theories of consensus, theories of conflict, and theories of action. Some writers have tried to explain this threefold distinction as corresponding to some timeless logical principle, e.g. the 'normative, force, and exchange solutions to the Hobbesian problem of order' (Ellis, 1971), or the 'communal, class, and institutional frames of sociological analysis' (Shanin, 1972). However, the classification is far from watertight from a logical point of view. It makes more sense to account for its prevalence by tracing it back to the great ideological movements of the nineteenth century— conservatism, liberalism and marxism (see below, p. 166).

Of the American theorists mentioned above, Parsons has moved from his initial position as an 'action theorist' to become almost the contemporary personification of 'consensus theory'. Homans and Blau as exchange theorists clearly espouse a variant of 'action theory'. Attempts at systematically elaborating 'conflict theories' have been relatively few since the generation of Pareto and Thorstein

Veblen, both of whom were already outsiders in the sociology of their own time. During the last ten or fifteen years, however, several sociologists have again claimed a place for conflict theory (cf. Coser, 1956; Dahrendorf, 1958; Horton, 1966). These claims were largely directed against the prevailing theoretical orientation in American sociology of the 1950s and 1960s, structural-functionalism, which in its most pronounced form represented a mixture of consensus and action theories.

One of the classic statements of structural functionalism in sociology is the essay 'Some Principles of Stratification' by two students of Parsons, Kingsley Davis and Wilbert Moore (1945). In this essay the authors set out to explain, in functional terms, why in every society positions are stratified so that some are accorded higher, others lower prestige and material rewards. The solution they offer is that 'the main functional necessity explaining the universal presence of stratification is . . . the requirement faced by any society of placing and motivating individuals in the social structure'. If a society is to survive, a number of tasks have to be performed, varying in degree of importance, difficulty, and unpleasantness. This challenge can be met through the development of a system of differential rewards:

> Social inequality is thus an unconsciously evolved device
> by which societies insure that the most important
> positions are conscientiously filled by the most qualified
> persons. Hence every society, no matter how simple or
> complex, must differentiate persons in terms of both
> prestige and esteem, and must therefore possess a certain
> amount of institutionalized inequality [Davis and Moore,
> 1945, p. 243].

The theory posits elements of both exchange and consensus: people make certain efforts in return for rewards, and they agree on the respective values of the services and rewards that are being exchanged. For Davis and Moore the elements of exchange preponderate; they hardly address themselves to the problem of how consensus arises. While this emphasis on exchange reflects in some part a perpetuation of the tradition of liberal thought (see below, p. 157), it is probably also inspired by the example of economics, with its neatly-formalized models based on the principle of supply and demand.

In the manner of economists Davis and Moore have succeeded in producing a remarkably simple and 'elegant' theory by adhering to a strictly analytical approach, in which they have deliberately eliminated all factors that might disturb their model. The result is a rather fictitious construction. 'Societies' are represented in a highly reifying way as regulative systems to which all sorts of active functions are ascribed: societies 'place and motivate' individuals in the social structure; they 'distribute' their members in social positions and 'induce' them to perform the duties of these positions; they must 'see to it' that less essential positions do not compete successfully with more essential ones; and so on. The fact that it is a figuration of interdependent individuals who form the society is never mentioned, nor is the possibility even remotely suggested that there may be differences of power chances between various individuals or groups of individuals which may account just as well, if not better, for inequalities in prestige and material rewards.

Such almost platitudinous objections have been raised numerous times (cf. Tumin, 1953). To refute them, Kingsley Davis (1953) haughtily replied that the model represents 'abstract, or theoretical, reasoning' and is not concerned with 'raw empirical generalizations'. The problem is to explain 'stratified inequality as a general property of social systems'—not to put forward descriptive propositions about any particular society. In other, less lofty, words he might well have said: 'Any resemblance to any real society is purely accidental'.

This sentence is, alas, applicable to many specimens of theoretical sociology. There is among sociologists a strong tendency to cultivate systematics for the sake of systematics. Original theorists such as Parsons, Homans, or Davis often display a lively interest in empirical topics. For many commentators, however, the theoretical issues thrown up by these writers soon become objects of interest in their own right. Only thus can it be explained that, for example, Arthur Stinchcombe, arguing in the spirit of Davis and Moore, has suggested as a hypothesis for serious research that 'the greater the importance of positions, the less likely they are to be filled by ascriptive recruitment' (1963, p. 805)—a hypothesis which, if it is to mean anything at all, would imply that such typically 'ascribed' positions as kingship, fatherhood, or motherhood are generally unimportant.

Formal theorizing can become wholly divorced from the original problems to which the theories allegedly refer. Thus, the author of a Dutch study on 'the explanation of conflict' (De Moor, 1961) has managed to devote a whole book to methodological issues without even touching upon one single real conflict. There are many books, like *Modern Social Theory* by Percy Cohen (1968), which contain nothing but formal arguments about sociological concepts with hardly any inkling of the actual problems of interdependent human beings. What Weber considered a painful necessity, that a certain 'estrangement from the world' is the price one has to pay for conceptual clarity and consistency, has become an easy justification for the far-fetched verbal acrobatics of many present-day sociologists. In recent years new inspirations for 'abstract, or theoretical, reasoning' have been found in such fields as the General Systems Theory (e.g., Buckley, 1967), linguistics, French structuralism and phenomenology (e.g., Filmer *et al.*, 1972). For a sample of some results, one may consult the volume *Theoretical Sociology: Perspectives and Developments,* edited by John McKinney and Edward Tiryakian (1970). In the introduction, the editors promise their readers a glimpse of a variety of approaches, both diverging and converging, and constituting, each in its own way, 'evidence of the gradual enrichment of theoretical sociology' (p. 26). Ploughing through the volume, one comes to know a very mixed company of theorists, the majority of whom keep up the appearance of being engaged in 'normal science' by fully excluding any criterion of empirical or practical relevance. Instead, they refer to an 'as-if' world constructed by academics with a strong philosophical penchant. Whoever expects that by reading these exercises in 'sociological theory' he will gain more insight into the problems of interdependent human beings had better prepare himself for the same disappointment that awaited the sailors in the American song:

> We joined the navy
> To see the world.
> But what did we see?
> We saw the sea.

Some critics of 'grand theory' and their alternatives

Rare is the sociologist who would not speak in favour of a closer integration of theory and research. The discrepancy between the verbal systems that pass for theory on the one hand, and the actual world of empirical facts and inquiry on the other, is generally recognized as one of the gravest problems in sociology; deploring it has become almost a standard ritual. Nevertheless, sociologists, once they start spinning theories, again and again get carried away by the figments of their own reasoning and lose their grip on reality. Among those who have criticized and tried to halt this tendency are Robert Merton, Herbert Blumer, C. Wright Mills, and more recently, Barney Glaser and Anselm Strauss.

According to Merton, sociological theory should consist of 'logically interconnected sets of propositions from which empirical uniformities can be derived' (1967, p. 39). This definition excludes various types of work which are often speciously labelled as theory—such as methodology, which deals with the logic of scientific procedure but not with substantive problems; or the formulation of general orientations without, however, setting forth specific hypotheses; or the analysis of concepts, an indispensable phase of theoretical work but not yet theory in the proper sense; or drawing up *post factum* interpretations or empirical generalizations neither of which meet the logical requirements of a theory (ibid., pp. 139-55). By Merton's strict standards sociology is not yet ripe for an all-embracing, unified theory. He rejects the ambitions of Talcott Parsons as being based on extravagant hopes. At the present stage sociologists had better devote their energies to theories of the middle range:

theories that lie between the minor but necessary working
hypotheses that evolve in abundance during day-to-day
research and the all-inclusive systematic efforts to develop
a unified theory that will explain all the observed uniformities of social behaviour, social organization and social
change [ibid., p. 39].

Curiously, when it comes to explaining middle-range theories
in some detail, Merton fails to provide one single example
of such a theory that meets the requirements of his own
definition. His argument unfolds in the same discursive
manner with which he finds fault in the writings of
comprehensive theorists. The most elaborate example he
gives is the theory of 'role set'. His exposition of this theory
amounts to little more than an analysis of the concept of
role, demonstrating that a given 'status' involves not just one
but several 'roles' in the sense of patterns of behaviour. Thus,
the status of a school teacher involves different patterns of
behaviour towards children, parents and colleagues. Although
Merton claims that his notion of 'role set' has fundamental
theoretical implications, all it actually does is to refute the
idea that the incumbents of a certain status will *not* behave
differently towards different people—a rather fantastic idea
which can occur only to sociologists who are so strongly
committed to certain concepts that they have lost sight of
the real world. In order to go to such extremes one must be
over-trained to think in terms of static abstractions rather
than of living human beings. Only after one has been led far
astray by formalistic reasoning may one be in a position to
appreciate Merton's discussion of 'role set' as illuminating.

Thus, while intended to counterbalance the attraction of
general systems of the Parsonian kind, Merton's plea for
theories of the middle range is of little help for freeing
sociologists from their infatuation with systematics. On
closer inspection, his argument serves primarily to preserve
formal rigour in sociological theory, at the cost of substantive
scope. The fact that his own examples fail to meet the
standards he himself sets does not change the programmatic
tenor of his words. The exclusion of general orientations,
concept analysis, *post factum* interpretations and empirical

generalizations from sociological theory pays homage to those philosophers of science who dictate that a theory, to be worthy of its name, has first to meet the canons of logic.

In this respect, Herbert Blumer has gone a step further than Merton. He has done so by carrying the posture of hypothetical-deductive reasoning to its extreme, and demonstrating that it is not feasible in sociology. Because of this strategy his own position is not always free from ambiguities. At times he writes as if he himself were committed to the stance which he uses as a vantage-point for his criticism. Especially in his more recent writings, however, he has moved toward greater consistency.

In 1954 Blumer, then at the University of Chicago, published a paper entitled: 'What is wrong with social theory?' A nodding acquaintance with this paper, as with LaPiere's early critique of survey research, has become part of the stock-in-trade of most sociologists. Nevertheless, most of Blumer's remarks are just as pertinent today as when they were first made. This holds true for his first point, the 'glaring divorcement' of sociological theory 'from the empirical world', as well as for his second and major stricture which is that, in spite of all pretensions to the contrary, the core concepts of sociology are unclear and imprecise and are, therefore, unsuitable for building neat theoretical constructions (Blumer, 1969, pp. 140-52).

Blumer's indictment is, on the whole, still justified. Sociologists continue to cherish an ideal of theory as a highly formalized set of definitions, classifications and propositions applicable at the most general level, whether that level be called 'society', 'social action', or 'social system'. If they attempt to link theory and research at all, they persist in their 'quest for universals' (Turner, 1953) by building timeless theoretical constructs into the design of their empirical inquiries. Specific situations are thus studied not for their own sake, but in search of the universal properties they supposedly manifest. Only those conclusions which can be rendered in the form of timeless propositions count as worthwhile from a scientific point of view. It is tacitly assumed that the concepts used in these propositions are both precise and empirically valid.

In a subsequent paper, dealing with variables in sociological research, Blumer has continued his critique of the way sociologists handle concepts in building theories. He distinguishes in this paper three types of concepts, referring to three sorts of 'variables'. The first type relates to such properties as voting preferences, school education and church membership. Obviously these concepts are bound to specific historical situations: 'Republican', 'high school', or 'Presbyterian' cannot be transmitted from an American to any other social setting. The second group consists of such sociological categories as 'social cohesion', 'social integration', and 'anomie'. These categories are usually defined as if their meaning is not restricted to any specific 'here and now'. As soon as they are related to empirical instances, however, they have to be 'operationalized', that is, they have to be fitted to particular features at hand which can serve as indicators. These indicators 'are tailored and used to meet the peculiar character of the local problem under study' (Blumer, 1969, p. 130). Even the third group of concepts, those referring to demographic attributes like age and sex, which are at first sight universally unambiguous, lose some of their self-evident generality when they are charged with empirical meaning. Most sociologists, however, find such subtleties too awkward. They proceed on the unwarranted assumption that concepts which can be defined in unequivocal terms will always refer to identical social phenomena, regardless of the context in which they are applied.

At the end of his paper Blumer voices some conciliatory notes, attributing to some unspecified uses of variable analysis 'a worthy status in our field' (ibid., p. 139). These mitigations come as an anticlimax in an essay that can be read as a consistently critical plea for realism rather than formalism in sociology. A first requirement for a realistic sociology is that its concepts be flexible—attuned to the protean nature of social figurations. A certain measure of standardization in methods and concepts is, of course, indispensable. What Blumer warns against is the widespread tendency to strive towards *complete* standardization and to be content with nothing less. As an antidote, he offers his notion of 'sensitizing concepts'. It serves as a contrasting alternative to 'definitive concepts' which are circumscribed by a definition in terms of attributes or fixed bench-marks. Since the social world cannot be dissected in such a definitive manner, it is best to study it by means of sensitizing concepts. This is a simple corollary of the recognition that 'what we are referring to by any given concept shapes up in a different way in each empirical instance' (ibid., p. 149).

Most sociologists fail to address themselves to the conceptual problems raised by Blumer. The literature of sociology abounds with monographs and papers written in the style of timeless, universal discourse. Whether it be 'the determinants of leisure behaviour' (Wippler, 1968), or 'the effects of vertical mobility on status inconsistency' (Jackson and Curtis, 1972), or the question of whether the structure of organizations is determined primarily by size or by technology (Child and Mansfield, 1972), time and again certain aspects of human figurations are conceptualized as if they can be studied in the same ahistorical manner as chemical elements or mechanical forces. The contexts from which the aspects are abstracted are treated tacitly as the 'other things' which supposedly remain forever 'equal'.

An awareness of contexts and levels of abstraction is one of the most important assets of what C. Wright Mills (1959) has called the sociological imagination. As Mills points out, this awareness is missing in both 'grand theory' and 'abstracted empiricism'. The practitioners of grand theory are too heavily preoccupied with the logic of their concepts to apply these concepts flexibly to social reality in its varying forms; their work is 'drunk on syntax, blind to semantics' (ibid., p. 34). The abstracted empiricists, narrowly engaged in methodological finesse, lose sight altogether of the larger historical scene from which the 'variables' they are studying derive.

It is in accordance with the style of work Mills is advocating that his programme for sociology cannot be summed up in a set of formal rules. His oft-quoted dictum, 'Every man his own methodologist! Methodologists! Get to work!' oversimplifies his position. Every chapter in *The Sociological Imagination* conveys, underneath the sometimes all-too-easy flow of rhetoric, a sense of the historical, or developmental nature of human societies, and of the need to grasp the context of broader social structures if we wish to understand the course of individual lives. If Mills fails to supply general rules on how to combine 'theory' and 'research', he does give some practical advice. The notes on intellectual craftsmanship with which he concludes his book are probably more helpful for students, and certainly more stimulating, than Merton's point-by-point paradigm for functional analysis (Merton, 1967, pp. 104-8).

In *The Discovery of Grounded Theory* (1967), Barney Glaser and Anselm Strauss have attempted to provide a more solid alternative to the prevailing models of logico-deductive theorizing. The best way to generate theories, they argue, is to do so in the process of research, in a continuous interplay with one's day-to-day observations. In an appealing metaphor they typify the armchair theorists as 'theoretical capitalists', setting the mass of 'proletarian testers' to work on their logically-derived hypotheses. The image aptly catches the spirit in which a sociologist can afford to publish a tome of 600 pages of pure 'theory', prefaced by the casual remark: 'The power of the propositions produced by this theory have [sic] to be tested in empirical research and social action' (Etzioni, 1968, p. x).

The Discovery of Grounded Theory is to be welcomed for its polemical thrust against the excess of deductive reasoning in sociology, and as a plea to relax the standards of quantitative verification. However, it should be noted, first, that the notion of theory espoused by Glaser and Strauss is not quite clear (they mention on p. 3 five 'jobs of theory' which are rather a hodge-podge), and, second, that the examples of grounded theory which they mention with approval are all restricted to what Merton would call 'the middle range'. In their general recommendations for sociology they refer almost exclusively to their own work in American hospitals (cf. Brown, 1973). Feeling no need for a more encompassing theory, they apparently consider all attempts to formulate such a theory as doomed to lapse into logico-deductive system-building. Thus, in contrast to Mills, they renounce the possibility of empirical-theoretical studies of a broad scope.

On the inconsistency of seemingly consistent systems

A critique of the frequent excesses of formal systematics may lead to a profound scepticism of all attempts at systematic theorizing in sociology. One may eventually conclude, with Nietzsche, that all systematicians are to be distrusted and avoided (1889, p. 946). Some sociologists have indeed carefully refrained from system-building. Erving Goffman, for example, seems in each new book to have started afresh with a new terminology. His patent indifference to systematic closure seems to be in line with a general refusal to be pinned down. It is highly questionable, however, whether such a cavalier handling of theory is to be recommended to sociologists in general. In spite of its aberrations into empty formalism, we need systematic theory, if only to clarify the concepts and theorems we use in classifying and explaining the events of the social world—to see how these concepts and theorems are mutually related, and to check their consistency.

Unfortunately there is a long tradition, already rooted in the teaching practices at medieval universities (cf. Ong, 1958), of treating theoretical reasoning as an autonomous activity, divorced from, or at least preceding, demonstration through empirical research. Deductive formalism is, in this respect, the mirror-fallacy of naïve inductionism. Whereas the latter is based on the assumption that 'the facts speak for themselves', according to the former, concepts and propositions have a logic of their own, which can be studied fruitfully without any reference to the empirical world.

This tradition continues to lead sociologists astray. They may become so enthralled by the seductive inner logic of their ideas that they mistake it for a structural property of the society they are studying. They accordingly design beautifully-ordered verbal schemes and diagrams, and let themselves be persuaded that these schemes represent the hidden order of reality. All too often, however, the schemes are only cerebral constructions. In so far as concepts and theorems which are largely devoid of empirical content are made to convey a suggestion of empirical significance, they belong to the category of what Gilbert Ryle (1951) calls 'systematically misleading expressions'. Such expressions enter into many sociological theories, of both the 'grand' and the 'middle-range' type.

To give just one illustrative example, Van Doorn and Lammers present in their textbook *Moderne Sociologie* (1959) the following definition of social control: 'By social control we shall mean: the totality of factors maintaining and restoring certain conditions of equilibrium within a social system' (p. 214). Like so many other definitions in sociology, this one consists in substituting for one term with unclear empirical referents a number of others which are equally ambiguous. Interestingly enough, the authors repeat the same set of words a little further on, this time in a different sequence: 'A certain condition of equilibrium in social life is always the result of the totality of interdependent mechanisms of social control' (ibid., p. 275). This reformulation sounds deceptively like an empirical generalization; all that has been accomplished, however, is a reshaping of the same elusive concepts into a new syntactical figure. Thus, underneath the surface of consistency, there are fundamental inconsistencies.

A system of concepts and theorems may be inconsistent and misleading, and yet have positive functions for those who adhere to it. For one thing, it may give them a sense of intellectual security and superiority. A well-ordered system radiates an aura of full comprehension and understanding; it is this promise which has made grand systems irresistible to many sociologists ever since Comte. For some, the verbal scheme may have served as a substitute for a lost religion, while others may have welcomed it in order to bolster their identity as practitioners of a science which appeared to have relatively little specialist empirical knowledge to boast of. For sociology as a profession, formal theories have undoubtedly served the same dubious purpose as for many other disciplines, viz., to constitute a corpus of esoteric knowledge. Outsiders may thus be impressed and kept at a distance; students will have to pass through a period of learning to know systems past and present in order to earn entrance into the profession.

In the practice of teaching, in particular, many sociologists like to rely on formal theories as objects for exposition, comparison and criticism, and as themes for essays and examinations. They have at their disposal a wide supply of introductory textbooks on theory; in addition, they can draw upon their own talents for 'didactic rationality'. Armed with pen and paper, or, to enlarge the effect, with blackboard and chalk, they can fill hour after hour outlining their own version of the social world to an audience of students. Many students, for their part accustomed in other courses to schemes and diagrams, and soon realizing that little preparation is needed to enter into discussions at this high level of abstraction, are only too eager to have sociology presented to them in the easily-digestible format of a closed theoretical system. Thus, what in other fields, such as physics, is generally recognized as the most difficult part of the discipline, high-level theorizing, is often treated in sociology as a free-for-all.

Too often sociologists have sought conceptual clarity and consistency by means of definitions. However, to quote Nietzsche again, 'definable is only that which has no history' (1887, p. 820). The subject-matter of sociology does not lend itself to itemization in a set of fixed and definitive categories. Working on the language of sociology is indeed a most worthwhile enterprise; we are badly in need of a 'semantics' providing guidance on how to deal with words, as 'statistics' shows us how to deal with figures. But for a sociological terminology to be adequate, it has to be attuned to a few substantive principles: that sociology is about people; that people form changing figurations; that the processes of change are by and large unplanned; and that the formation of knowledge is itself a social process the results of which are necessarily relative. These principles are not to be treated as 'axioms' from which other propositions follow deductively; they are to serve as reminders of what sociology actually is about, of the order of reality to which any set of sociological concepts and theorems is to refer.

Viewed in this light, several theoretical movements of today are to be regarded with suspicion, because they proceed from assumptions which violate these fundamental principles. In structuralism, to name one well-known trend, there is a strong tendency to study 'structures' as constituting a level of reality in its own right which can be reduced to static binary oppositions (cf. Glucksmann, 1974). Similarly, in phenomenology, the emphasis tends to fall so heavily on man as an individual subject who experiences the world that neither social interdependence nor social development can be adequately conceptualized. If structuralists or phenomenologists try, nevertheless, to take these obvious features of the social world into account, it is at the price of inconsistency, for at the very core of their theories is a built-in systematic bias against viewing societies as the forever-changing figurations formed by interdependent human beings.

4

Problems of Scope
in Sociology

Early developmental theories: Comte and Marx

Specialists, so the saying goes, are people who know more and more about less and less. Sociologists, if they wish to count as serious experts, are exposed to strong pressures to specialize, either in some branch of empirical research, or in a particular type of theorizing. To most contemporary sociologists, 'scope' will sound a slightly antiquated and unprofessional ideal of knowledge, evoking irony or nostalgia as the case may be. They will consider it the inevitable outcome of an irreversible trend that sociology has become one academic specialism among others, a specialism that is itself being split up into an increasing number of sub-specialisms.

Probably the first to formulate clearly a sociological theory of the division of labour and specialization was Adam Smith. Today it is often forgotten that, before the eighteenth century, neither the concept 'division of labour' nor any sociological theory dealing with it was available. It is quite customary nowadays to attribute such a theory to Plato (e.g., Sabine, 1951, pp. 57-8; see also Marx, 1867, pp. 387-88). However, the central concept in Plato's theory of inequality is 'justice'; nowhere does he use the concept 'division of labour'. The gist of his theory, moreover, runs counter to modern sociological ideas. According to Plato, men are born with different aptitudes, fitting them for different occupations: some are born to rule, others to fight, still others to toil. The differences between rulers, soldiers, and slaves, performing their respective duties for the state, correspond to natural, inbred talents. The most just state is that in which the diverse talents can unfold to their best mutual advantage. For more than two thousand years this Platonic doctrine has prevailed in political philosophy. Against this background, Adam Smith's formulations on the same subject form a great innovation (for other aspects of Smith's modernity, cf. Medick, 1973, pp. 244-6).

> The difference of natural talents in different men is, in reality, much less than we are aware of; and the very different genius which appears to distinguish men of different professions, when grown up to maturity, is not upon many occasions so much the cause as the effect of the division of labour [Smith, 1776, p. 19].

Today, economists usually claim Adam Smith as one of the founders of their science. Smith himself never used this label. He called his own profession moral philosophy, and contributed liberally to areas which today would be reckoned to belong to psychology, sociology and political science. In his time there was only a rudimentary division of labour in the field of social studies; for a man of Smith's capacities it was still possible to encompass most of it.

Auguste Comte embraced an even wider range of subjects. With his positive philosophy he intended to provide a new synthesis for all human sciences, from mathematics through astronomy, physics, chemistry, and biology to sociology. As a justification for this ambitious undertaking he pointed to the very process of specialization. It was by virtue of specialization that human knowledge had grown prodigiously; but this very same beneficial process also threatened to destroy the unity of knowledge and the mutual understanding between the practitioners of the various sciences. The time had come to carry the process of specialization one step further, to fill the obvious remaining gap by adding one more class of specialists: the generalists, devoted to the study of the relations and interconnections between the various particular sciences. Their task would be

to restore the broken synthesis, by examining and demonstrating how the results of the special sciences hang together.

The over-arching perspective within which a synthesis
could be built up was to be found in sociology. The most
fundamental point to be grasped in order to understand the
development of the sciences was, according to Comte, the
fact that men as social beings have the capacity to learn from
each other. Through the ages humanity has moved through
a process of intellectual evolution in which, from one
generation to the next, a great stock of knowledge has been
accumulated. Men's physiological preconditions for learning
can be explained biologically; the actual growth of human
knowledge, however, is a sociological phenomenon. A sociological theory is needed not only to explain how humanity
has moved through the theological and the metaphysical
stages to reach the present positive stage, but also why
specialization has proceeded most quickly in those sciences
dealing with the least complex phenomena of physical
matter, while it has lagged in the most complex areas of
human thought and action.

The study of human society confronts us with great
problems owing to the vastness, the heterogeneity and the
complexity of the subject. Elaborating an aphorism of Pascal,
Comte states that sociology 'represents men in the mass as
constituting in the present, past, and future, both in place
and time, one immense social unit, whose various individual
or national organs, in their intimate and universal solidarity,
necessarily contribute each according to its mode and degree
to the evolution of humanity' (1838, p. 177). The development of humanity as a whole is 'the real scientific subject'
(ibid., p. 167). Unless this insight is fully grasped, sociology
cannot come into its own. What happens in the present can
only be understood in the context of what has happened in
the past. What is happening here can only be understood in
the context of the interdependencies with human beings
elsewhere. Therefore, 'no social fact can have any real
scientific significance unless it is immediately associated with
some other social fact; isolated, it necessarily remains in the
sterile state of mere anecdote, capable at most of satisfying a
vain curiosity, but incapable of meeting any rational need'

(ibid., p. 183). Since it is above all in their development that the different social elements are necessarily interdependent and inseparable (ibid., p. 193), a historical method is needed, proceeding from a general conception of social evolution. The study of society rests on two basic tenets: first, there is always 'the obligation, in social studies, of making the spirit of the whole predominate, by always proceeding from the system to its elements' (ibid., p. 184), and second, in order to emphasize how each generation is linked to its predecessors (and its successors), the historical method is the best means of sociological investigation (ibid., p. 198).

Leaving aside Comte's premature efforts to canonize his own ideas into a rigid system, we can only admire the power of synthesis with which he brought together many aspects of knowledge that in his own time were already rapidly drifting apart into disconnected departments. The conception sustaining his synthesis was the conception of social development. It was by reconstructing the fragmentation of knowledge as a social process that Comte was able to discover the underlying connections among the divergent sciences of his day.

Similarly, a developmental perspective informed the synthesis achieved by Marx and Engels. As they wrote in *The German Ideology* (1847, p. 346): 'We know only one single science, the science of history'. In the great majority of commentaries much more has been said about the obvious differences between Comte and Marx (cf. Marcuse, 1955) than about certain basic similarities which can be observed as well (cf. Fletcher, 1974). Of course, while according to Comte 'ideas rule and transform the world', Marx sought the key with which to explain social development in the modes of material production. Moreoever, although Comte was by no means blind to the struggles through which humanity had to pass—combatting the theologians and metaphysicians of his own time was one of his vital concerns—he emphasized consensus as a precondition for progress. Any such accentuation of ideas and consensus was anathema to Marx: if social development was to be understood in terms of changing modes of production, the first point to be grasped was that for long periods the course of human history had been, as it still continued to be, determined by the bitter struggle for control over the means of production and the social product.

Already in his early, unpublished writings Marx had made a firm stand against philosophical idealism. Most philosophers, he argued, suffered from professional deformation. They were so immersed in books and ideas that they mistook the world of ideas for the real world. They saw human beings as moved only by thought; they forgot that in order to think, men must eat. Human beings were made of flesh and blood, and only after their basic physical needs were fulfilled, could they begin to philosophize. That German philosophers could spend their lives writing books and delivering lectures was made possible by virtue of material conditions not of their own making. These material conditions were the outcome of a long and continuing development, encompassing countless generations, and tainted with strife and misery. A society's mode of production, including the division of labour and the distribution of property, was at the core of people's social existence; it entered into their whole experience of the world in ways the philosophers did not dare to fathom.

There were, of course, such philosophers as Feuerbach who called themselves materialists. For them, however, materialism was still just another philosophy, the far-reaching implications of which they failed to grasp. If, as Feuerbach allegedly said, 'man is what he eats', the truism should be added at once that, in contemporary society, no single person produces all the food he eats. The satisfaction of hunger and other vital needs is more than an individual affair; and far from being ahistoric, timeless givens, both the structure of the needs and the potential for satisfying them depend on the particular stage in the development of the forces of production. No one can hope to understand human beings and human societies unless he clearly recognizes this fundamental principle. As Marx later stated in the preface to the *Critique of Political Economy* (1859), this was the general conclusion to which his early studies had led him, and which continued to serve as a guideline for all his further investigations:

In the social production of their life, people enter into

relations that are definite, indispensable and independent
of their will; these relations of production correspond to a
definite stage in the development of their material pro-
ductive forces. The totality of these relations of
production constitutes the economic structure of society,
the real basis, on which rises a legal and political super-
structure and to which correspond definite forms of social
consciousness. The mode of production of material life
conditions the social, political and spiritual process of life
in general. It is not the consciousness of men that
determines their being, but, on the contrary, their social
being that determines their consciousness [Marx, 1859,
pp. 8-9].

This is probably the most frequently quoted, and commented
upon, passage in sociology. Its implications for the study of
society are far-reaching. In it Marx breaks once and for all
with the tradition of viewing various aspects of society—such
as religion, philosophy, law and morality—as autonomous
spheres. Instead he holds that these aspects are all interconnected and bear the imprint of men's struggle for the
means of subsistence—which includes not only a struggle
against the forces of nature but, no less important, among
men themselves. As Norbert Elias remarks:

Marx perceived as structured and thus gave scientific
standing to the fact that men have to make efforts in order
to satisfy their elementary needs and to find the
wherewithal of life, and that the changing conditions for
getting or producing them . . . are aspects of their social
lives which one has to include in one's studies if one wants
to account for the long-term development of societies as
well as their structure and momentum at any given time.
This changed view of societies was a great step forward on
the road of discovery of the specifically *social* character of
that which binds people to each other in the form of
societies and which often enough by binding them also
antagonizes them and drives them against each other
[Elias, 1971, p. 153].

However, as Elias also indicates, in his battle against the

intellectual traditions of philosophy and history writing, Marx tended to take a stand of literal opposition which was still tied to the very opinions he strove against. Take for example the sentence: 'It is not the consciousness of men that determines their being, but, on the contrary, their social being that determines their consciousness'. In the polemical context from within which this statement was written it makes good sense. Nevertheless, it posits an untenable contradiction between 'social being' and 'consciousness'. How are we to conceive of 'social being' *without* 'consciousness'? The moment that we realize the impossibility, it becomes clear—although we may be in full sympathy with the statement's intended meaning—that it is inconsistent and self-contradictory. It points to a most important relationship, but in a conceptually inadequate way. (As if one were to say: 'It is not breathing which determines life, but, on the contrary, life determines breathing'.)

It was one of Marx's great insights to perceive the economic features of capitalism as fundamentally social: to see that 'capital' did not exist independently in itself, but only as a relationship between persons, 'mediated by objects' (Marx, 1867, p. 793). Yet, at the same time, he saw everything social as so thoroughly permeated by economic factors as to be, in the last resort, conditioned by them. This led him to use, in many characteristic passages, the language of law-like formulations employed by the economists of his age. He emphatically stated that *Capital* was about 'the natural laws of capitalist production' (ibid., p. 12); if it dealt with persons, it did so only in so far as these persons were 'the personification of economic categories, the representatives of definite class relationships and interests' (ibid., p. 20). Individual capitalists were treated only as 'capital, endowed with will and consciousness' (ibid., p. 168); capital was described as having its own inexorable momentum, driven by a 'vital urge to multiply itself' (ibid., p. 247).

Because of its uncompromising emphasis on the interweaving of economic and other social conditions, Marx's approach has proved very effective in opening up an enormous range of problems for empirical investigation: how to relate the religion, morality, law and science of particular groups in particular eras to the prevailing mode of production. This approach has been followed by many writers, and not only those who have placed themselves within the Marxist tradition. At least as many sociologists, economists and historians—ranging from Weber and Pareto to J.A. Schumpeter and Alexander Ruestow—who are highly critical of Marx, have profited greatly from his insights and have never made a secret of their indebtedness to him.

Still, as more than one critic has remarked, 'man is producer, thinker, warrior, and each must be taken into account if we are to do justice to him' (Leff, 1969, p. 134). The singular form 'man' in which the criticism is expressed may be somewhat inappropriate, and the list 'producer, thinker, warrior' is certainly not exhaustive—it does not cover, for example, people's libidinous or affective valencies ('man' as 'lover'). Yet the upshot is clear and compelling. Besides the social organization of production, there are other aspects of human figurations which command the sociologist's attention, such as the organization of physical security, the organization of knowledge and the organization of affections and affect controls. In each of these respects the history of human societies reveals certain patterns. The great achievement of the sociologists of the nineteenth century has been to point to these patterns, and to try to explain them. They have demonstrated clearly that human societies are involved in processes of structured development. However, in trying to explain the nature and causes of social development, they have tended to attribute too strong an autonomous impact to certain processes, such as the growth of knowledge or the development of the means of production. But all these aspects are so deeply inter-related that it seems impossible, given the present state of our knowledge, to separate any single one of them and brand it as *the* universal driving force.

Durkheim's definition of sociology

'Unboundedness is the curse of sociology'. These words by the Dutch sociologist Rudolf Steinmetz (1927, p. 2) voiced the opinion of many first-generation academic sociologists. For most of them the far-reaching claims made by their nineteenth century predecessors were a source of embarrassment. They found themselves faced with a twofold problem: first, to demonstrate that sociology need not be speculative system-building, but could rather be based on proper scholarship and scientific method, and, second, so to define its subject-matter as not to infringe on already-established disciplines. The two sets of problems were narrowly related; together they gave rise to intensive discussions about the scope and methods of sociology.

Among the founders of sociology as a university subject, Durkheim came closest to continuing the expansionist tradition of nineteenth-century sociology (cf. Lukes, 1973, pp. 392-409). In his writings, language, morality, religion, law, education and all other manifestations of human culture are viewed as 'social facts', explicable only in connection with other 'social facts'. The human condition thus appears *sub specie societatis*: the beliefs people adhere to, the ideals and ambitions they cherish, and their chances of realizing these ideals and ambitions are all seen as depending on the collectivities to which they belong. Only one aspect of human social life is excluded: individual psychology. In line with this approach, little attention is paid to biography or to history in any personal sense. This probably reflects the composition of Durkheim's intellectual interests as well as his reluctance to trespass on the territory of psychologists and historians.

The study of suicide (1897) well exemplifies Durkheim's approach. The problem he posed was not new: how to explain the regularities in suicide rates for various countries. Various factors had been proposed, including mental illness, race and heredity, climate, season, and the tendency toward imitation. By discarding these factors one by one in a clever statistical analysis, Durkheim cleared the way for his own, sociological, account—which he presented as superior to the rejected psychiatric, genetic, climatological and social-psychological theories. The *raison d'être* of sociology was thus established by demonstrating the failure of other disciplines to account for the registered facts.

Durkheim's own interpretation has not proved to be immune to criticism, however (cf. Douglas, 1967). The theoretical concepts he used (egoism, altruism and anomie) are lacking in clarity and consistency; these concepts are, moreover, too easily superimposed upon the empirical materials, the suicide statistics; and even the statistics themselves may not be fully reliable. Nevertheless, in spite of these criticisms, no-one has yet succeeded in providing a more satisfactory explanation of suicide rates. Durkheim's general idea, that the propensity of people to end their own life is related to the integration of the social units to which they belong (or, in other words, to the sort of solutions they have found for the problems of living together), is an insight that has not lost its plausibility. It is difficult, however, to express it in a way that is both internally consistent and in keeping with all the known empirical facts.

While paying due respect to his colleagues in psychology, Durkheim left it beyond any doubt that in his perspective sociological factors predominate over psychological factors. What human beings are capable of, what they allow or forbid themselves and each other, what they desire and what they detest–all this is determined primariy by the groups to which they belong, and by the pressures and the constraints which these groups exert upon them. Seeking psychological explanations for social phenomena is putting the cart before the horse, for psychological factors are shaped in the process of living together, in society. As individuals we are, to a far larger extent than we usually realize, 'products of society':

> there is in us a host of states which something other than ourselves—that is to say, society—expresses in, or through us. Such states constitute society itself, living and acting in us. Certainly society is greater than, and goes beyond, us, for it is infinitely more vast than our individual being; but at the same time it enters into every part of us. It is outside us and envelops us, but it is also in us and is everywhere an aspect of our nature. We are fused with it. Just as our physical organism gets its nourishment outside itself, so our mental organism feeds itself on ideas, sentiments, and practices that come to us from society [Durkheim, 1902-1906, p. 71].

This passage clearly demonstrates the conceptual difficulties which Durkheim's sociological train of thought leads us into. 'Society' is here made to appear as something existing over and above individuals, enveloping them and penetrating into them. In the fervour of dethroning the image of man as a separate individual, wholly the product of 'psychological' forces, Durkheim seizes upon the notion of society as an entity in its own right, surrounding men and imbuing them with its spirit. Instead of conceptualizing human figurations in terms of interdependent individuals exerting intended and unintended influences upon each other, he is led to regard society as something apart from the individuals who compose it. The image of the penetration of society in the individual has remained popular in sociology to the present day. It has been adopted by Talcott Parsons among others, and it has become one of the standard metaphors of sociology. Thus Peter Berger, somewhat oblivious of its origin, writes with deceptive fluency:

> Society, then, is not only something 'out there', in the Durkheimian sense, but it is also 'in here', part of our innermost being . . . Society not only controls our movements, but shapes our identity, our thought and our emotions. The structures of society become the structures of our own consciousness. Society does not stop at the surface of our skins. Society penetrates us as much as it envelops us [Berger, 1963, p. 121].

In the sociology of Durkheim the tendency to reify the concept of society goes with an emphasis on those factors that strengthen the unity and the integration of societies. In this respect Durkheim follows the tradition of Comte and not Marx. In America Talcott Parsons has greatly contributed to the reception of precisely this aspect of Durkheim's work. Parsons has put the problem of order into the centre of sociology; and he has allotted to sociology in particular the task of investigating the normative-integrative aspect of social systems. If this is indeed the central subject for sociology, one can only agree with the lament voiced by Robert Bierstedt toward the end of the turbulent 1960s:

We have in sociology a discipline that can deal with an
orderly society—there are canons and criteria, laws and
norms, statuses and roles, customs and institutions, that
explain the social order—but not with a shattered society,
torn with dissension, rent by violence, and tending to a
disorder that leads to anarchy and ultimately to anomy
[Bierstedt, 1969, p. 152].

It is somewhat paradoxical that Bierstedt delivers an
unambiguous sociological commentary (and even a
prediction) on developments which, according to his own
words, lie beyond the reach of sociology. This seemingly
incompatible combination of scholarly scepticism and bold
generalization occurs all too often, especially among those
who speak out strongly against the claims of a far-reaching
sociology. They apply severe canons of science by which they
condemn any attempt to design sociological theories of a
large scope; at the same time they freely indulge in sweeping
statements about what is going on in the world.

Durkheim's writings compare very favourably with the
vagaries of these contemporary social scientists. There is a
direct continuity between his sociological theory and his
comments on morality, education and politics. Because of its
wide implications his work has inspired practitioners of
various social studies and has imbued them with a sociological way of thinking. When, in 1935, Célestin Bouglé drew
up a balance-sheet of French sociology, he could demonstrate
the radiation of Durkheimian ideas to psychology, ethnology,
history and political economy. Of particular interest are the
writings of the historians grouped around the journal
Annales; although explicit references to Durkheim may be
few, they display an interest in social bonds (Marc Bloch) and
collective representations (Lucien Febvre) that is closely akin
to Durkheim. Only gradually is a similar 'sociologization' of
historiography gaining ground in England and the United
States.

The 'social action' approach and its limitations

Next to Durkheim, the most influential definition of the

domain of sociology has been that given by Max Weber. In the methodological introduction to *Economy and Society* (1922) Weber takes as his point of departure individual action, and thence proceeds very cautiously towards concepts which refer to larger social structures and institutions. Individual action is visible and intelligible; it lends itself to sociological observation and understanding. Social structures, on the other hand, are much more difficult to grasp. We cannot see them; all we can do is assume that they are operative in bringing about certain observable effects which we cannot otherwise explain. Social institutions, according to this argument, merely exist in the complementary actions of single individuals; the only way to understand the functioning of large organizations such as states, churches, business corporations or political parties is by considering the question:

> Which motives *prompt*, and *have prompted* the single functionaries of this 'corporation' to act in such a manner that it has come into existence and continues to exist? [Weber, 1922, p. 13].

This question, pointing to the motives of individual human beings, is indeed an important one. It can serve as a warning against the tendency exhibited by sociologists both of a Marxian and a Durkheimian persuasion to reify social structures, to treat them as existing independently of the will of individual people. Taken literally, however, the stance known as 'methodological individualism' (cf. Agassi, 1960) leaves very little scope for sociology. Instead of regarding social institutions as 'things' Weber reduces them to 'ideal types', mental constructions invented for the sake of systematic explanation. From the denial that social structures as such can be known other than as ideal-typical abstractions from individual motives, it is but a small step to a highly formalistic conception of sociology: for if our concepts do not in the last resort refer to any recognizable historical reality, the sole test of classifications and theories lies in their internal logic. The result may be a quest of systematics for the sake of systematics (cf. Moore, 1958, pp. 89-110).

If sociologists are to focus upon individual action and

individual motives, the question arises how to distinguish sociology from psychology. Weber's answer to this problem is that the subject-matter of sociology is not individual behaviour in general but only meaningful social action, that is, action consciously directed toward other people. As illustrations of actions falling outside this definition he mentions an individual prayer and, today a slightly antiquated example, the unintended collision between two cyclists. Both examples are unfortunate in that they suggest that praying or riding a bicycle are activities which can be understood independently from the social development of religion and technology. Weber's formulations obviously run counter to Durkheim's, for they imply that an act of suicide is not to be regarded as a social action (and a proper subject for sociological study), unless it can be firmly established that the deed has been consciously 'directed toward others'. The very difficulty of establishing this demonstrates how elusive the distinction is between 'individual' and 'social'.

These problems were seen very clearly by Weber's contemporary, Georg Simmel. Yet, in spite of great sophistication in treating the issue, his writings also display a bias towards regarding 'the individual' as more real than 'society':

> Society is merely the name for a number of individuals, connected by interaction . . . Groping for the tangible, we find only individuals; and between them, only a vacuum, as it were [Simmel, 1917, pp. 10-11].

This seemingly obvious idea that individuals are more tangible than societies is deceptive. The tangible aspects of human beings, those by which people can be weighed and measured in physical terms, are the corporal aspects. Concepts like 'individual' and 'personality' serve to indicate, just as the concept 'society', aspects of human beings that are only partially tangible; they refer, so to speak, to a psycho-social universe with more dimensions. In their material aspects, societies are no less tangible, visible, and audible than individuals. Of course one is well advised to avoid the fallacy of misplaced concreteness. This advice applies equally, however, to the concepts 'individual' and 'society'; neither one is more 'concrete' than the other.

Like Durkheim, Simmel was well aware that human culture is 'social' in every fibre. As the inevitable corollary of this insight he concluded that if sociology were to be the science of the 'social' in all its ramifications, it would have to include the study of language, religion, law, art and every other aspect of human social life. In order to rescue sociology from this overwhelming assignment Simmel suggested that it should focus on one general aspect of social reality: the forms of social interactions. Structures of domination and subjection, competition, division of labour, party formation, delegation, solidarity and hostility–these would constitute a proper subject for sociological investigation. Such a definition would clearly demarcate sociology from, on the one hand, the substantive study of language, art and so on, and, on the other hand, individual psychology.

In their methodological writings both Weber and Simmel tried to single out a range of phenomena to be designated as specifically 'social'. Their notions of social action and social interaction have continued to play an important part as core concepts in the further development of sociology. In addition, the notion of social role, first introduced by George Herbert Mead, has become very important. Referring to the standard patterns according to which individuals in particular positions and situations model their behaviour, this concept makes it possible to combine the tenets of an 'action approach' with a distinctly Durkheimian idea of normative social constraint. Its implications have been clearly outlined by Ralf Dahrendorf in his well-known essay on *homo sociologicus.*

Homo sociologicus is, according to Dahrendorf, the counterpart of *homo economicus* or 'psychological man'. It represents the one-sided image of man on which sociology is built: the image of man as an actor, a performer of roles, whose behaviour is explicable and predictable on account of the social positions he occupies and the role patterns incumbent on those positions. Characteristically, *homo sociologicus* appears in Dahrendorf's exposition as an image in the singular form. As a single individual, a person in our contemporary society may often experience the restraints of rules and norms as coming from outside himself, as alien to his own inner being. These experiences confront him with what Dahrendorf calls 'the vexatious fact of society'. It is in this vexatious fact of society, forcing man to play the part of a role-performer, that Dahrendorf sees the subject-matter for sociology. By the same token, the limits of sociology are set. For sociological analysis cannot reveal man in his capacity as a unique, autonomous individual, 'free from any bond to society' (Dahrendorf, 1967, p. 183). The knowledge that a person is a man, a father, a protestant, a schoolteacher gives us a fair impression of the setting within which he spends his days; but it is a picture that remains incomplete:

> Whether he is a good or a bad teacher, a severe or a gentle
> father, whether he manages to come to terms with his
> emotional conflicts or not, whether he is satisfied with
> his life or not, what sort of opinions about his fellow men
> he holds for himself, where he would like to spend his
> holidays—all this and much more we cannot come to know
> on the basis of his social positions and what we can deduce
> from them [ibid., p. 142].

This interpretation is, in spite of a certain surface plausibility, highly questionable. It suggests that society consists of sets of fixed, formal role definitions which do not really affect the inner lives of the individuals performing the roles. This is a very static and unrealistic view. It simply takes for granted that the roles are there, without examining how they have originated and developed as the more or less standardized ways in which people have learned to cope with certain recurring problems of social existence. A study of the sociogenesis of roles is likely to reveal, underneath the 'mutual expectations', power contests and emotional tensions (cf. Elias, 1950). The separation of social roles from individual feelings is in accord with deeply-rooted traditions of literary romanticism and political liberalism. But it is none the less thoroughly unsociological. It ignores the basic fact that human beings are interdependent, not just in the satisfaction of materials wants and cognitive needs, but also in their emotions. An image of *homo sociologicus* which omits this fact can be no more than an empty abstraction, a shallow 'construction of the intellect' (Dahrendorf, 1967, p. 187).

Further restriction of scope

Sociologists today are exposed to a variety of pressures impelling them to restrict the scope of their work. It is impossible for anyone to keep up with the enormous literature of sociology; any attempt to do so is doomed to fail miserably. Out of sheer self-protection, sociologists feel forced to specialize in the study of some particular area or aspect of society. Consequently the field as a whole tends to fall apart, as there is no generally accepted overall perspective within which the various specialisms can be integrated. The few men who called themselves sociologists in the nineteenth century all worked on problems of a very large scope; today only a very small minority of the profession do so. Although it is not difficult to explain this trend, there are plenty of reasons to regret it, and to look for possibilities of arresting and reversing it. The absence of an overall perspective is clearly to the disadvantage of the practitioners of the various specialisms, who are deprived of the means of accounting for the multiplicity of forces at play within their own field of investigation. They may possess very effective tools of analysis; but they lack the power of synthesis, of relating their findings to the continuing development of larger figurations (cf. Elias and Scotson, 1965, pp. 1-12).

The so-called experiments in the Relay Assembly Test Room at Hawthorne provide a telling illustration. By concentrating exclusively on one problem, the relation between morale and productivity within a single workshop, the investigators failed to see that the women working in the test room formed a part of wider social figurations, and that the pressures of these wider figurations impinged upon the situation on the shop floor. Besides neglecting the home circumstances of the workers, the investigators also showed hardly any interest either in the Hawthorne plant as a whole (they never mentioned in their major report, *Management and the Worker*, that trade unions were forbidden) or in the world outside the plant. Their research was terminated in 1932, not because it was completed, but because of the Depression. Roethlisberger and Dickson reported this as a mere 'external fact', having nothing to do with the actual problems they had been studying. An industrial sociology which is so narrowly confined to the specific situation within a factory can yield little more than precise factual information of a very limited scope. The same is true of other empirical specialisms: if they are not informed by a broader orientation, their findings are necessarily impaired by the illusion that longer-term developments and further-reaching interdependencies are of no importance.

Similar restrictions apply to those sociologists who specialize not in a particular institutional area such as industry, education or medicine, but who concentrate solely on certain aspects of social life, like face-to-face communication. The work of Erving Goffman is a case in point. Goffman is generally admired for his acute observations of the strategies people employ in their routine dealings with each other. He has succeeded in capturing his observations in salient turns of phrase, a mixture of colloquial idiom and academic jargon. All his writings exhibit a peculiar elusiveness, however. In his first book, *The Presentation of Self in Everyday Life* (1959) he employed what he called a dramaturgical perspective, looking at interaction *as if* it consisted of theatrical performances. In a concluding chapter he disclosed that his whole approach was just one way of looking at interaction—others being the technical, the political, the structural and the cultural points of view, a quartet clearly reminiscent of Parsons' AGIL system. How the various approaches were inter-related, Goffman did not reveal. In subsequent books he never returned to the issue; in fact, each new book was written as an attempt from scratch to capture interaction processes in a particular metaphorical terminology. The metaphors are often illuminating, but they remain disconnected. Moreover, since Goffman's attention is devoted entirely to the occurrences within a given social setting, he never bothers to inquire how that setting has developed within wider networks of power. Consequently, in spite of its occasional brilliance, his sociology remains rather flat. At his best, Goffman approaches the aphoristic lucidity of La Rochefoucauld; but especially in his later writings he is often sidetracked in the kind of learned academic digressions that too many sociologists habitually mistake for 'theory'.

Harold Garfinkel's 'ethnomethodology' is another example of the widespread tendency to restrict the scope of sociology. The basic problem to which Garfinkel originally addressed himself is undoubtedly an important one: in presenting avowedly 'rational' accounts of the social world, sociologists are engaging in activities that are not essentially different from what laymen are doing—on what grounds then do they justify that their versions of social reality are superior? Garfinkel's persistence in raising this fundamental issue is quite understandable as a reaction against the spurious mood of self-confidence that dominated sociology in the 1950s. In tackling it, however, Garfinkel has moved to the other extreme, to a stance where nothing is taken for granted any more. Durkheim, who also advocated suspension of all pre-existing notions about social reality, is criticized as not having practised what he preached. In a radical fashion, no structure of social interdependence, no process of social development is acknowledged as 'known'. Instead, it is deemed necessary to see every situation as constituting a 'here and now', displaying perhaps to the innocent sociologist an appearance of familiarity, but actually completely alien and un-understood in its underlying nature. From these starting-points Garfinkel and his students have moved as theorists to elaborate philosophical analysis, and as empirical researchers to minute examination of interaction. In both respects they are deliberately oblivious of long-term developments and wide-ranging interdependencies. As so often, behind their stance of extreme scepticism and subjectivity there seems to be a quest for certainty and objectivity: to find unchanging 'deep structures' of interaction analogous to the 'deep structures' allegedly underlying human speech (cf. Garfinkel, 1967; Garfinkel and Sacks, 1970).

Emulation of modern linguistics is not confined to the school of ethnomethodology. Several other attempts have been made lately to redefine the subject-matter of sociology in such a manner as to reduce it to static elements, comparable to phonemes and morphemes. Thus the avowed aim of a group of sociological structuralists is to discover 'the structures [patterns] formed by . . . fundamental behaviours':

> Fundamental behaviours parallel morphemes in linguistics; similarly, the status and role construction tasks in structuralism parallel the sentence construction task in linguistics. The ways in which status roles articulate into structural systems of roles parallel syntax. Structuralists interpret the relationship(s) of unit behaviours to one another as providing an explanation for behaviour within specific social systems [Mullins, 1973, p. 257] .

As Claude Lévi-Strauss has abundantly shown, an orientation toward linguistic structuralism does not preclude one from covering a wide range of problems. However, the bias towards static reductionism already apparent in Lévi-Strauss' own writings has become predominant in the works of some of his followers. Like the ethnomethodologists, they retreat into a world of their own, occupied by minute empirical investigations and subtle scholastic disputes. They are so immersed in their schematic 'structures' that they forget about the world of living human beings.

Again, it should be stressed that the restriction of scope in contemporary sociology is not a matter of caprice on the part of certain nameable groups. The movement to restrict scope has been going on for at least half a century. Since Rudolf Steinmetz (1927) called lack of boundaries the curse of sociology, sociologists have felt compelled again and again to lift that curse, if not for the field as a whole then at least for themselves, and to narrow down their competence to those areas where they can feel sure of working with reasonably solid facts and reasonably consistent concepts. Together, these individual sociologists have brought about the development of sociology to its present state of fragmentation.

Figurations: human beings in the plural

Under the pressures of academic specialization sociologists

have come to relish impressively abstract definitions of their discipline, such as 'sociology is the study of systems of action and of their interrelations' (Inkeles, 1964, p. 16). Such definitions are a far cry from the original idea that the aim of sociology is to provide us with means for orientatir͡g ourselves in the social world of human beings. They represent society in terms of depersonalized 'its', social systems, instead of living people, of 'we, you and them'.

Perhaps a more lively formulation is to be preferred. *In sociology we study the ways in which people cope with the problems of social interdependence.* Like the definition by Alex Inkeles, this statement combines a description and a programme. In a descriptive sense it is somewhat vague, but it is not wrong. More important, however, is its programmatic thrust: an explicit reminder that in sociology we are concerned with people, for whom social interdependence never ceases to be a source of problems with which they must somehow cope.

It may be noted that the formulation is in agreement with the four points of departure mentioned in Chapter 1. The plural 'people' does full justice to the fact that people are bonded to each other in figurations (1). Coping with the problems of interdependence is a process which never comes to an end: every 'solution' people hit upon is bound to create new problems, for themselves and for others; in this respect the formulation directly implies that human figurations are in flux (2), and that their dynamics are by and large unplanned and unintended (3). The term 'problems' also helps to bring out the important part played by knowledge in the development of figurations (4).

Not quite superfluously, the plural 'people' underlines that sociology is about men, women, and children, and not about man in the singular. People can only survive and develop in groups; this is even confirmed by the few documented cases of men who have lived by themselves for several years (cf. Kroeber, 1961). After having lost or severed virtually all human contact these men could survive only thanks to the knowledge and skills they had already acquired 'as a member of society' (cf. Tylor, 1871, p. 1).

There is, however, a time-honoured tradition to speak of 'man' in the male, singular form. More than twenty-five hundred years ago Protagoras remarked: 'man is the measure of all things', an excellent insight which could be expressed more cogently, however, in the plural. Descartes' *cogito ergo sum* is emphatically couched in the singular form: *I* think, therefore *I* am,—as if it were possible to conceive of this thought and to express it without ever having been in contact with other people. Pascal's famous sentence 'man is a thinking reed' is more realistic, for in spite of its grammatical form it evokes an image of a plurality: a reed stalk rarely grows in isolation.

Many sociologists have taken up the habit of talking of 'man' in the singular. The singular is used in the titles of journals (*Man and Society* being a favourite in various languages, from Russian to Dutch) and books like *Culture Against Man* (Henry, 1963) or *Man in Society* (Van den Berghe, 1975). Ralf Dahrendorf (1967, pp. 128-93) has even suggested that the central category of sociology is *homo sociologicus*, man as a role player, and in a similar vein Alfred Schutz (1964, p. 82; 1967, p. 41) has argued that all sociological inquiry is informed by the idea of a *homunculus*, a fictitious character to whom the investigator ascribes certain motives. Thus, in various forms, 'man' recurs again and again, as a depersonalized Adam. In so far as a gender is bestowed upon this abstraction it is, as grammar prescribes, male (cf. Schneider and Hacker, 1973); the age, we are led to suspect, is, without further specifications, 'adult'.

Obviously, if we wish to bring out the diversity and the interdependence of human beings, the plural 'people' is more adequate. One probable reason for the persistent use of the singular is that it corresponds to a very common self-experience, and to an old widely-professed ideal. Many members of industrial societies—and in particular their most articulate members, men of letters and academics—are familiar with the experience of oneself as an isolated individual, cut off in one's innermost thoughts and feelings from all others. This experience, which can be very painful, is closely connected to an ideal that people have learned to hold up to themselves as well as to others: the ideal of the self-possessed, autonomous person, capable of standing on his own feet, not quickly perturbed by what other people say or do. Both the feeling of isolation and the longing for autonomy are liable to spread at a time when people find themselves increasingly caught up in ties of interdependence which they cannot, and perhaps do not even wish to, comprehend. Ours is such a time. As Norbert Elias has noted, 'the same process which has made men less dependent on the vagaries of nature has made them more dependent on each other':

> More and more groups, and with them more and more
> individuals, tend to become dependent on each other for
> their security and the satisfaction of their needs in ways
> which, for the greater part, surpass the comprehension of
> those involved. It is as if first thousands, then millions,
> then more and more millions walked through this world
> their hands and feet chained together by invisible ties. No
> one is in charge. No one stands outside. Some want to go
> this, others that way. They fall upon each other and,
> vanquishing or defeated, still remain chained to each other.
> No one can regulate the movements of the whole unless a
> great part of them are able to understand, to see, as it
> were, from outside, the whole patterns they form together.
> And they are not able to visualize themselves as part of
> these larger patterns because, being hemmed in and moved
> uncomprehendingly hither and thither in ways none of
> them intended, they cannot help being preoccupied with
> the urgent, narrow and parochial problems which each of
> them has to face. They can only look at whatever happens
> to them from their narrow location within the system.
> They are too deeply involved to look at themselves from
> without. Thus what is formed of nothing but human
> beings acts upon each of them, and is experienced by
> many as an alien external force not unlike the forces of
> nature [Elias, 1956, p. 232].

The singular 'man' often serves as the counterpart to a very abstract notion of 'society' as an anonymous, wholly depersonalized constellation of forces. It is in this vein that newspaper editorials and political speeches point to 'forces', 'structures' and 'systems' which restrict 'man' in his freedom. The same contrast underlies a great deal of sociological thinking. Thus, in his well-known interpretation of anomie and deviant behaviour, Robert Merton has treated 'culture' and 'social structure' as actively-operating forces which in mutual interaction seem to determine people's behaviour:

> It is only when a system of cultural values extols, virtually above all else, certain *common* success-goals *for the population at large* while the social structure rigorously restricts or completely closes access to approved modes of reaching these goals *for a considerable part of the same population*, that deviant behaviour ensues on a large scale [Merton, 1957, p. 146].

Two abstract forces are postulated here: a 'system of cultural values' and a 'social structure' both of which are supposed to act upon people's behaviour. When they act in unison, apparently all goes well; when they conflict, the result is deviance.

As Alvin Gouldner has pointed out, many sociologists work on the tacit assumption that men are powerless to control the social world they live in: they are its products, not its masters. Society is seen as the result of interplaying forces, not as the willed creation of men. Gouldner holds this to be an incomplete and morally unacceptable view. According to him, 'the core concepts of society and culture, as held by the social sciences, entail the view that their autonomy and uncontrollability are a normal and natural condition, rather than intrinsically a kind of pathology'. These concepts give expression to, and endorse, 'an historical defeat: man's failure to possess the social world that he created'; they represent therefore 'the repressive component of sociology'. Against this, Gouldner stresses the 'liberative potential' inherent in 'the subsidiary conception of man as the maker of society and culture' (Gouldner, 1970, pp. 53-4).

Clearly in this way the original contrast is not overcome; only its accents are reversed. The same procedure has been followed by other sociologists opposed to the dominant trend of turning sociology into a 'reifying', 'de-humanized' science. Thus Ernest Becker (1968, p. 65) has stated that only those sociological theories are acceptable in which an explicit choice is made 'for man over above the constraints of social institutions'. Condemning and banishing social constraints from one's theories, however, seems more like magic than like proper sociology.

The singular form 'man' blocks some simple but important sociological insights. Societies are pluralities of inter-dependent people. The 'constraints', allegedly exerted by 'social institutions', are in fact exerted by people. The very same persons who may feel terribly 'constrained' are at the same time actively 'constraining': they exercise pressures on other people, and on themselves.

There are a few sociologists who more or less consistently use the plural 'people'. The custom of using the plural is most alive among those who reckon themselves to be proponents of the Chicago tradition, such as Herbert Blumer, Everett Hughes and a number of their students. Some typical titles already form an indication: *Men and Their Work* (Hughes, 1958), *Boys in White* (Becker *et al.*, 1961), *Outsiders* (Becker, 1963). Theoretical explanations why the plural is to be preferred are rare, however. Marx and Engels, in *The German Ideology* (1847), are among the few who addressed themselves to the problem. More recently, Lucien Febvre (1925, p. 201) and Marc Bloch have criticized the notion that the object of history is, as is usually assumed, man:

> Let us say, rather, men. Far more than the singular, favoring abstraction, the plural which is the grammatical form of relativity is fitting for the science of change. [Bloch, 1953, pp. 25-6] .

One could probably dig up a few more scattered statements to the same effect. Most sociologists, however, appear to find the whole matter of little consequence: why not just speak of 'man and society' or 'man in society', if it is plain enough that when we *say* 'man' we actually *mean* 'men'? They do not seem to realize that in taking this attitude they are displaying a carelessness about words such as they would never allow themselves with regard to figures. Yet sociology is made out of words and figures; and, of the two, words are the more important.

Figurations in flux

One of the difficult semantic problems sociologists have to face is the problem of conceptualizing development. It is in a way comparable to the problem with which chemists had to wrestle for centuries in their search for a 'language of chemistry' (Crosland, 1962), fitted to the description of inanimate processes and free from anthropomorphic allusions. Our whole vocabulary is attuned to a static conception of the social world; it tends to reduce all processes to conditions. Terms expressing process like bureaucratization and industrialization are only derivatives from 'bureaucracy' and 'industry'; the static concepts come first. For the most elementary terms of sociology like role, position, norm and value we do not even have dynamic derivatives. There have been a few attempts to put dynamic concepts at the centre of sociology. Simmel (1917) has proposed 'sociation', Berger and Luckmann (1966) have introduced a whole series of words like 'nihilation' and 'objectivation', but none of these attempts has had any profound effect on the standard vocabulary of sociology. The language of sociology itself demonstrates that social structures may have a very slow rate of change.

The very slowness of many changes reinforces the idea that 'structure' in a static sense precedes 'process'. Of course, no-one can deny the omnipresence of change in society. Individual people are born, they grow up, they die. As they grow older they change, and their relations with other people change. However, while individuals come and go, the social positions they occupy in the course of their lives apparently remain the same: father, mother, daughter, son—these and similar roles, together comprising the institution of the family, survive the succession of the generations. Therefore, as Robert Nisbet (1970b, pp. 304-9) and many others have argued, persistence and fixity may be regarded as no less important aspects of social life than change. As an example, Nisbet points to the university:

Although *what* is taught today is very different from what was taught eight hundred years ago, we cannot, as sociologists, overlook the persistences of the *ways* things are taught. Now, as then, we find the university organized in terms of colleges, faculties, institutes; we find its work parcelled out in the forms of curricula, courses, and lectures. Today, as then, the prime protagonists are groups called faculty and students. And as surely today as eight hundred years ago, the permission of the faculty is required before a student may receive what was then and is now called a degree or license. The norms of academic consensus remain much the same, as do the criteria of advancement, whether faculty or student advancement [Nisbet, 1970b, p. 305].

Apart from the question whether Nisbet's generalizations about the past eight hundred years are quite correct, he fails to mention that there was a time when there were no universities. Even then, one may argue, teaching and learning took place. And indeed these are, in some form or other, universal features of all human societies. However, human societies themselves are not an eternal given; and in the few hundred millennia of their known existence, they have undergone such profound changes that it makes little sense to try to account for any given social structure without considering its developmental nature.

Of course it makes a great difference whether we measure time by seconds, minutes, hours, days, weeks, years, centuries or millennia. Processes that are merely repetitive from day to day change gradually over centuries. It may clarify discussion of social change and development if we distinguish roughly between three types of change which are measurable by different time scales: (1) the life courses of individuals, (2) the development of societies, and (3) the evolution of the human species (cf. Elias, 1969b, pp. 25-33).

Most obvious are the changes taking place in the course of life of any individual. These changes are partly 'biological' processes of growth and ageing. To a large extent, however, they have to do with a person's relations towards other people. Thus, for any boy, growing up implies a shifting balance of power between himself and his father. The changes may be articulated in *rites de passage*; but even when they are not expressed so dramatically, they continue to take place, be it ever so slowly. The course of individual lives forms the subject-matter of biography and autobiography. The study of recurrent patterns of individual development is a concern of psychologists and psychiatrists alike. In biography as well as in developmental psychology, the social figurations of which an individual forms a part tend to be treated as external background. The psychologist Robert White, for example, in his interesting book *Lives in Progress*, speaks of the need to study individual development 'amid natural circumstances' (1966, pp. 2 and 22); although his intentions are laudable, his choice of words reflects a very static conception of the 'social conditions' affecting people's lives.

It has often been pointed out that Freud as a psychologist focused so strongly on individual development that the dynamics of social figurations remained beyond his orbit. His grand speculations about the first origins of taboos are not informed by a sociological theory of development. In his later writings he did show an increasing interest in such a theory; he continued to think, however, that it was merely 'applied psychology', since 'strictly speaking there are only two sciences: psychology, pure and applied, and natural science' (1932, p. 194). Since Freud wrote these words many psychoanalysts have turned to the study of individual lives within the context of specific periods and groups (cf. Erikson, 1962; Coles, 1970). They have hardly ever attempted, however, to inquire at once empirically and systematically into the development both of individual persons *and* the figurations formed by these individuals.

Studying the development of human societies was, in the nineteenth century, one of the major aims of sociology. Without exception, the great sociologists saw their own society in transition: from the theological through the metaphysical to the positivist stage (Comte), from conditions of great inequality to conditions of greater equality (Tocqueville), from a military to an industrial society (Spencer), from feudalism through capitalism to socialism (Marx). Their interpretations diverged strongly, if only because they were all imbued with something of their authors' hopes and fears. One feature they all had in common—a sense of the necessity with which social development moved in a particular direction. Tocqueville, pointing to the ubiquitous advent of democracy, and the decline of monarchies and aristocracies, attributed the whole process to Providence. Comte, Spencer and Marx, less inclined to use theological language, spoke of the 'laws' of social development; in doing so they almost inevitably incurred the reproach of engaging in teleological thinking. The lack of consensus among theorists, their blending of analysis and opinion, the suspicion of teleology—these characteristics of nineteenth-century developmental sociology all combined to bring it into disrepute among later generations. By 1937 'Who now reads Spencer?' had become a moot question, to which the answer was known: 'Spencer is dead' (Parsons, 1937, p. 3). Social development became a matter of secondary importance to sociologists; typically, textbooks would deal at great length with structures and institutions, only to conclude with a separate section devoted to 'social change'. The representation of society was thoroughly static; problems of change were mentioned almost as an afterthought. The prevailing sentiment was one of hodiecentrism: the contemporary world of advanced industrial nation-states served simply as the self-evident prototype of 'society'.

During the last fifteen years the tide has been turning. Probably in response to the shifts in the global power-balance, interest in long-term development has reawakened. Even Talcott Parsons (1967; 1970) has turned to this subject. Once again, there are textbooks written from a developmental perspective (Lenski, 1970; Hurd, 1973), and the number of monographs is steadily rising. But resistance against developmental sociology still continues to be strong. Many critics apparently assume that contemporary developmental theories are identical to their nineteenth-century predecessors, and contain the same ideological and teleological biases. Such, indeed, is the impression created by Robert Nisbet's polemics against 'developmentalism': erudite and eloquent, but too indiscriminating in their overall attack.

According to Nisbet, developmental sociologists overlook

the following points: (1) most social processes lead to persistence, not to change, (2) the sources of change are mostly external, (3) social change tends to be discontinuous, (4) there is no autonomous change, and (5) the study of social change is inseparable from historical events (1970a, pp. 199-204). None of these points, however, is necessarily at odds with a developmental perspective. Most of Nisbet's objections arise from a notion of social development that is too narrow and too deterministic. If we broaden our time perspective it is hard to conceive of recurrent processes that do not eventually lead to change; and if we survey human figurations in their full size, we can see that most changes originate within the figurations themselves. Nisbet refers to Max Weber's essay on the rise of capitalism as demonstrating 'that this major change in the European economy proceeded not from factors within the economy, but from factors— changes in religious evaluations of work—outside the economy' (ibid., p. 201). This, however, is a misguided use of the word 'external'; the so-called 'economic' and 'religious factors' are both aspects of the figurations which the rising entrepreneurs (about whom Weber wrote) formed, together with landowners, peasants, guildsmen, patricians and many others. The discontinuities emphasized by Nisbet also become less marked when viewed from a greater distance; there is continuity in so far as any given stage in a society can only be explained as having developed out of earlier stages. To mention but one example, current processes of decolonization in Africa and Asia cannot be explained without reference to the preceding phase of colonization. Again, the scope of the figurations to be taken into account is important; for most social developments taking place today the figuration to be studied is, as Comte has already intimated, not any particular nation, but the figuration of nations, that is mankind (cf. Wallerstein, 1974). Single unpredictable events are indeed inseparable from the stream of development—as inseparable as rapids and floods from a river. The divorce of history and sociology is detrimental to both: it make historians needlessly allergic to the very idea of structures, and sociologists afraid of dealing with single events.

The least noticeable process of development in which people are involved is the evolution of the human species. Perhaps 'the assumption that biological evolution moves at a desperately slow pace is made patently obsolete by our biological technology' (Van den Berghe, 1974, p. 788). Still, although we all partake in it, we rarely recognize evolution in our daily lives. It is not surprising that it has been discovered relatively late: it takes a great detachment to notice a process extending over many millennia, of which one forms a part oneself. The emotional resistances aroused by Darwin's publications are quite understandable. The evolutionary perspective implies a radical transformation of the human self-image: instead of one single deed by which the whole world with all its inhabitants has been created in a clear hierarchical order (crowned by 'man' made in God's own image), one is forced to think of a blind process, with no discernible beginning or end, a process into which mankind made a very late and inconspicuous entry.

Although the evolutionary perspective is generally accepted today, it plays a very minor part in the literature of sociology. Evolution is delegated to biologists and only occasionally do sociologists or anthropologists venture into this field, mainly on speculative forays (cf. Tiger, 1969; Tiger and Fox, 1971). However, it is useful to bear the evolutionary perspective in mind, if only as an antidote against static thinking. There is no distinct dividing line between biological evolution and social and individual development; it is possible to view the latter as continual processes of human self-domestication.

On the development of social dependencies and controls

In order to see how processes of 'individual' and 'social' development intermesh, it is instructive to realize the close connection between three types of fundamental problems with which people have to cope again and again, namely: (1) problems arising because they are dependent on the physical world within which they live and of which they are a part; (2) problems arising because they have to live with, and are therefore dependent on, other people; and (3) problems arising because they have to live with, and are dependent on, their own energies and impulses (cf. Elias, 1970, pp. 176-7). At first sight these three types of problem are clearly distinguishable. In conventional parlance they belong to the categories of, respectively, technology, social relationships and psychology. They may also be designated briefly but loosely as referring to people's chances of control over 'nature', over 'society', and over their own 'selves'.

Of the three types of problem, the first appears to be the least difficult to recognize. People live everywhere in dependence of 'nature'. They need it for food, for shelter. As the very word shelter indicates, 'nature' contains not only resources but dangers as well. Very early in the development of human societies, even before people had begun to engage in the 'production' of food and clothing, they had to find certain modes of 'protection' from the dangers among which they lived. They also had to develop some means of 'orientation' enabling them to find their way, to distinguish food from bait and poison (cf. Burke, 1954, p. 5), to decide upon the best time for hunting and gathering. The triad of functions—production, protection, and orientation—has continued to be central to people's control of nature.

For each of these functions people are dependent on others. They learn from each other, they form common attack-and-defence units, they produce food together and exchange goods and services. Their interdependence is a condition they have not freely chosen but one which is as inevitable a fact of human life as their dependence on nature. As we all know, both conditions are also highly flexible and subject to change. Through the development of technical skills and tools men have learned to increase their control over nature tremendously, and thereby to add to their own security and comfort. As a result, for people living today in the industrialized centres of the world, several basic problems of life have become hardly noticeable. The threat of floods in a country like the Netherlands is a good example: most Dutchmen nowadays never bother about such dangers, nor do they pay any attention to the technical apparatus which keeps their country dry. However, the fact that, for the time being, the problems of flood control have been solved satisfactorily, by no means implies that they have disappeared. Millions of people nowadays live in safety in areas which have been made inhabitable through the steady control of rivers and tides. For their continued social existence, all these millions are dependent on the few who are in charge of these controls.

The entire material network of dikes and sluices in Holland has been built up and continues to be maintained by means of a complex social organization. Over the centuries central controlling agencies have developed which have amassed so much power that today the governmental department responsible for flood control is generally known in the Netherlands as 'a state within the state'. The history of how the Dutch have mastered the surrounding sea is a history of co-ordination of the activities of increasingly large groups—a co-ordination which required, besides co-operation, submission. Individuals had to subordinate some of their own interests to the demands of communal organizations; local and regional groups had to submit to national authorities. The overall process has not been altogether peaceful; the struggle against the sea has also been a struggle between men.

The history of advanced technology, from the building of the pyramids to space travel, abounds with examples demonstrating the interlocking of controls over 'nature' and 'society'. Sending up a spaceship is an impressive feat of control over natural forces; it can be accomplished only thanks to the ability to co-ordinate minutely the activities of many thousands of people. In this sense, social organization is a precondition of technical mastery. At the same time, the very process of 'mastery' or 'domination' of nature can often only be understood in the context of groups of people trying to increase their control over others. This connection is most evident in arms races; as both pyramids and spaceships testify, however, the domination of nature may also serve the domination of men in other, more symbolic ways. The fact that the same words are used to express control over 'nature' and control over people is in this respect significant (cf. Leiss, 1972).

Controls over nature as well as controls over other people are closely connected with self-control. The first great steps in the mastery of nature—the conquest of fire, the invention of hunting weapons, the domestication of cattle, the early development of horticulture and agriculture—all involved a certain mastery of self, an overcoming of fears, a giving up of immediate satisfactions for the sake of 'deferred gratification'. In the course of social development most of these elementary controls have become built so deeply into each new generation as to become seemingly part of man's natural endowments. They are, however, results of a long process of civilization.

The capacity of 'mastering' one's emotions, of not being 'a slave' to them, can be an effective means of controlling others. As George Orwell (1936, p. 269) noted, the British empire rested to no small extent on the British capacity 'to appear resolute, to know his own mind and do definite things'. Before they were used to impress Asians and Africans these same qualities had been cultivated for centuries by noblemen and gentlemen at home, in subtle mutual power contests and in condescending humiliation of servants and tenants. Of course, a different kind of self-possesion is required in a society of hunters than in one dominated by courtiers or mandarins. Yet self-control in its many variations, including the ability to allow oneself caprices at properly chosen moments, appears to be a generally positive asset in commanding respect and exercising authority. It was probably a lack of appropriate self-control to which Lenin alluded in his Testament when, observing how the Soviet régime became bogged down in 'bureaucractic misrule and wilfulness', he complained: 'We lack sufficient civilization to enable us to pass straight on to Socialism although we have the political requisites' (quoted by Conquest, 1971, p. 21).

In every respect, with regard to controls over nature, over society, and over self, people's capacities have developed in different directions in different societies. Each phase in the process has been brought about by the intentions of the people involved; the development as a whole, however, has been unplanned and unintended. Thus, there has never been a blueprint of today's technology; to a large extent it is, so to speak, a product of wild growth. Likewise, the way mankind is divided according to language, religion, race, class, or nationality does not correspond to any previously devised plan. Nor is there any evidence that the major social institutions in which people's lives are organized—families, states, cities, factories, offices, armies—were first rationally designed before they developed into their present manifold shapes. Throughout the ages, certain groups of people have managed to gain control over others for longer or shorter periods; the others have learned somehow to cope with the condition of submission. On the whole all these processes have been guided mainly by short-term ambitions and by the exigencies of day-to-day survival. It is all the more remarkable that, in the long run, they show some persistent tendencies. First, by fits and starts, ever larger social units have been formed and brought under central control. Second, within these large units struggles have arisen to make the central controls more accessible to representatives of various segments of the population. Today no-one can tell how these struggles will continue to develop; among the many possible 'scenarios' are the nightmarish visions of *Brave New World* and *1984*.

One reason why social processes in the long run take an uncontrolled and blind course lies in the unintended interdependence of human beings. Superior control over certain natural forces may enable some groups to dominate others for a time, while they themselves live in relative security. Thus, in 1945, possession of the atomic bomb seemed to confirm the position of the United States as the leading world power. In a few decades, however, a proliferation of nuclear arms all over the world has taken place which is most unlikely to have been intended by Presidents Roosevelt and Truman and their advisers. The threat of nuclear disaster is, like the uneven and irrational use of natural resources and the prodigious growth of population (cf. Heilbroner, 1974), the result of dynamics at work in a world figuration which is still largely beyond human control.

Paradoxically, many human controls themselves strike us as 'wild' and destructive. As producers, men have destroyed forests, and turned them into deserts. As conquerors and rulers, they have oppressed and exterminated their victims. The histories of the great human migrations and of all great empires past and present read like so many horror stories (cf. Ruestow, 1950); even if today there are some governments whose internal policies are more humane than those of any regime in the past, they too are caught up, no matter how sincerely they may wish for peace, in a world figuration that is poised in a precarious 'balance of terror'.

The development of self-controls is embedded in, and part of, the largely unplanned processes in the course of which human groups have extended their controls over nature, and in which have emerged central governments capable of exerting a considerable control over increasingly large numbers of people. The functions of what Freud has called ego and superego have not been planned or designed any more than have languages or social classes. Coping with their own specific problems of social interdependence, successive generations in various societies developed self-controls which they transmitted to their children in a more or less 'conscious' fashion. In advanced societies, priests and philosophers have contributed to this process by holding up moral ideals; these contributions are, however, easily over-rated. For one thing, as Max Weber among others has clearly shown, moral ideals are never entirely autonomous: they are modelled after the life-style of specific social stata. Moreover, in order to be effective, they have to appeal either to the established ruling groups in a society or to groups who are ascending.

There is a world of difference between the ideals of virtue and self-control of Homeric warriors (cf. Finley, 1967) and those of Puritan merchants (cf. Weber, 1904-5). This contrast between a society dominated by warriors and one dominated by a rising entrepreneurial class shows how closely the ways in which people control others and control themselves are inter-related. In the one society, the central means of control is violence; in the other, money.

With the means of control, that which is being controlled is also likely to change. Thus in the process of exploitation of natural sources, these resources may change to the point of total exhaustion. The subordination of one group of people by another is bound to affect both groups, for better or for worse. The same is likely to apply to processes of self-control. In the classic literature of psychoanalysis there is a tendency to treat the agencies of control, ego and superego, as susceptible to change, whereas the substratum that is being controlled, the id, is conceived as unchanging. However, in the course of human development (both ontogenetic and phylogenetic), it is not merely the controls that change but the whole constellation of drives *and* controls. As Norbert Elias observes, the actual structure of drives and needs is 'no more separated from society, and no less historically changeable, than the structure of ego and superego functions' (1969a, II, p. 390). It is perhaps characteristic, Elias concludes, of our own phase of civilization—in which the ego and superego functions have become rather sharply differentiated from the id functions—that some regions of self are largely inaccessible to consciousness, and consequently tend to be regarded as belonging to an ahistoric and immutable 'human nature'.

Norbert Elias on the sociogenesis of civilization

Norbert Elias's two-volume *Ueber den Prozess der Zivilisation* is an excellent specimen of a sociological study of large scope. The first edition of this book appeared in 1939 in Switzerland. Since then, it has slowly gained a growing reputation among psychoanalysts, historians and sociologists. In 1973 a French translation of the first volume was published. An English translation is still to come.

Apart from the unfortunate date of its initial appearance, perhaps the main reason why the book has remained unknown for so long is that it does not fit into a clearly recognizable academic tradition. It deals with an historical process, but it is not 'history'. There is much in it about psychological structures; yet it is not 'psychology'. It comes closest to sociology; but in its whole manner of approach it deviates strongly from the current sociological literature. There are no diagrams, no definitions, no tables; there is no formal parade of numbered hypotheses; except for one or two methodological footnotes there are no explicit arguments about the ideas of other authors; thus, all in all, the usual signs of 'sociology' are missing.

The absence of these signs is not an accidental, external facet. It reflects a somewhat different commitment, to a different conception of science than that which we usually find in sociological monographs. In the preface to the first edition Elias wrote that he had come to his investigation not so much from a distinct scientific tradition, but much more out of a concern with the problems of his time. The Europeans of the 1930s considered themselves 'civilized' in comparison to other peoples and also to their own ancestors. They derived a certain feeling of superiority from their 'civilization'; but at the same time they experienced it in many ways as imperfect, incomplete, and worse yet, as troublesome, a burden, a source of tensions and neuroses. How was this ambivalence to be explained? What exactly did this 'civilization' imply, and how and because of what had it become what it was?

The challenge Elias took up was to trace the course of the European civilizing process in a disciplined, scholarly manner without indulging in the speculative and highly evaluative style of an Oswald Spengler or Arnold Toynbee. In doing so he drew from a variety of intellectual resources: historical studies, psychoanalytic theories, sociological concepts, such as were for instance to be found in the works of Johan Huizinga, Sigmund Freud and Max Weber. But, as is already evident from these three names, the diversity of viewpoints in the literature was so wide that in order to find a synthesis, pioneering work was required. The methodological and theoretical innovations needed, however, were not intro-duced for their own sake, but in connection with the empirical problems at hand. As Elias noted in his foreword:

> I did not set out to build a general theory of civilization in
> the air and then test whether it fit the evidence. On the
> contrary, it appeared to me that the immediate task was
> threefold: first, to win back, at least for a limited area, the
> lost view of the process of the specific changes of human
> behaviour; then to seek a certain understanding of their
> causes; and, finally, to gather whatever theoretical insights
> might offer themselves on the way [1969a, I, p. lxxix].

The design of the book reflects a sequence of interlocking problems. The opening chapter raises the question of how the concepts of *civilisation* and *Kultur* have acquired their particular significance. Unlike mathematical concepts, these notions cannot be separated from changing historical situations; they cannot be pinned down by formal definitions. Elias shows how the development of the concept *Kultur* is closely connected with the developments of a politically impotent bourgeoisie in the kingdoms and principalities of eighteenth- and early nineteenth-century Germany. The concept *civilisation* has had a quite different social career; it arose at the court of Versailles, where it served to express an increasing refinement in manners and feelings. This observation immediately leads to another problem: If the word *civilisation* signified the delicate life-style of the French court nobility, how has this mode of living come into being?

This problem sets the theme for the bulk of Volume One, which provides a documented survey of the development of rules of etiquette. Obviously, there is no 'zero point' in the history of codes governing eating, drinking and sleeping; but, from the thirteenth century onwards, a new development is visible in which the elementary activities of life become more and more stylized, or even withdrawn entirely from public view. This development begins among the highest European nobility; the resulting codes of behaviour have become diffused, particularly in the nineteenth and twentieth centuries, over broader and broader strata of the population.

The next problem is: How is this development to be explained? How is it to be explained that a worldly élite came to impose ever more severe restraints on its behaviour, and that other groups have taken over these same prohibitions? This question leads from the history of manners to a more encompassing analysis of social developments of which the changes in codes of behaviour were only a part. It turns out that the new rules of etiquette were formed in the princely courts of late feudal Europe and were brought to their highest refinement at the absolutist French court of the seventeenth and eighteenth centuries. The process of civilization, then, is closely connected with the process of state-formation, in the course of which the warrior aristocracy was transformed into a court nobility—a process which, though by no means evenly, took place all over Europe.

The process of state-formation forms the subject of the greater part of Volume Two of Elias's study. The immediate problem is to explain how, in the sixteenth century, such a great dynastic state as France could emerge, ruled by one man whom all (including the highest aristocrats) obeyed as his subjects. This question, in turn, leads back to a more remote past, in which the origins of the state-formation process are to be found. Again there is no 'zero point'; but this much is clear: in the tenth and eleventh centuries the former Carolingian empire was fragmented into a plethora of relatively small domains each with its virtually sovereign ruler, who was almost continually entangled in violent struggles with his peers. From the twelfth century onwards, a handful of princely houses managed to acquire enduring control over ever wider territories. Their control was based on a dual monopoly over the means of violence and taxation—a monopoly which came to be of such vital importance to the continued social existence of all dominant groups that, after long and bitter fights, they acquiesced in its consolidation.

Before the establishment of state monopolies over the means of violence and taxation the ruling class in France, as elsewhere in Europe, consisted of warrior knights. Compared with the members of later élites, such as the court nobility and the bourgeoisie, these men lived a relatively free existence, unhindered by such duties as always having to be considerate of the feelings of others or having to pay taxes regularly. When feudal decentralization was at its peak, every lord was master on his own land and could afford to vent his emotions more or less as he pleased. This is not to say, however, that the warriors were 'free' in any absolute sense. On the contrary, they lived under strong social pressures, pressures emanating from the figurations they formed together. They were all engaged in an unceasing struggle for the expansion of their own territory. As the very name 'warrior' indicated, warfare was the social occupation from which they derived their power and *raison d'être*: did they not protect by military prowess their own peasants against the attacks of alien invaders? Protection and oppression are closely related social functions; in a warrior society they are quite openly associated.

In feudal Europe, the pressures of the military-agrarian figuration were so great as to leave the individual lord no choice between fighting and not fighting. He who was unable or unwilling to take part in the struggle for land, was lost. He lost his possessions, his honour, and possibly his life. The compelling force which the figuration exerted on each warrior individually derived from the desire present in them all to acquire more land. At the same time, the compelling intensity of this desire in each individual was a consequence of the figuration they formed together. That the warriors spent their lives in a grim struggle for territory, was not the result of a consciously-made decision. Rather, the reverse was true: their military spirit sprang from the strong pressures exercised on them from their early youth. It would also be mistaken to explain the bellicosity of warriors as an inborn aggressive instinct; the sociological analysis demonstrates how the very way in which the warlords were related to their fellow human beings predisposed them to a life by the sword. It is equally unlikely that the subsequent 'courtlification' of the aristocracy in the following era is to be attributed to biological degeneration; once again a sociological analysis seems more promising:

> A transformation occurs in the social relations between people; therefore their behaviour changes; and, therefore, their consciousness and emotional economy as a whole are transformed. The changing 'circumstances' are not something which, as it were, comes upon people from 'without'; they are nothing but the changing relationships between people themselves [Elias, 1969a, II, p. 377].

Elias's enquiry culminates in the last chapter of Volume Two, where the successive problems are systematically connected. Here the sociological model, whose outlines have been drawn ever more sharply in the course of his argument, is spelled out in full. Put briefly, it goes like this: people are interdependent; they form social figurations. The genetic equipment of man is not such that these figurations are fixed once and for all: they are subject to change, and as they change, the constituent individuals change as well. Remarkably, the entire complex of intermeshing processes of change eludes the control and even the comprehension of the individuals who partake in it. And thus

> out of the interweaving of innumerable individual interests and intentions—be they compatible, or opposed and inimical—something eventually emerges that, as it turns out, has neither been planned nor intended by any single individual. And yet it has been brought about by the intentions and actions of many individuals. And this is actually the whole secret of social interweaving—of its compellingness, its regularity, its structure, its processual nature, and its development; this is the secret of sociogenesis and social dynamics [ibid., II, p. 221; italics deleted].

The reader who recognizes the model outlined here as the one underlying the present book may be slightly abashed by the note of certainty on which the quotation ends. One may be led to think that for Elias the discovery of this 'secret' might have exorcized all riddles from the world and magically have solved all problems. Such an interpretation, however, would fail to recognize that the meaning of this passage is paradigmatic. The 'secret' alluded to belongs to the category of what Thomas Kuhn would call the 'fundamental problems'. Its disclosure implies that we see all social phenomena as 'becoming': they have not always been the way they are at present; nor have they been 'caused' by some immutable principle; nor have they been 'made' in the sense of being the unmediated result of a conscious design—instead, they have emerged as part of a structured process of development, the course of which can be studied precisely and systematically.

Of course, the idea of unintended consequences of intended human actions is a familiar one in sociology, running from Adam Ferguson to twentieth-century writers as diverse as F.A. von Hayek and Robert Merton. Thus, in a typical statement, Karl Popper observes that 'the main task of the theoretical social sciences ... is to trace the unintended social repercussions of intentional human actions' (1963, p. 342; italics omitted). It is worth noting that in this formulation only the repercussions are 'social', not the human actions themselves. Consequently, it fails to convey the essential fact that, in the development of human societies, yesterday's unintended social consequences are today's unintended social conditions of 'intentional human actions'. As Karl Marx wrote in *The Eighteenth Brumaire*: 'Men make their own history, but they do not make it just as they please; they do not make it under circumstances chosen by themselves, but under circumstances directly encountered, given, and transmitted from the past' (1852, p. 115).

To see people are interdependent is to see them as partaking in the processes of development of social figurations. Important changes in the social figurations—such as increases or decreases in the length and complexity of interdependencies or shifts in power balances between groups—necessarily imply changes in the constituent individuals. A sense of these encompassing interconnections may better enable us to explain certain problems which seem incapable of any solution as long as we approach them with static classificatory schemes. Take, for example, the following statement by the sociologist, Amitai Etzioni:

> ... the institutionalized control of the means of violence is largely a macro-variable; it has minimal application in micro-theory and next to none in intra-role and intra-personality analysis [1968, p. 48].

Instead of connecting and explaining, this tidy classification into 'micro' and 'macro' variables has a disconnecting, and therefore an obscuring effect. It prevents one from seeing how deeply the social relationships and the personality structure of individual people are affected by the degree to which these people are protected and excluded from the exercise of physical force. Through his developmental, figurational, approach Elias has managed to make these connections visible, and to show something of their structure. Far from merely being an interesting foray into history, the study of the sociogenesis of 'civilization' points to some

fundamental relationships which no analysis of the contemporary world can afford to ignore.

The development of sociology as a social process

As with the development of increasingly complex means of
production, and the formation of ever larger and more
formidable military units, so the acquisition of knowledge
has proceeded without an all-embracing long-term plan. It is
not due to any conscious design that physics and genetics
have reached their present high level, while the scientific
knowledge of the social world is fragmented and confused.
The general attitude toward these discrepancies in scientific
development seems to be to regard them as 'facts of life'
which one may regret and perhaps even seek to remedy—
however, like other features of contemporary civilization,
they also stand in need of an explanation (cf. Elias, 1956).

About the social development of knowledge, astonishingly
little is known. There is no dearth of descriptive accounts;
but as far as an explanation is concerned of the growth of
human knowledge as a long-term process we are still very
much in the dark. Comte's law of the three stages, Spencer's
idea of evolution and the survival value of knowledge, Marx's
emphasis on the primacy of production, Durkheim's conception of knowledge as a reflection of social structure—these
still seem to be the most seminal general notions. They are,
however, too heterogeneous and too vague to provide
explanations for the actual course of development of
knowledge with its specific spurts, stagnations and set-backs.
Obviously the entire process is closely linked with the
development of controls over nature, society and self. To
provide a developmental theory showing these connections is
one of the problems of intellectual synthesis for sociology
today (cf. Elias, 1971).

It is sometimes said that the very task of sociology—the
scientific study of human society, of which we ourselves
form a part—is impossible. This assumption is clearly too rash.
People are also part of 'nature', and yet they have learned to
investigate it with considerable success. They have done so,

not by placing themselves in some mysterious manner 'outside' nature, but by changing their relationships to it. Natural scientists have gradually managed to achieve a level of institutionalized detachment from the objects studied which enables them to investigate those objects in such a way as to let their own personal wishes and anxieties interfere only minimally with their observations and conclusions. Thanks in part to the impressive results of this strategy they have also succeeded in emancipating themselves to a high degree from the dominating ideas of ruling groups. Submission of scientific opinion to political or ecclesiastical authority is rare nowadays, the Lysenko affair being a notorious deviant case (cf. Joravsky, 1970).

Social scientists, on the other hand, still find themselves caught between cross-pressures which penetrate deeply into their work. Curiously enough, one set of pressures with which they have to wrestle arises from the very requirement to be scientific. As pointed out above, the success and prestige of natural scientists has led many sociologists to a vain quest for universal lawlike propositions. Much self-styled 'value-free' sociology is permeated by at least this one value, the epistemological ideal of Newtonian physics. Ever since the days of Saint-Simon and Comte, sociologists have had to come to terms with this dominant idea, either by adopting and modifying it, or by opposing it with another conception of knowledge.

The other set of pressures is no less strong. Sociologists, even if they aspire to be 'socially unattached intelligentsia' (Mannheim, 1936, p. 137), belong to certain groups whom they need, not only for material production and physical protection, but also for their emotional satisfaction and intellectual orientation. Even if the members of these groups do not exert directly noticeable pressures on them, the sociologists may spontaneously feel compelled towards solidarity. They may wish to support their own group, to supply it with suitable means of orientation—suitable because those means are in accord with the group's prevailing self-images and capable of reinforcing its collective sense of self-righteousness, and possibly because they entail promises of a better future. In response to the demands of loyalty sociologists have explored a variety of stances, ranging from full identification with the cause of a class or a nation to attempts to be completely 'detached'. Whereas problems of factual precision, of theoretical consistency, and of scope lie at the heart of sociology as a 'scientific' enterprise, here we touch upon the 'ideological' issue of the ways in which, and for which groups, sociology can be made relevant.

5

Problems of Relevance in Sociology

The concept of relevance

Relevance has of late become rather a fashionable term. It is often used as if its meaning were self-evident. Thus in the twin readers edited by Jack D. Douglas, *The Impact of Sociology* (1970a) and *The Relevance of Sociology* (1970b), nothing is said to elucidate either the concept of 'impact' or of 'relevance'. Although in an earlier publication (1967) Douglas has stressed the importance of problems of meaning, he apparently assumes that in this case we are dealing with a pair of clear and unequivocal terms. On closer inspection, however, 'relevance' turns out to be a rather slippery concept, the meaning of which comes fairly close to 'impact'.

Both 'impact' and 'relevance' refer to the effects, the 'functions' of knowledge. The main difference appears to be that 'relevance' covers, besides the actual, also the potential and the desired effects, the uses to which knowledge *is* being put as well as the uses to which it *might* be put. The latter connotation renders the concept somewhat elusive. A further cause for confusion lies in the tendency to use the word in a dichotomizing sense suggesting that some knowledge is, and other knowledge is not, relevant—in the way that some numbers are odd and others even. It seems more sensible, however, to speak in terms of degrees, and to qualify as clearly as possible to what extent certain items of knowledge

153

may be relevant for which groups. Not all knowledge is equally relevant for all of the people all of the time.

Relevance became one of the key terms in the 1960s, among the movement for a sociology that would direct itself in a more committed manner against the unequal distribution of wealth and power in the world today. Against this movement more academically-orientated sociologists have declared 'relevance' to be an unscientific concept, belonging in the political arena but not in sociology. This, however, seems an unwarranted restriction. Are we to conceive of the development of an academic discipline like sociology as having run a wholly autonomous course, unaffected by its actual and potential functions? Sociologists more than any other professional group should be ready to acknowledge that this is very unlikely. It is more in line with sociological wisdom to work on the hypothesis that problems of relevance have been, and continue to be, of great importance to the development of their own discipline, and that these problems may enter even into high-level discussions on theory and methodology which are ostensibly of purely 'scientific' interest.

The primacy of ideological relevance in 19th century sociology

We believe that it is possible for scientific research to learn something about the reality of the world by which we can increase our power and according to which we can arrange our lives [Freud, 1927, p. 379].

These words of Freud might well have served as a motto for the founders of sociology. They intended sociology to be the study of society in the widest sense: 'society' meaning not just a 'realm' ruled by a king, but the encompassing social reality in which all human beings, kings and subjects alike, take part. In their vista, the study of society would not merely be disinterested scholarship; it should also have a higher purpose: to serve the progress of humanity.

As indicated in Chapter 1, the modern conception of society was developed in the late seventeenth and eighteenth centuries. Writers in Britain and France pointed out how individual human lives, which traditionally had been seen as destined by 'character' or 'fate', were to a large extent shaped by social conditions, by 'society'. These writers also set forth that the social conditions of their own time had come about largely as the result of blind secular processes—processes which far exceeded the powers of any single king or government but which seemed at the same time, at least in principle, controllable, if only the 'laws' underlying them could be known and this knowledge wisely applied. These thoughts, first succinctly expressed by such writers as Adam Ferguson and Condorcet, were triumphantly elaborated in the nineteenth century. Herbert Spencer neatly summed up the high hopes for sociology in the subtitle of his first book, *Social Statics: The Conditions Essential to Human Happiness Specified, and the First of Them Developed* (1850).

The high hopes were not immediately fulfilled. In 1887 the economist, Henry Sidgwick, commenting on the fundamental disagreements between some of the most prominent sociologists, could remark with some justice:

> With equal confidence, history is represented as leading up, now to the naïve and unqualified individualism of Spencer, now to the carefully guarded and elaborated socialism of Schaeffle, now to Comte's dream of securing seven-roomed houses for all working men . . . Guidance, truly, is here enough and to spare; but how is the bewildered statesman to select his guidance when his sociological doctors exhibit this portentous disagreement? [quoted by Abrams, 1968, p. 82].

To Sidgwick, and to many others, the lack of unanimity among its practitioners proved that the whole enterprise of sociology was doomed to fail. Instead of immediately jumping to that drastic conclusion, however, we may discern from a further distance in time some interesting problems in the seemingly chaotic state of affairs in nineteenth-century sociology. Was the situation indeed merely chaotic? Were there no common traits in the various theories apart from the general claim to have discovered 'the laws of social motion'? The very co-existence of various incompatible theories of society seems to reflect the degree to which the societies in which these theories originated were segmented and divided against themselves. The spectrum of theories was not as arbitrary as Sidgwick intimated; it is possible to discover some structure in it, and to see not only how the various views differed but also how they were mutually related and how they were linked to specific groups. This interpretation then leads us to a question which is highly pertinent to us today: if nineteenth-century sociology can be shown to reflect the ideologies of different social classes, to what extent do these one-time ideological influences continue to play a part in contemporary theory? In other words, can an examination of the relationship between sociology and ideology in the nineteenth century throw light upon some central problems of sociology today?

Most sociologists in the nineteenth century wrote for the flourishing section of the literate public known as the bourgeoisie. Some, however, acted as spokesman for the industrial working class, while others still identified with strata whose social functions were declining as commercial and industrial groups gained ascendency. They all shared an acute awareness, however, that the present in which they lived constituted a phase in a continuing process. Their primary concern was to understand this process, to trace the forces which shaped it, and to predict its future course—in order to cope in a more enlightened manner with the unprecedented problems of their contemporary world. Thus each writer provided a diagnosis, a critique, and a provisional prognosis. The bourgeois sociologists tended to conclude that humanity was on its way to a better future; progress would continue if not impeded by governmental (or, as Spencer put it, 'military') obstacles. Among the writers who addressed themselves to the industrial proletariat there was a strong sense of the inevitability of crises and strife as the 'labour pains' of a better society. In the famous words of Marx and Engels: 'the history of all hitherto existing society is the history of class struggle'; this 'diagnostic' statement, that societies are made up of oppressors and oppressed, implies at once a critique and a call for action: live by this insight, and fight your oppressors. Factual diagnosis and political persuasion were no less closely wedded in the writings of the aristocrat Tocqueville who tried to convince an audience of privileged readers that the French Revolution had been only a beginning: a continued levelling of social conditions lay ahead, leaving no choice but to accommodate and to learn to live with democracy.

In their subtle mixture of 'descriptive' and 'prescriptive' themes the various forms of nineteenth-century sociology were all impregnated with 'ideology'. At first, this may sound like a wholly negative qualification. The word ideology is often associated with false consciousness or deliberate distortion; 'ideology' then stands in direct contrast to 'science' or 'truth' (cf. Geiger, 1953). However, the distinctions suggested by such antinomies as 'descriptive' versus 'prescriptive', or 'ideology' versus 'truth' are often far from clear; more often than not, these distinctions themselves appear to be slightly 'ideological'. Certainly when we consider such broad theories of society as expounded by, say, Spencer, Marx or Tocqueville, it seems hardly appropriate to classify these views wholesale as either 'ideology' or 'truth'. A more promising approach is to regard ideologies as intellectual attempts 'to render otherwise incomprehensible social situations meaningful, to so construe them as to make it possible to act purposefully within them' (Geertz, 1964, p. 64). This formulation implies no immediate judgment with respect to the 'state of truth' of the ideas in question; the emphasis is on their social functions for those who hold them. It remains an important intellectual challenge to see if it is possible to find out in particular cases whether the need for accurate orientation in the social world (the need for 'knowledge') has been served well or ill by the pressing need for 'meaning' and 'purpose'. The configuration of ideologies in the nineteenth century—liberalism, marxism and conservatism—can be taken as a case in point.

Liberalism and sociology

Liberalism, the oldest of the three, represented as a typical ideology in all its ramifications a view of society as it *is* and as it *should be*. According to this view, every man is by nature gifted with reason, capable of unfolding his talents, and of acquiring possessions by his labour and industry (Macpherson, 1962). People's inborn capacities for self-improvement and for bettering their material conditions are best served if each person can freely pursue his own enlightened self-interest, not hampered by restrictions set up by any authority. The division of labour is the most obvious example: although it has greatly contributed to the quality of human life, it has not originated out of human foresight but out of the narrow propensity present in every man to exchange goods to his own advantage. As Adam Smith expressed it in a striking, still faintly anthropomorphic metaphor: the egoistic strivings of individuals will, if left to themselves, be 'led by an invisible hand' so that out of the private actions of many, a common good will result that was not consciously designed by any individual (Smith, 1776, pp. 477-8).

No less memorable was Adam Ferguson's observation that 'nations stumble upon establishments, which are indeed the result of human action, but not the execution of any human design' (Ferguson, 1767, p. 222). The power of this remark lay in its emphasis both on the blind, uncontrolled momentum of social forces and the fact that these forces can only be understood as springing from individual 'human action'. This twofold recognition, of the relative autonomy of social development on the one hand, and of its ultimate basis in individual action on the other, has remained central to the liberal tradition. Only in some later vulgarized versions was the significance of the individual extolled to the virtual neglect of social forces (cf. Lynd, 1937, pp. 401-86).

In the original liberal view, society appeared as a network of ties by which independent and equal partners are mutually connected on a voluntary basis, each led by his own interest as he himself perceives it. Other social bonds, such as those which are primarily based on coercion or on sentiment and tradition, remained in the background. Thus the liberal view reflected something of the way of life and the self-experiences of its adherents, the members of a bourgeoisie that owed its prosperity to the thriving of commerce and industry. Hard-working entrepreneurs, whose lives were dedicated to 'business', saw voluntary contract relationships—with suppliers, clients, workers, perhaps also competitors—as the cement of society; they were ready to regard all talk of other social bonds as sentimental rubbish. In the writings of the Social Darwinist, William Graham Sumner, this mentality was worked out into a sociological perspective:

> In the Middle Ages, men were united by custom and prescription into associations, ranks, guilds, and communities of various kinds. These ties endured as long as life lasted. Consequently, society was dependent, throughout all its details, on status, and the tie, or bond, was sentimental. In our modern state, and in the United States more than anywhere else, the social structure is based on contract, and status is of the least importance. Contract, however, is rational—even rationalisitic. It is also realistic, cold and matter-of-fact. A contract relation is based on a sufficient reason, not on custom or pre-scription. It is not permanent. It endures only so long as the reason for it endures [Sumner, 1883, p. 113].

It is, Sumner contended, out of the question 'to go back to the sentimental relations which once united baron and retainer, master and servant, teacher and pupil, comrade and comrade'. These words are interesting not so much for the highly romanticized and 'sentimental' colours in which they paint the past, as for the avowedly 'realistic' picture they convey of the present—as if modern society is held together by nothing but utilitarian contract relations, based on 'a sufficient reason'.

In a less outspoken but still clearly recognizable fashion the liberal view has been expressed by such twentieth-century writers as F.A. Hayek and Karl Popper. Hayek's arguments in particular are reminiscent of Ferguson and Smith. Like Ferguson, Hayek mentions language as the most salient example of an ingredient of society that is structured without having been consciously designed; his general conclusion is that 'the independent actions of individuals bring forward an order that in no way lay in their intentions' (Hayek, 1952, p. 40). The moot point in this formulation is the word 'independent', which somehow suggests that individuals are in no way mutually connected until they decide to enter into specific 'interactions'. It seems more accurate, however, to recognize that 'underlying all intended interactions of human beings is their unintended interdependence' (Elias, 1969c, p. 143). The fundamental relatedness of people, which begins with being born, tends to be lost sight of in the liberal image of man as an adult individual freely deciding his own course of action, only to be confronted later by 'unintended consequences'.

Marxism and sociology

As an ideology providing orientation in the modern industrial world, Marxism developed in direct opposition to liberalism. In an eloquent passage in *Capital* (Vol. I, 1867, pp. 189-91), Marx dissected the idyll of a liberal society, dominated by 'freedom, equality, property and Bentham'. In this peaceful world, freedom consisted in buying and selling labour power at market value, equality in the 'equal' exchange of this human commodity, property in the phrase 'every man his due'. Against the liberal idea, here attributed to Jeremy Bentham, of a society composed of freely interacting individuals, Marx emphasized the ties by which people are connected not out of their own will, but because they have no choice.

In modern society based on a capitalist mode of production men's lives are moulded by and large by their respective social classes—of wage-labourers, capitalists and landowners (Marx, 1894, p. 892). We cannot hope to gain an understanding of modern society if we proceed from an abstract notion of 'economic man' endowed with a general tendency 'to truck and barter'. To conceive of the economy in terms of isolated individuals is an absurdity (Marx, 1859, p. 268); what people perceive as their self-interest, and what chances they have of pursuing it, depends primarily on their historic class position.

In its emphasis on social class, Marxism departs radically from liberalism. Both ideologies share the central notion that society is moved by anonymous forces with a momentum of their own, stronger than individual wills. Marx and Engels, however, refused to identify with the prosperous bourgeoisie, for whom the social forces seemed by and large beneficial; instead, they stood up for the wretched industrial wage-workers. In this perspective, the central feature of the modern world was not communal progress for all, but fundamental and inevitable antagonism. As they stated in the *Communist Manifesto* (1848, p. 464), in modern times 'no other bond between man and man' was left 'than naked self-interest, than callous "cash-payment" '. If liberals such as Sumner were to hail this development as the liberation of man from the fetters of feudalism, for Marx and Engels it signified the liberty for capitalists to exploit workers on a scale unparallelled in history. In liberal imagery, society was reigned benignly by the 'invisible hand' governing the division of labour; in marxist imagery, the history of all societies was the history of class struggle, engendered by struggle for the control over the means of production:

> The specific economic form in which unpaid surplus labour is pumped out of the direct producers determines the relation of domination and servitude, as it grows directly out of production itself and in return reacts upon it as a determinant. Upon this, however, is founded the entire formation of the economic community which grows up out of the production relations themselves and therewith simultaneously its specific political form. It is in each case the direct relation of the owners of the conditions of production to the direct producers—a relation whose prevailing form always by nature corresponds to a definite stage in the development of the kind and mode of labour and therefore of its social productive power—in which we find the innermost secret, the hidden foundation of the entire social construction and therefore also of the political form of the relation of sovereignty and dependence, in short, of the prevailing specific form of the state. This does not preclude that the same economic basis—the same as regards its main conditions—can, due to innumerable different empirical circumstances, natural

conditions, race relations, external historical influences,
and so on, show infinite variations and graduations in
appearance, which are only to be understood through
analysis of these empirically given circumstances [Marx,
1894, pp. 799-800].

The focus in this passage, as in numerous others, is on the
mode of production as the fundamental social structure
which—although it does not directly 'determine' the whole
variety of 'superstructures'—nevertheless stands out as the
only aspect of society about which a solid general theory can
be formulated. As Norbert Elias (1971, p. 152) points out, in
this respect Marx 'took over the basic conceptual scheme of
the liberal ideology, but infused it with negative values'. The
primacy attributed to economic relationships over all others
is as typical of Marx as it is of Sumner. Consequently, in
marxism as in liberalism, relatively little attention is paid to
the ways people are bonded emotionally to their families,
tribes, churches or nations. Nor has either tradition produced
an adequate sociological theory of the most over-ridingly
powerful organizations of today, states.

In the extreme liberal version, virtually the sole function
of the state was to protect property rights. As Sumner (1883,
p. 101) put it bluntly: 'At bottom there are two chief things
with which government has to deal. They are the property of
men and the honour of women. These it has to defend
against crime'. This straightforward opinion finds its counterpart in statements to the effect that 'the executive of the
modern state is but a committee for managing the common
affairs of the whole bourgeoisie' (Marx and Engels, 1848,
p. 83). Engels in particular is noted for the ease with which
he has prophecized that with the abolition of capitalism the
state would 'wither away' (cf. Lichtheim, 1964, pp. 367-79).
Later writers in the marxist tradition, most notably Antonio
Gramsci, have tried to fill this obvious lacuna in marxist
sociology. But it still remains a weak spot, especially in
Soviet orthodoxy which cannot possibly face up to the
realities of state power in the USSR —where the first stable
totalitarian régime of the twentieth century rules over the
last fully surviving European empire (cf. Amalrik, 1969).

Conservatism and sociology

According to several commentators (Salomon, 1955; Spaemann, 1959; Nisbet, 1966) the decisive inspiration for sociology sprang from conservative thought, with its strong emphasis on community and authority as the fundamental social bonds. After the foregoing it should be clear that this interpretation gives insufficient credit to the contributions of liberalism and marxism. Therefore, rather than speaking of a single 'sociological tradition' in the nineteenth century, as does Nisbet (1966), it would be more appropriate to refer to several traditions in the plural (cf. Habermas, 1971, pp. 290-306). Among these traditions conservatism has played an important part.

As Karl Mannheim (1927, pp. 408-508) has pointed out, conservatism as an articulate ideology was formulated in reaction against liberalism and socialism. In their polemics with liberals and socialists, the conservatives argued that societies were not based upon individual self-interest, nor upon organized coercion; on the contrary, every society was grounded in consensus, in the common acceptance by its members of an order that had grown historically, and which was legitimized by tradition. Conservative writers from various countries—such as Edmund Burke in England, Joseph de Maistre in France, Adam Müller in Germany, Guillaume Groen van Prinsterer in Holland and George Fitzhugh in America—all followed this same line of reasoning. They all argued that societies have an order and a pattern of development of their own; this order should not be disturbed, nor the development hastened. Abstract and speculative ideas are dismissed as dangerously upsetting the delicate structure of social bonds; the real, the 'concrete' is stressed instead: 'only what *is* has proven its value'.

Burke's *Reflections on the Revolution in France* (1790) was one of the first and fullest documents of conservative thought. It presented a picture of society as a partnership, 'not only between those who are living, but between those who are living, those who are dead, and those who are to be born' (pp. 194-5). Continuity is of the greatest value to society, inconstancy its greatest peril. Without the collected wisdom of the ages, men are doomed to lapse into egoism and barbarism; they need this wisdom to provide for their own wants:

> Among these wants is to be reckoned the want, out of civil society, of a sufficient restraint upon their passions. Society requires not only that the passions of individuals should be subjected, but that even in the mass and body as well as in the individuals, the inclinations of men should frequently be thwarted, their will controlled, and their passions brought into subjection. This can only be done *by a power out of themselves*; and not, in the exercise of its function, subject to that will and to those passions which it is its office to bridle and subdue. In this sense the restraints on men, as well as their liberties, are to be reckoned among their rights. But as the liberties and the restrictions vary with times and circumstances, and admit of infinite modifications, they cannot be settled upon any abstract rule; and nothing is so foolish as to discuss them upon that principle [Burke, 1790, p. 151] .

A century later, words of the same tenor–except for the disdain of reason–were written by Emile Durkheim in his theory of anomie. The resemblance is all the more striking since Durkheim was certainly not a political conservative. Yet his theory of anomie abounds with themes emanating from conservatism. All living beings, Durkheim argues, must in one way or another be able to strike a balance between needs and satisfactions, or else their cravings will never end, and they will always suffer. In animals this capacity is innate; when a need like hunger is fulfilled it no longer vexes the organism. But human beings, by virtue of the unbounded powers of their imagination, know many cravings for which there are no natural limits. The only way for them to bridle such passions is to accept the boundaries set by their society. This is a primary function of social norms; and when, as in times of crisis, this regulating function fails, a condition of anomie ensues. In modern societies the normative ties between men have weakened; there is a chronic anomie, resulting among other things in high suicide rates. Such is the general perspective from which Durkheim derived his critique of the contemporary world:

> As a matter of fact, at every moment of history there is a dim perception, in the moral consciousness of societies, of the respective value of different social services, the relative reward due to each, and the consequent degree of comfort appropriate on the average to workers in each occupation. The different functions are graded in public opinion and a certain coefficient of well-being assigned to each, according to its place in the hierarchy . . . A genuine regimen exists, therefore, although not always legally for- mulated, which fixes with relative precision the maximum degree of ease of living to which each social class may legi- timately aspire . . . Under this pressure, each in his sphere vaguely realizes the extreme limit set to his ambitions and aspires to nothing beyond. At least if he respects regu- lations and is docile to authority, that is, has a wholesome moral constitution, he feels that it is not well to ask more [Durkheim, 1897, pp. 249-50] .

This passage can typically be called both 'sociological' and 'ideological'. The first line, 'at every moment in history', reads like a counterpart to the famous sentence in the *Communist Manifesto*: 'the history of all hitherto existing society is the history of class struggle'. Both statements offer sweeping generalizations for which it is not difficult to find empirical support. But precisely because these contrasting interpretations of the social world are each in a sense 'correct', it can be concluded that they both fail to convey, as unqualified formulations, the full complexity of the social world.

In conservatism there is a tendency to view human nature as a dark and perennial force which always needs to be held in check. Even Durkheim, noted for his 'sociologism', displays something of this tendency. In his theory of anomie he strongly emphasizes that human beings, since they have no innate 'physiological mechanisms' to set a limit to their appetites, can only be saved from insatiate desire by accepting the moral authority of their society. He does not in this context develop the obvious point that not only the constraints, but the seemingly limitless longings of men are sociogenetic as well. People are not born with a biologically programmed drive for money or glory; the fact that these drives may strike very deep roots in the adult personality does not mean that they stem directly for the unchanging nature of 'man'. Here the marxist tradition is more explicitly sociological in stressing that 'history is not only the story of the satisfaction of human needs but also the story of their emergence and development' (Avineri, 1968, p. 79; see also O'Connor, 1974, pp. 1-15).

Nineteenth-century ideologies and twentieth-century sociology

The threefold division into liberalism, marxism and conservatism, although too schematic to do justice to the subtle variety of viewpoints of individual authors, brings into focus the major means of sociological orientation: the prototypes of looking at society which were available in the nineteenth century. Today, in retrospect, we may be struck by the obvious similarities between these prototypes. Just as armies engaged in a battle display many time-bound resemblances in armament and strategy, so the nineteenth century ideologies show some remarkable common traits. The armies are ranged against each other; their movements can only be explained from the total figuration they form together. The same holds true for the nineteenth-century ideologies.

There is, to begin with, the shared assumption that societies are more than just the personal properties ('realms') of princes. The nineteenth-century ideologies all contain a quite different perception of power. Not personal rulers, but anonymous forces are seen as directing the course of history: the invisible hand of the market mechanism; the forces of production and class struggle; or the gradual process of generational succession. It is supposed to be possible to formulate general principles explaining these mechanisms or forces or processes—principles which are in most cases presented as resting on a sound 'scientific' basis. The statements about how society 'is', and how it 'works', are subtly blended with statements expressing hopes and expectations about how society 'should be' and how it 'should work'. In each ideology certain bonds between people are stressed, to the neglect of others; the emphases vary with the social angle from which society is seen. General principles are expounded regarding the well-being of society as a whole; behind these ostensibly general principles loom the particular concerns of specific groups whose interests seem to be served best by, respectively, the protection of civil liberties; the revolutionary overthrow of the capitalists; or the preservation of established ways of life.

In most twentieth-century sociological writings the ideological ingredients have become less manifest. Sociology by and large has become an academic discipline with less explicit concern for the larger questions of life, but more attuned to specific professional interests: developing systematic theories, testing hypotheses, refining the means of gathering empirical evidence. Among these professional interests are both epistemological inquiries into the nature of theorizing and studies of the history of sociology. These two lines of inquiry, however, are seldom combined—Parsons' *The Structure of Social Action* (1937) being the most notable exception. As a result, the links between the major ideologies of the nineteenth century and the main types of contemporary sociological theory remain insufficiently noted. When today sociological theories are classified according to their substantive content, a distinction is usually made between (a) action theories; (b) conflict theories; and (c) consensus theories. This threefold classification recurs again and again, although in different terms, e.g., as normative, force and exchange solutions to the Hobbesian problem of order (Ellis, 1971), or as institutional, class and communal schemes (Shanin, 1972). If these are indeed the main sociological models, the analogy with the basic schemata of the nineteenth-century ideologies is indeed striking. Until now, however, this analogy has received little attention. The few authors who have dealt with continuities between nineteenth-century ideologies and contemporary sociology have confined themselves to tracing the influence of one particular ideological tradition—in most cases conservatism, in a few others marxism (cf. Zeitlin, 1968).

Sociologists have not deliberately set up their discipline in such a manner that it would offer the choice between three major orientations. The co-existence today of action theories, conflict theories, and consensus theories is not the outcome of a well-thought-out scientific strategy; rather, it has come about in the same way as social phenomena in general: as the largely unplanned and unforeseen result of the actions and thoughts of consecutive generations of interdependent individuals. There is a widespread tendency, not only among sociologists, to consider the intellectual problems of today as timeless givens; this 'hodiecentric' tendency can easily lead to the belief that the threefold scheme which currently appears to dominate sociological theorizing reflects some sort of unchanging logic. A greater awareness of the sociogenesis of these schemes may offer an escape from the seemingly compelling predicament that any theoretical stance will necessarily commit us to a choice between these three models.

A developmental perspective may help us to regain a sense of how the three models are interrelated. Each of the three highlights, from a particular perspective, certain general ties of interdependence between human beings: ties of individual self-interest, of organized coercion, of common sentiment and tradition. We do not know whether this rough classification of social bonds is the most appropriate, nor even whether it is approximately exhaustive. We do know something, however, about how it originated. This may be of help in the further development of sociology.

'Sociology' versus 'ideology'

Ideological strands in sociological thinking are more likely to become manifest in theories of a wide scope, like those of Marx or Spencer, than in the abstract schemata and factual analyses which have been produced in such abundance in the twentieth-century. The nineteenth-century pioneers, by trying to gain an insight into the forces determining social development, aimed at ultimately controlling and directing those forces. As their writings formed a part of intellectual discussions which passed directly into political debates and activities, they contained no sharp distinction between 'theoretical' and 'practical' problems. In the twentieth-century, however, sociologists became increasingly convinced of their own incapacity (which they objectified into 'the impossibility') of arriving at practical evaluation through scientific analysis. For Max Weber, this was still a deeply-experienced personal problem; for many of his followers it has almost become a dogma—the separation of 'sociology' and 'ideology'.

The desire to erase all traces of ideology has probably been one of the reasons for the restriction of scope in con-temporary sociology. In this respect, too, Weber and Durkheim mark the transition from pre-academic to academic sociology. Both men were quite close to the world of practical politics and had statesmanlike ambitions; yet in their role as sociologists they made a valiant effort to reach a level of detachment at which their conclusions would remain valid irrespective of any particular group interests. Although Weber's methodological, and Durkheim's theoretical writings bear the unmistakable imprint of, respectively, the liberal and the conservative tradition, they were expressly designed as 'pure sociology'.

Sociologists of subsequent generations have continued this quest. By emphasizing factual precision and systematic reasoning they have tried to steer clear from the perils involved in formulating theories of a wide scope, one of the chief perils they perceived being the exposure of an ideological viewpoint. As Seymour Lipset and Neil Smelser put it in their introduction to a selection of American sociological papers from the 1950s, proudly announced as *Sociology: The Progress of a Decade*:

Sociology, in its brief history, has evolved gradually toward a concern with scientific canons and away from social philosophy and social problems. The two advance guards in this movement have been the development of systematic research *methods* and the exploration for adequate systematic *theory*. While this process of differen-

tiation of the scientific aspects of sociology from its
ethical and practical background has been gradual and
irregular, it has been powerful and unrelenting as well
[Lipset and Smelser, 1961, p. 7].

This passage (which incidentally also testifies to 'a process
of differentiation of sociology' from its 'literary background') is probably not meant to imply that sociology, in
moving away from ethical and practical preoccupations, has
become less relevant. On the contrary, in all likelihood the
authors would argue that sociological knowledge can only be
relevant at all if it is *real* knowledge, well-established in
empirical observation and logical inference. They would
interpret the growing concern with scientific canons as
evidence that sociologists have successfully freed themselves
from the pressures of extraneous groups.

Now that sociology has become an established academic
discipline, most sociologists no longer write for a diffuse
audience of readers who wish to be ideologically
informed—they write only for colleagues. In their daily work
they have to deal mainly with colleagues again, with students,
and, in research, possibly with sponsors. Most sponsors for
whom sociologists carry out research are primarily interested
in precise factual information; they do not ask for ideological
advice. Applied sociological research typically provides an
inventory of 'factors' at work in a given area, and a statistical
analysis of the interrelations between these 'factors'. The
study on leisure behaviour quoted in Chapter 2 (Wippler,
1968) is a characteristic example: it reports the relationships
between a number of 'dependent variables' (sport activities,
attendance at theatres and so on) and 'independent variables'
(age, sex, education etc.) in a particular setting. Any
commitment to a general theory of society is carefully
avoided. A similar reduction of problems has occurred in
teaching. The usual practice of teaching consists of lecturing
and examining on the standard repertory of research methods
and systematic theories. As two disgruntled former students
commented:

Those who entered graduate school with the intention of
acquiring skills to deal with *social* issues found themselves

obligated instead to deal with scholastically derived *socio-logical* issues; those who were motivated by a sense of *social* responsibility found themselves being socialized into a coterie in which *professional* obligations claimed precedence [Colfax and Roach, 1971, p. 7] .

Although at first sight research and theory have become far removed from ideology, the relationship is not so simple as the textbooks (e.g., Johnson, 1960) have sometimes suggested. Such critics as T.W. Adorno and C. Wright Mills have cogently pointed out that the tendency to focus research on technically measurable 'variables' has made more fundamental problems disappear from view. Empirical researchers have taken society as a given, supposedly well enough known to be treated as the familiar context within which the relationships between specific variables can be studied. Most of them have hardly paused to realize that in doing so they have tacitly endorsed the prevailing ideological images of society.

Those sociologists who worked on general theories could not help exposing their ideological leanings to a rather greater extent. They had to cope with an intellectual heritage thoroughly impregnated with ideas from nineteenth-century liberalism, marxism and conservatism. Even if such a theorist as Talcott Parsons emphatically intended to continue the Weberian tradition of not mixing science and values, he forged his general system from an amalgam of action theory and consensus theory, reminiscent in its basic assumptions of liberal and conservative thinking. Consequently his critics have had little difficulty in laying bare the strong ideological undercurrents below the surface of pure sociological theory (cf. Gouldner, 1970).

Just as Parsons combined items from action and consensus theory into one theoretical synthesis, so one of his major adversaries, Ralf Dahrendorf, made an alloy of action and conflict theory. As an intellectual system, Dahrendorf's work is less impressive than Parsons'; it is worth mentioning, however, as one of its ideological counterparts. In contrast to Parsons', Dahrendorf's theoretical stance seems to correspond to a generally more militant approach to social issues, and a distrust, akin to Weber's, of the authority vested in large modern organizations.

As a third, rather monstrous combination, a mixture of marxism and consensus theory emerged in Eastern Europe in the Stalin era, when the notion of 'non-antagonistic classes' was introduced to efface officially the tensions and inequalities in Soviet society (cf. Ossowski, 1963, pp. 100-120). Since then Eastern European sociologists have made repeated attempts to reconcile the militant rhetoric of marxism with a view of society marked by order and consensus within, and by peaceful co-existence between nation-states.

It would be too hasty to conclude from these few sketchy observations that the ideological impregnation of sociology is so thorough and persistent as to be virtually inevitable and unchangeable. If any conclusion can be draw, it is rather that sociological ideas reflect a balance between 'knowledge' and 'fantasy', the ratio of which has to be investigated in each instance. As Norbert Elias has remarked:

> Probably few sociologists would claim that the primacy of object-orientation over an ideological subject-orientation is already as great in the basic assumptions and theories underlying sociological research as it is in those underlying physical or chemical research. And, again, probably few sociologists would maintain that the ascendency of subject-oriented ideologies or mythologies over object-oriented knowledge is as great in sociological theories as it is in the political propaganda of parties or nations—that in other words sociology is nothing but another form of national or party propaganda. If one wants to determine the position of sociology as it is in relation to both physical knowledge and the knowledge represented by the great party creeds such as conservatism, communism, socialism, liberalism or by the great national ideologies, then relatively undifferentiated all-or-nothing models, such as that which leaves one only the choice between science *à la* physics or ideology, are not quite up to the task. Here too a more differentiated model is needed linking non-scientific and scientific knowledge to each other and allowing for alloys of different degrees of object- and

subject-centeredness in our knowledge of society as in that of nature [Elias, 1971, p. 368].

Parochial perspectives and semantic problems in sociology

Sociologists studying 'society' do not have the same degree of institutional protection and self-discipline as natural scientists studying 'nature'. In a chemical laboratory the processes studied have been brought sufficiently under control to pose no threat to the person of the investigators. Although they may be highly involved in their research, the investigators have learned not to let their hopes and fears affect their observations and conclusions. For sociologists, the situation is quite different. As people have increased their control over nature, they have become more dependent on ever greater numbers of other people. Groups of people who count each other as belonging to different nations, classes or races are still bonded to each other. The mutual ties put manifold constraints on them, constraints which they may resent strongly without seeing any way of relieving them. Also, within and among smaller groups like families and work-teams, problems of living together, arising from mutual dependencies, form recurrent sources of tension and strain, scarcely accessible to conscious control. Sociologists often find themselves too deeply entangled in these very problems to be capable of studying them in the detached manner in which natural scientists observe the behaviour of enzymes or galaxies.

The precarious relationship between 'subject' and 'subject-matter' leads, among others, to semantic problems. The concepts we choose for discussing problems of human interdependence usually bind us in advance to certain viewpoints. Take, for example, the area of problems variously known as social inequality, hierarchy, stratification, mobility, or class structure. The very terms we select as a general heading for this area already predicate certain assumptions; and even if we ourselves are careful to avoid making these assumptions, we cannot prevent the associations others are likely to make between our choice of concepts and our ideological position. The close relationship between words and valuations is clearly evident in Robert Nisbet's *The Sociological Tradition.* According to Nisbet, there are five 'unit ideas' comprising the core of sociology: community, status, authority, the sacred and alienation. Obviously these concepts belong to one 'word-family'; they express affinity with a distinct 'form of life' (Wittgenstein, 1953). Far from being emotionally indifferent, these terms convey nostalgia for the pre-revolutionary, pre-industrial era and discontent with current processes of individualization, centralization, democratization, secularization, and, of course, alienation.

Many have been the attempts by sociologists to design a vocabulary that would not be committed in advance to a particular perspective. A good example is the concept of 'latent functions' developed by Robert Merton (1957, p. 51). Time and again sociologists and social anthropologists have encountered social institutions which are seemingly anomalous since they do not appear to serve any useful purpose in the society of which they are a part. Do these institutions then have no functions at all? Or will closer inspection reveal certain 'latent' functions—which may explain why they are maintained? By way of example Merton has addressed himself to the problem of the political machines in the United States. The practices of these political machines run counter to widely-held ideas about democracy and constitutional government; yet they play an important part in American politics. More specifically, political machines form a link between centres of wealth and power and various sections of the population which are cut off from these centres. By integrating these groups in an admittedly devious way, political machines contribute to the functioning of American society; but, Merton (pp. 71-82) argues, this contribution is latent and can be made visible only by sociological inquiry.

The question is, latent for whom? The Hawthorne investigators discovered by painstaking research in the 'bank wiring observation room' that daily production was deliberately restricted, something the workers themselves of course knew all along. Similarly Merton discovered by means of theoretical analysis that political machines perform useful services for certain social groups and thus contribute to the functioning of society at large. Again, this is a conclusion that would hardly surprise the people involved: they knew it, and, as evinced by remarks that Merton himself quotes, some of them were capable of explaining the whole mechanism quite vividly. Sociologists who perceive the positive functions of political machines obviously show a better understanding than those who can only pass moral judgment on the corruption of bosses and precinct workers. However, by calling these functions 'latent' sociologists continue to identify with the official point of view according to which only penetrating analysis will disclose the 'positive' side of political machines. The concept of latent functions turns out to be an abortive attempt to break through the restrictions of a naïve perspective that is *partial* in the twofold sense of the word: incomplete and partisan.

This is only one example of the problems involved in developing a sociological vocabulary which is not tied to a particular group perspective. The concept of 'dysfunction' is another, even more obvious illustration (cf. Gouldner, 1970, pp. 336-7). These and similar instances confront us with the problem: is it possible to make the language of sociology less bound to preconceived evaluation? The concept of function may serve as a test case.

The concept of function reconsidered

The concept of function can be used in two ways: (a) something *is* a function *of* something else, or (b) something *has* a function *for* something else. Statements of type (a) refer to the past, to conditions out of which the item that concerns us has come forth. Statements of type (b) refer to the future, to 'consequences', 'effects', 'results', 'impact'. By virtue of these twofold possibilities the term 'function' may serve as a reminder that every social event has been determined by events in the past and is directed toward future events. Because it can so clearly express the time dimension, the term fits very well in a developmental perspective.

What is usually known as functional analysis in sociology consists of a way of reasoning which relies on a particular variety of statements of type (b)—statements pointing to the functions which 'elements' or 'parts' are supposed to have for larger 'systems' or 'wholes'. This approach is summed up in Merton's well-known definition: 'Functions are those observed consequences which make for the adaptation or adjustment of a given system' (1957, p. 51). In most cases the 'system' which serves as the ultimate unit of analysis is a nation-state—as witnessed by such functionalistic pronouncements as: 'Perhaps the best example of a societal goal is national security' (Johnson, 1960, p. 53).

The logic underlying the dominant functionalist approach derives largely from biology (cf. Hempel, 1965, pp. 279-330). For the survival of a living system, an organism, certain conditions are necessary; in so far as these conditions are produced by parts (organs) of the total system, one can speak of functional contributions or functions. A functional explanation of this type 'begins with a postulated state of affairs, and refers *back* to the necessary antecedent or underlying conditions' (Parsons, 1970, p. 33). In biology this procedure yields plausible enough results: one starts from the organism as a given unit, the continued existence of which is secured by the workings of the lower organs; the structure of these lower organs can be explained by referring to their function *for* the organism as a whole. But in sociology it is much more problematic which units are to be taken as explanatory. Often, it seems feasible to reverse the entire procedure, and to seek to explain larger structures by examining their functions for smaller ones: thus, the existence of single nations is not to be explained by their functions for the United Nations, but rather the United Nations is explained in terms of its functions for the member-states.

The habit of thinking in terms of parts and wholes, of systems and subsystems, easily leads one to inquire more readily for 'what' than for 'whom' something has functions. The theory of stratification by Davis and Moore, criticized above (p. 94), is an example. It is deliberately formulated in terms of positions, not of people. It assumes a closed, static system, and deals with 'external circumstances' and 'developmental stages' as mere contingencies, unimportant to the rational kernel of the theory. In contrast, it is worthwhile to try to broaden the scope of the concept of function, to make it at once more 'human' and more 'dynamic', by relating it to people forming changing figurations with each other.

As an example we may take Norbert Elias's (1969b) analysis of the social functions of etiquette and ceremony at the court of Versailles during the seventeenth and eighteenth centuries. Practically all activities at the court were governed by ceremony; the problem is, why? According to the traditional functionalist model an answer would have to be sought by referring to some over-arching 'system' which 'required' etiquette for its continued existence. As Elias shows, however, there is no need to postulate such a system; an explanation can be found by examining the specific functions of etiquette for various members of the court. For the king, it was at first a means of suppressing the nobles, who had to obey the rules of etiquette instituted by the king in order to stay in his favour; for the nobles, it was a means of exhibiting their superiority over and above the bourgeoisie. As the balance of power in the society at large shifted, both king and aristocracy increasingly found themselves prisoners of the protocol of etiquette which hung as a spectre over their lives. They resented the strain under which it put them, but they could not free themselves from it without upsetting the very fundaments of their social existence. In spite of all feelings of ambivalence they continued to observe the rules of ceremony because these had for them the function of lending social distinction. Even if they detested ceremony, the very figuration in which they found themselves caught made them dependent on it.

For another example of functional analysis in terms of dynamic figurations of human beings, one may think of the by no means hypothetical case in which a country settled by farmers is invaded by nomads attracted by the rich produce of agriculture. The farmers have no choice but to fight or to surrender. Either alternative implies a drastic reorganization of their lives. The nomads on their part, if they succeed in subjugating the farmers, and if they wish to maintain the continued enjoyment of the agrarian surplus, are forced to reorganize their own lives, too. Thus, from the moment of their first encounter, the original settlers and the invaders are interdependent, and are caught up in a process which neither group can control fully. It would be a mistake to describe the relationships of the subdued peasants toward those who have become their masters as a relationship of unilateral dependence. The peasants are indeed dependent; but so are the masters. Together they form one figuration, and the way of life of any group or any individual within this figuration can only be understood in the context of the network of interdependencies. It can be asked of every participant to what extent his activities are explicable by referring (a) to his personal interests, (b) to the personal interests of other people, (c) to the collective interests of groups to which he belongs, and (d) to the total figuration of which all people concerned are a part.

Of course this train of thought can be pursued without using the word 'function' at all; but it has to be admitted that the word fits the argument very well. The train of thought itself is one on which sociologists have to rely again and again; in this respect, one can only agree with Kingsley Davis (1959) that sociological analysis *is* functional analysis. In the social world we always find people engaged in activities through which they are serving partly their own interests ('I'-functions), partly the interests of others ('you'- or 'they'-functions) and partly common interests ('we'-functions). These activities take place within figurations which are in flux, without fixed boundaries, and without any ulterior 'goal' from which all functions can be explained.

To mention one more example: in his study of *mafia* in a Sicilian village between 1860 and 1960, Anton Blok discusses the institution of *omertà*, according to which a man is respected for keeping silent over what he happens to know about the deeds of *mafiosi*. Blok writes:

It is important to see the code not in isolation, but as an aspect of the real interdependencies between people who formed the community. *Omertà* was not something abstract, floating in the air so to speak, reinforcing or influencing actual behaviour. On the contrary, . . . it constituted a very concrete and real part of the behaviour of people who depended on each other in specific and fundamental ways [Blok, 1974, p. 212] .

In other words, *omertà* had some clearly evident functions for those directly involved. For the witness of a murder, to talk or not to talk was a matter of life and death. For the *mafiosi*, secrecy was just what they needed. For other parties concerned, it was the disadvantages that were predominant: for family members who might want to revenge the victim, or for the police authorities who were supposed to prosecute the killers. *Omertà* was a function of the balance of power between the several parties with divergent interests in it. In order to explain *omertà*, as Blok does, one has to specify the stakes which specific groups had in it, and to show how the figuration of Sicilian society during a long period of incipient but arrested state-formation gave rise to these specific interests. Far from being contingencies, the stage of development of Sicilian society, and its relationship to Italy at large, were essential conditions for *mafia* in general, and for *omertà* in particular. *Omertà* was an integral aspect of a society in which people's military, political, economic and judiciary functions had not become as clearly demarcated as they are today in the industrialized-state societies of Western Europe.

The differentiation into 'I'-, 'you'-, 'we'-, and 'they'-functions may also help to conceptualize contemporary social processes. It may be noted, for example, how the 'I'-functions of individual directors of large companies in capitalist societies are gradually receding in favour of corporate 'we'- and 'they'-functions, leaving smaller scope for personal aggrandizement. Again, it may be observed how the encounters between governmental agencies and citizens engender recurrent tensions because of the tendency on the part of the officials to let 'we'- and 'I'-functions prevail over the 'you'- and 'they'-functions they are supposed to perform. Gouldner's (1959) observations on functional reciprocity and autonomy are pertinent in this context. Functional differentiation can only proceed on a basis of reciprocity; but each party in such a process will strive to increase its functional autonomy, or, in other words, to diminish the demands of 'you'- and 'they'-functions, and to attain larger scope for 'we'- and 'I'-functions. The concept of 'it'-functions may add yet another aspect to the analysis. Social actions are often legitimated as having been performed in the service of a symbolic 'it'—a creed or a flag, the honour of a family or the glory of a nation. Although in the last resort such 'it'-functions always refer back to people, their symbolic appeal is not to be underestimated.

It should be clear that the foregoing is not intended to reduce social reality to an exchange of 'interests'. If in the four-fold scheme (a) and (b) draw attention to private interests and (c) to commom interests (the two need not be at odds), (d) demonstrates how relative the whole notion of 'interests' is. 'Interest', like 'motive', refers to the meanings people ascribe to their own and each other's actions (cf. Gerth and Mills, 1953, pp. 112-29). As a general proposition, the statement 'people act out of self-interest' is just as empty as 'people act out of motives'. Without specification such statements are meaningless.

'We'- and 'they'-perspectives and the problem of Verstehen

In studying any social figuration one is well-advised to try placing oneself within the world of experience of the various groups of people who make up the figuration. 'If the scholar wishes to understand the actions of people it is necessary for him to see their objects as they see them' (Blumer, 1969, p. 51). A sociologist has to understand the language, to recognize the meanings of the people he is studying. Objects are for him not just physical matter, actions not just movements in space. Identifying with the 'we'-perspectives of different groups may enable him to understand something of the sense in which certain actions and objects are 'meaningful' to these groups. At the same time he should heed Durkheim's advice not to rely solely on the interpretations people themselves give of their own doings, for no matter how sincere, these interpretations can, as a result of ignorance and self-deceit, be highly misleading. Comparison of different 'we'-perspectives will usually soon reveal that the same events and institutions can give rise to wholly contradictory interpretations. Thus, while 'we'-perspectives are indispensable in sociological analysis, so are 'they'-perspectives which show the figuration from a greater distance, and may thereby offer a fuller view of how the intentions and actions of the various groups are interlocked.

The ideal of a detached 'they'-perspective is at least as old as sociology. As early as 1783 Condorcet proposed to study human society in the same spirit in which naturalists study beavers and bees (cf. Hayek, 1952, p. 108). This idea has been repeated in countless variations. It can be found almost literally in *The Rules of Sociological Method* (1895) and *Suicide* (1897) by Emile Durkheim.

In *Suicide* Durkheim set out to study a subject loaded with taboos and emotions in a purely scientific manner, by cool statistical analysis. Yet, as several commentators have noted, the book contains more than a mere mechanical processing of facts and figures. It is full of allusions, either explicit or implicit, to meanings. Such allusions enter into Durkheim's very definition of suicide according to which 'the term suicide is applied to all cases of death resulting directly or indirectly from a positive or negative act of the victim himself, which he knows will produce this result' (p. 44). If the investigator working with this definition is to discriminate between suicides and other deaths, he has to be capable of deciding whether the deceased person has wished his own death, and whether he has known that his 'positive or negative act' would bring it about. This presupposes a faculty for somehow assessing 'inner states' and understanding motives. Similarly, in the interpretations of his statistical material Durkheim continually resorts to plausible accounts of what may prompt people either to endure or not to endure their fate. In the official statistics the threefold distinction of egoistic, altruistic and anomic suicide is nowhere to be found. Yet Durkheim appears to have had little difficulty in assigning every group of registered suicides to one of his categories. The arguments with which he explains his procedure of categorization abound with highly debatable truisms about how, for example, Jews or widows cope with the problems of social life (cf. Douglas, 1967, esp. pp. 65-70).

The idea that all references to 'inner mental states' should be eliminated from social studies has become the guiding principle of the so-called behaviourists. Refusing to let any non-scientific notions enter into their work, they claim to restrict themselves to the study of behaviour in the strict sense of 'any temporo-spatial movement in or of any object capable of being observed by any device and recorded instrumentally' (Linschoten, 1964, p. 397). Behaviourism has struck root especially among psychologists; but its appeal has also extended to several sociologists such as George Lundberg (1939). More recently, some sociologists have turned to behaviourism under the influence of B.F. Skinner (cf. Ritzer, 1975, pp. 141-86). They appear to be impervious to the kind of critique brought forward very convincingly by Noam Chomsky (1959) in his review of Skinner's book *Verbal Behaviour* (1957). As Chomsky points out, at the crucial points in his theory Skinner (like Durkheim) has to resort to a mentalistic psychology, to a tacit understanding of how human beings select and interpret the 'stimuli' to which they 'respond'. The impossibility of generalizing beyond strictly-controlled laboratory situations circumscribes behaviouristic psychology to a very narrow scope. As soon as one tries transferring the laboratory findings to other, 'real-life', settings one has to introduce a sense of meaning, for the simple reason that all social settings are endowed with meaning as a part of their structure. A seemingly elementary social act like casting a vote at elections might perhaps be described as a 'temporo-spatial movement'. The description would be very cumbersome, however, and it could never convey what voting is actually about—that it means expressing a political preference within a specific institutional setting.

Here lies the crucial weakness of behaviourism. Even though it may be possible, in principle, to describe behaviour in purely physical terms, such descriptions, if consistent, would remain devoid of meaning altogether. But meaning is an ineradicable dimension of the social world, and in order to bring this out we have to rely on an interpretation of human behaviour as more than just 'spatio-temporal movement'. A first-person perspective, an 'I'-perspective or a 'we'-perspective, is needed if we wish to convey something of the meanings inherent in all social actions–meanings that are more or less clearly articulated by the persons themselves, and more or less recognizable and understandable for other people.

The manifold problems in understanding meanings are often designated by sociologists as problems of *Verstehen*. It is no coincidence that a German word is used as a label for this field, since problems of understanding (or hermeneutics) have for a long time been a favourite theme among German social scientists. The discussions about *Verstehen* originated from the philosophical contrast between mind and matter, a contrast engendering the idea that there were two separate modes of knowledge, respectively the mode of natural science and the mode of the human or cultural sciences. Whereas matter was assumed to be subjected to strictly-determined chains of cause and effect, mind was regarded as in essence free and indeterminate. The end of natural science was seen to lie in discovering regularities and general explanations; the cultural sciences, on the other hand, were to deal with events and patterns that were essentially unique and not accessible to causal explanation.

One of the great intellectual exploits of Max Weber was his attempt to incorporate both 'causal explanation' and 'interpretative understanding' into sociology. In the first paragraph of *Economy and Society* (1922, p. 3), Weber bridged in one sentence the seemingly insurmountable cleavage between the two methodological traditions by defining sociology as 'a science which seeks to understand social action interpretively, and thereby to explain it causally in its course and its effects'. This apparently innocuous opening is actually a rather daring innovation. Like Durkheim, Weber announces that sociology is directed at finding general causal explanations; but unlike Durkheim, he explicitly adds that, to this end, the procedure of *Verstehen* is indispensable. He even goes so far as to call the possibility of *Verstehen*, of direct access to motives as a special class of causes, an advantage social scientists have over natural scientists—although the price to be paid for this advantage is high: the results of social science are of necessity less certain and less systematic (ibid., p. 11).

In spite of Weber's emphatic concern for 'subjective meanings' his design for interpretive sociology is actually rather 'objectifying' and formalistic. His approach to meanings is by way of formal categories, the most important of which are the four general types of affective, traditional, value-rational and goal-rational action. Like Durkheim's types of suicides, these are constructs invented by a sociologist, and not categories in which certain groups of people order their own experiences. The same holds true of the classificatory schemes devised by Talcott Parsons: although they have been developed in a frame of reference which is unmistakably *Verstehen*, these schemes are dictated by the logic of the theorist; they do not spring from an attempt to enter into the 'we'-perspective of particular groups.

The artificiality of these constructions was very clearly shown by Alfred Schutz. *Verstehen*, Schutz noted, is first of all 'the particular experiential form in which common-sense thinking takes cognizance of the social cultural world' (1962, p. 56). Subsequently, it may be evolved into a problem for epistemologists, and a method for social scientists. The latter use it to build 'constructs of the second degree', in order to interpret systematically the common-sense constructs by which the people under study interpret the reality of their own everyday lives. The world of social scientists is a world inhabited by a purely abstract type of man, a 'homunculus':

> The homunculus was not born, he does not grow up, and he will not die. He has no hopes and no fears; he does not know anxiety as the chief motive of all his deeds. He is not free in the sense that his acting could transgress the limits his creator, the social scientists, has predetermined. He cannot, therefore, have other conflicts of interests and motives than the social scientist has imputed to him. He cannot err, if to err is not his typical destiny. He cannot

choose, except among the alternatives the social scientist
has put before him as standing to his choice . . . He is
nothing else but the originator of his typical function
because the artificial consciousness imputed to him contains merely those elements which are necessary to make
such functions subjectively meaningful [Schutz, 1962,
p. 41].

This description reads almost as a caricature of the static,
isolated *homo sociologicus*; but its intention is wholly
serious. If indeed a gulf is posited between the social scientist
as an inquiring subject and ordinary people as the objects of
his inquiry, this seems to be the only way in which he can
come to grips with this alien world. Schutz carries to its
extreme the position of 'methodological individualism' as
outlined by Weber. The world of science and the world of
everyday experience are seen as separated by an invisible
barrier; the scientist appears to be doomed to shuttle to and
fro forever between the two. Schutz seems to draw the
picture with a certain gloom, as it it were an inevitable fate
that 'the social scientist has no "Here" within the social
world' (ibid., p. 39). But the picture comes closer to resem-
bling an unattainable ideal. In most cases, for practitioners of
the social sciences, the boundaries between their 'scientific'
and 'non-scientific' activities are far from clear; it is one of
their major problems that these activities continually impinge
upon, and spill over into each other.

In the actual practice of research, writing and teaching,
sociologists rely on *Verstehen* all the time. They do so no
matter which method of inquiry they use: reading documents, coding questionnaires, observing what people do—all
these activities imply 'understanding'. The method of theoretical reflection, represented by such writers as Simmel and
Wittgenstein, is of course 'interpretive' *par excellence*. In
writing and lecturing one cannot help ascribing at least some
potential for understanding to one's audience.

One of the reasons why 'the operation called *Verstehen*'
(Abel, 1948) continues to appear so mysterious—in spite of
the fact that we never cease using it to cope with the
problems of social existence—is probably that most methodo-

logical attempts at explaining it are made in terms of a singular 'I'-perspective. The gist of the problem then is: how can I, as one single individual, understand the utterances of other people, of so many other 'I's? Stated in these terms, the problem may indeed be insoluble: the longer one ponders over it, the more enigmatic it becomes. It is not very realistic, however, to conceive of oneself as a wholly isolated 'I'. The very fact that we are capable of saying 'I', and of understanding others when they say 'I', indicates that as talking human beings, as *homines sapientes*, we take part in a universe in which we can also significantly speak of ourselves as 'we'. The key to understanding what is involved in *Verstehen* seems to lie in the recognition that *Verstehen* is not just a matter of 'I'- but also of 'we'-perspectives.

Identification as a problem in sociological inquiry

The belief that 'the sociologist has no "Here" within the social world' is an obstacle to understanding how closely the development of sociology has been, and continues to be, linked with the position of sociologists *vis-à-vis* other groups in their figurations. One cannot appreciate the problems with which sociologists have grappled if one does not see how they have absorbed or resisted influences from numerous other groups, both within and outside the universities. The alternative ideals of proper scientific method—the models of the 'natural' and the 'cultural' sciences—have not originated within sociology; nevertheless they have entered into its very core. The same holds true for the views of society inherent in liberalism, marxism and conservatism.

The intellectual problems of sociologists are, then, to no small extent problems of choosing among, and coming to terms with, reference groups. Should they take intellectual advice from philosophers, psychologists, linguists? Should they identify with literati, with ruling élites, with 'the oppressed'? Depending on their social position, sociologists are more or less free to select their own standpoint within the figurations of their own time. No standpoint places them outside or beyond the social world. Every standpoint has implications for their work.

All sociological work requires both involvement and detachment. The kind and degree of either involvement or detachment are not just matters of personal caprice; they are heavily dependent on socially-developed standards. Standards of detachment are today much higher in the physical than in the social sciences. But then one of the problems confronting social scientists is that a certain measure of involvement or identification is an essential ingredient of their work:

> They cannot cease to take part in, and to be affected by, the social and political affairs of their groups and their time. Their own participation and involvement, moreover, is itself one of the conditions for comprehending the problems they try to solve as scientists. For while one need not know, in order to understand the structure of molecules, what it feels like to be one of its atoms, in order to understand the functioning of human groups one needs to know, as it were, from inside how human beings experience their own and other groups, and one cannot know without active participation and involvement [Elias, 1956, p. 237] .

For an example, we may briefly return to one of the first modern social scientists, Adam Smith. It may be claimed, somewhat over-dramatically, that Adam Smith 'discovered' the division of labour. Obviously he did not invent it, any more than his contemporary Lavoisier invented oxygen. Yet, in a way, both discoveries *were* also inventions: Lavoisier invented a way of isolating a specific chemical substance, while Smith invented a way of discerning a specific feature of social structures. The fact that they could make these discoveries or inventions was, of course, due to each man's genius. But, as Adam Smith himself was careful to point out, this 'genius' was largely the result of the division of labour, by virtue of which some people could become scientists and scholars.

Although a man of letters himself, Adam Smith was quite prepared to identify with the entrepreneurs of his time, to see the world from their 'I'- and 'we'-perspectives. He was familiar with their way of life, he respected them, and he shared many of their views. Yet he never became so engrossed in the world of commerce as to take all its features for granted. On the contrary, the workings of trade and industry kindled his curiosity. *An Inquiry Into the Nature and Causes of the Wealth of Nations* (1776) is therefore a book of a wholly different calibre from, for example, Benjamin Franklin's *Advice to a Young Tradesman* (1748). What Franklin did was to explain the secrets of the trade, as an old merchant would do to an aspiring apprentice. His manual still forms a valuable document expressing 'the spirit of capitalism'. But *The Wealth of Nations* is much more than that: for, in writing it, Smith added to his intimate knowledge a sense of puzzlement and a philosophically-trained faculty for systematic reasoning at a very high level of abstraction.

Franklin's *Advice* has provided source-material for Max Weber's famous study of 'the protestant ethic and the spirit of capitalism' (1904-5). This study is another striking example of detached scholarship, informed by a great capacity for understanding through identification. In it, Weber evokes the 'I'- and 'we'-perspectives of hard-working small entrepreneurs, with little or no capital of their own, stubbornly trying to make their way in the world through industry and thrift. He demonstrates convincingly how, for these people, economic exigencies—the need to save for investments, to lead a virtuous life in order to be regarded as worthy of credit—and religious duties converged; how, in other words, there was 'affinity' between the ethics of capitalism and Calvinism.

While *The Protestant Ethic* fully deserves its reputation as a masterpiece of well-documented 'interpretative under-standing', it is hopelessly inconclusive when it comes to the problem of explanation. In some passages Weber asserts that he is only concerned with examining 'one side of the causal chain' (p. 27), leaving altogether open how the role of Calvinism in the emergence of capitalism is to be assessed other than in terms of 'affinity'. In other passages, however (without naming Marx) he diametrically opposes the Marxist explanation of the rise of capitalism:

The question of the motive forces in the expansion of modern capitalism is not in the first instance a question of the origin of the capital sums which were available for capitalistic uses, but, above all, of the development of the spirit of capitalism. Where it appears and is able to work itself out, it produces its own capital and monetary supplies as the means to its ends, but the reverse is not true [Weber, 1904-5, pp. 68-9].

The inconsistency may be partly accounted for by the perspective from which Weber wrote his essay. This perspective is typically 'partial', based as it is on the vantage-point of one particular group within the figuration in which capitalism emerged. In a few passing remarks, Weber makes it understood that he is not writing about the rich patriciate of bankers and merchants (who often supplied the capital with which the small entrepreneurs went to work); nor is he concerned with wage-workers or peasants, or any other group. The subjects of his treatise are a relatively small group, wedged in between the grand bourgeoisie and the proletariat, motivated not only by a desire to become rich but, even more strongly perhaps, by a deep-rooted fear of sinking into desolate poverty. For these people, a work ethos could indeed, as Weber put it, yield a high premium. Systematic self-control, allowing not even an occasional lapse into frivolity; a calculating spirit always aware of the device 'time is money'; diligence and frugality—these qualities had strongly positive functions for this stratum in its struggle for social survival and advancement.

This is the aspect highlighted by Weber in his essay. He consciously disregarded the figuration of which the work ethos was a function—the wider figuration encompassing all social classes, and extending geographically way beyond the enclaves of Calvinism. Why he chose to do so is a problem in itself. It has to do with his interest in the development of a peculiarly Western type of rationality, and also with the implicit polemic with Marx which runs through much of his work, and which, in turn, cannot be seen in isolation from his own social position. (If, incidentally, the wider figuration is taken into account, at least one other point of affinity between capitalism and Calvinism becomes apparent. The belief that one's success in business forms an indication of one's 'state of mercy before God' may seem irrational; but it corresponds in a striking way to an irrationality of capitalism: no matter how hard one works, and how well one organizes one's affairs, one cannot ultimately guarantee one's own success, for eventually the market determines whether one succeeds or fails. 'Mercy' may thus be read as a religious metaphor for 'success'. For the petty capitalists, the only certainty in life was a negative one: without hard work, one would be lost.)

While problems of identification enter into every genre of sociological inquiry—whether it be theoretical reflection, study of documents or questionnaire research—they are most easily recognized in participant observation. In the other genres the sociologist may be said to participate only in his imagination; but in participant observation his participation is real. As the Redfield-Lewis controversy (referred to above, pp. 66-67) illustrated, this increases the temptation to become emotionally involved, and to let one's emotions colour one's report. Of course, involvement as such need not be disastrous. In *The Road to Wigan Pier* (1937) and other writings George Orwell showed how much more enlightening a report can be if, in addition to his observations, the author also gives an account of the emotional problems he has confronted in the process of living among the people he has studied. The important thing is that the problems have to be faced.

A familiar problem for participant observers is what is known among anthropologists as 'going native'. This need not take the extreme form of a liability to stay in the field and never return to the academic world; it may also mean, in a milder sense, the tendency to adopt the point of view of the people whom one studies. Cases illustrating this tendency abound in sociology; one of the better-known is Howard Becker's *Outsiders. Studies in the Sociology of Deviance* (1963).

Outsiders is a very perceptive study, based on intimate familiarity with two sorts of groups in particular, marijuana users and dance musicians. Both groups are regarded as outsiders or deviants, by others as well as by themselves.

Becker, taking the deviants' own point of view, notices nothing inherently strange or objectionable in their behaviour. He therefore concludes that 'deviance is *not* a quality of the act the person commits', but 'deviant behaviour is behaviour that people so label' (p. 9). This is, in a nutshell, what has come to be known as the 'labelling theory', one of the most widely-popularized products of modern sociology. It obviously contains a kernel of truth; but it is also partial and superficial. According to Becker, 'social groups create deviance by making the rules whose infraction constitutes deviance' (ibid.). This statement reflects all the naïveté of a voluntaristic action model. It glosses over the problem why certain groups have developed certain rules discriminating between deviant and non-deviant behaviour, and how they have managed to maintain these rules. What functions do rules against stealing or murdering have *for* various groups? Of what figurational developments *are* these rules and their enforcement a function? When one concentrates solely on the 'we'-perspective of selected 'deviant' groups, these problems recede into the background; for those people labelled as 'deviant' the rules appear as givens, as facts of life dictated by those who 'have power'. A sociology anchored on this basis runs the risk of developing a one-sided, incomplete view of society.

At the end of his book Becker admits that, besides the viewpoint of the deviants themselves, we also need to study the other viewpoints involved (p. 174). This, however, comes as an afterthought in a book written rather consistently from within the perspective of 'deviants'. In a subsequent essay (1967) Becker has stated that every sociological inquiry is bound to be partisan; this imposes on the sociologist the moral duty to take the side of those who are at the bottom of the social hierarchy, who have to suffer most from this hierarchy, and whose voices are not represented in the official 'definitions of reality'. Alvin Gouldner (1968) has vigorously combatted this notion of sociological partisanship. There is, as he has argued, no compelling reason why underdogs should be better intellectual guidesmen than those in power; they may command our sympathy, but not our credulity, for the chances are that their ideas are nothing but the ill-informed and resentful reflections of the dominant opinions of the dominant groups.

The challenge for sociologists, then, lies in combining identification and detachment. The 'we'-perspectives of various groups in a figuration are to be examined, not because any one of them may reveal the 'truth', but because they are all constituent parts of the figuration. The next step has to be an inquiry into how these constituent parts are interconnected.

Relevance and irrelevance: the problem of trivialization

Sociologists are not only exposed to strong pressures to make their work 'relevant', but also to counter-pressures of 'trivialization'. As W. Baldamus (1971) has pointed out, by accepting the current standards of professional competence, researchers are almost bound to restrict the scope and relevance of their inquiries. First of all, they have to deal with the constraints of inter-disciplinary specialization. They may start out with a broadly conceived problem touching upon many inter-related areas; but in approaching this problem they will be drawn irresistibly into the orbit of a specific discipline, with its own vocabulary, theoretical assumptions and research procedures. The process of 'inter-disciplinary attenuation' is irreversible, since once a problem has been reformulated to suit the framework of a specific discipline, the results of an analysis carried out within this framework cannot be translated back into the vocabulary of other disciplines. Such are the consequences of specialization in the social sciences.

But this is not all. Noting that the same tendencies towards problem reduction can be observed within each particular discipline, Baldamus proceeds to distinguish no less than three different types of 'intra-disciplinary attenuation' within sociology. First, there is the widespread custom of changing from a 'macro' to a 'micro' perspective by converting original concepts such as anomie or class to empirical referents. The second, related type is the transition from 'objective' to 'subjective' factors, manifested in the common practice of reducing the study of social structures to a study of attitudes. Thirdly, there is the frequent tendency to superimpose 'static' schemes upon 'dynamic' processes. For an example, Baldamus refers to the first volume of *The Affluent Worker* (Goldthorpe *et al.*, 1968). This study is presented as part of a project whose main objective was to test empirically the far-reaching thesis that the working classes in Western Europe are involved in a process of *embourgeoisement*. However, as the authors point out in their introduction, the first volume has a different focus: it deals mainly with workers' attitudes to their jobs. Baldamus interprets this shift of focus as a typical example of intra-disciplinary trivialization: the 'macro' problem of 'class structure' is brought down to the 'micro' setting of industrial relations within a plant; the dynamics of 'class struggle' are reduced to the wage bargainings between employers and employees; and the 'objective' conditions of 'exploitation' are replaced by the 'subjective' variables of 'orientation to work'.

It may be objected that Baldamus has employed a set of marxist concepts to criticize an investigation attuned to a different sociological tradition. Interestingly enough, his analysis applies equally well to a celebrated study which, in its initial stages, was strongly inspired by a marxist orientation: *The Authoritarian Personality* (Adorno *et al.*, 1950). This study, undertaken in California towards the end of the Second World War, had among its major instigators and collaborators Max Horkheimer and T.W. Adorno, of the exiled Frankfurt Institute of Social Research. In retrospect these two men have described the original aims of the project in the following words:

> The objective was to gain a picture, at once reliable and significant, of the human forces and counter-forces which are mobilized whenever and wherever totalitarian movements and their propaganda are successful. Thoroughly empirical in design, the project started from a question of uttermost gravity—racial hatred, especially anti-semitism. One had to overcome one's aversion to the endeavour of penetrating, as a so-called objective, detachedly observing

researcher, the horror to which the lives of millions of harmless victims had been sacrificed. Those who nevertheless engaged in these investigations were moved by the conviction that only differentiated social-scientific knowledge offers certain possibilities of effectively countering a repetition of the calamity, wherever it may be imminent, and whomsoever it may menace [Adorno and Horkheimer, 1956, p. 151].

The actual scope of *The Authoritarian Personality* is considerably less wide than this statement intimates. The bulk of the report consists of psychological material, based upon questionnaires, personality tests and clinical interviews, and culminating in the famous F-scale, a psychological instrument designed for measuring individual proneness to a fascist mentality. (Curiously, the title of the report suggests that one might find in it an A-scale for measuring authoritarianism; this unexplained inconsistency looks like one more symptom of sociologists' indifference to words.) Most of the conclusions had already been anticipated in bolder terms by Horkheimer and Erich Fromm in their contributions to the German volume *Autorität und Familie*, published by the Institute of Social Research in 1936. Subsequent to the publication of *The Authoritarian Personality* numerous attempts have been made to refine the F-scale and to acquire more systematic knowledge about the sociogenesis of authoritarianism. However,

> the number of college students who have filled out one or more versions of the F-scale must be astronomical, but the results are no closer to proper generalization than ten years ago [Kirscht and Dillehay, 1967, p. 31] . . . No single social theory now encompasses the major findings on authoritarianism, nor has a comprehensive set of hypotheses ever been tested and revised [ibid., p. 132].

Although Kirscht and Dillehay cannot help stating, with the characteristic optimism of professional scientists, that 'yet, our knowledge of authoritarianism has moved toward greater maturity and differentiation' (ibid., p. 127), the overwhelming impression to be gained from their survey of the literature is one of confusion and futility. An important reason why continued research on the F-scale has yielded so few tangible results may well lie in its trivialized design, in the reduction implied in it of sociological to psychological problems. The decisive step in this direction was made when the original investigators took as their guiding principle the hypothesis that 'what people say against Jews depends more upon their own psychology than upon the actual characteristics of Jews' (Adorno *et al.*, 1950, p. 57). Although Adorno made some slight reservations about this proposition ('we do not deny that the object plays a role', p. 607), he also endorsed it as the working hypothesis for his own contribution to the project. The argument was indeed plausible. Evidence abounded that no matter what Jews did, an anti-Semite could find fault with it; if they assimilated to Gentile ways, he would accuse them of being pushy; if they did not assimilate, of exclusiveness. What, then, was more advisable than to concentrate research not on the objects of prejudice, but on its subjects, the anti-Semites?

This seemed the obvious course to take on moral grounds as well. The victims of prejudice were innocent; their prosecutors were guilty. Was it not a moral duty to expose the prosecutors, to lay bare their motives, with the objective of combatting them? The investigators consciously took sides; identifying with the victims, they studied the anti-Semites as 'them', in order to discover a fatal 'it', the fascist syndrome.

What the investigators did, for quite understandable reasons, was to isolate prejudice, trying to account for it wholly in terms of the functions it had *for* the prejudiced individuals—without examining to what extent it was a function *of* a wider figuration in which both the prejudiced individuals and their victims took part. Actually, the latter approach would have been in line with the idea of 'totality' espoused by the Frankfurt school; that it was not pursued was due partly to considerations of research economy (a psychological format kept the inquiry within manageable size), partly to identification with the victims who, since they 'had nothing to do with it', were altogether left out of the study.

As Norbert Elias and John Scotson have noted in a much more truly sociological study of prejudice, *The Established and the Outsiders:* 'once people have become interdependent, research is bound to be sterile if one studies them in isolation' (1965, p. 167). This is precisely what was done in *The Authoritarian Personality*: the prejudiced and their victims were separated, and prejudice was not studied as a social relationship but as a personality trait. Taken solely as a personality trait, however, 'prejudice' loses its significance. Uttering, and acting upon, prejudice presupposes power. People who are in a position to discriminate against others effectively and with impunity, have power over those others, while those who suffer discrimination lack the power to put up resistance against it. A relationship of prejudice just cannot be understood without reference to the underlying power balances.

Adorno and his collaborators were right in attaching a good deal of weight to the consideration that whatever the 'objects' of prejudice did would be interpreted to their disadvantage. But when they drew the conclusion that the origins of prejudice were to be found in the personalities of the prejudiced, they did not go far enough. They stopped halfway towards the sociological recognition that prejudice, like any other social phenomenon, can only be understood if it is also seen as a function of the figuration in which it occurs.

Sociology and problems of
human interdependence

As the dilemma of trivialization shows, sociologists are faced with a set of goals that seem at times incompatible. They are expected to produce knowledge which is precise in its factual references, systematic in its manner of classification and explanation, of far-reaching scope, and relevant to a variety of purposes. Although the adherents of various schools may differ on the interpretation and the degree of priority to be given to each of these requirements, no sociologist can afford to ignore them. Everyone has to articulate this vague conglomerate of expectations into a feasible work programme. In varying combinations, these expectations form the major criteria by which both individual contributions and the field of sociology as a whole are evaluated.

In the successive chapters of this book I have tried to focus on these four general aims of sociology one by one. Repeatedly it has become clear that they are closely related: they can be distinguished, but not separated. The issue of trivialization shows how the various demands of sociological knowledge conflict; it should be realized, however, that they are also in many respects complementary. No matter how great the difficulties of pursuing the four ideals together, pursuing any one of them in isolation is bound to be futile.

If I denote the respective problem-areas for the sake of brevity with the single terms 'precision', 'systematics', 'scope', and 'relevance', advocates of conceptual formalism will probably require that these terms be defined. This, however, would give only an illusion of clarity. The terms are intended as sensitizing concepts, to be used in a developmental framework. The notions they convey have played an important part in the development of sociology, and continue to do so; but they can only be grasped adequately by realizing that they have meant different things for different people. The margin of vagueness admittedly implies a lack of systematic rigour; but it increases the scope of these concepts considerably. In principle, they can be applied to every school or movement, since in spite of all divergences, every group of sociologists has tried to come to terms with each of these problems.

It may also be objected that my classification does not correspond to such well-known methodological or epistemological categories as validity, reliability, generalization and abstraction, or, to name another set, truth, validity and content. I have avoided allocating central importance to these more familiar terms because they tend to lead us away from the actual problems of sociology and into areas where authority is claimed by philosophers. Rather than plunging into the debates between 'contemporary schools of meta-science' (Radnitzky, 1973) I have distilled from the actual literature of sociology itself this set of four persistently recurring issues. While there is certainly no reason for sociologists to evade methodological discussions with philosophers, we should be prepared to take the initiative of deriving methodological notions from our own discipline instead of first turning for guidance to putative experts. The latter do not pick their precepts out of the air; they are strongly influenced by conceptions of how the most prestigious scientists, the physical scientists, proceed.

Directions for a genuinely sociological methodology and epistemology can be found in classical sociology, from Comte and Marx to Durkheim. Curiously, in the very period when sociology presumably came of age and was proclaimed a mature science, its practitioners seemed to have lost their methodological self-confidence, and either relied on philosophers of science or over-reacted with the simple and unsociological rhetoric of 'every man his own methodologist' (Mills, 1959, p. 123) or 'abandoning method' (Phillips, 1973). Among this confusion, the writings of a few men such as Herbert Blumer and, most notably, Norbert Elias, stand out as containing a sociologically argued rationale for a sociological methodology.

In a sociological sense, there is nothing 'timeless' or 'metasocial' or 'metatheoretical' about the concepts of precision, systematics, scope and relevance. They refer to real problems experienced by real people: problems of acquiring precise information; of finding clear and consistent principles of classification and explanation; of grasping the wider implications of events; of knowing how to make their knowledge of some avail in arranging their lives. They refer, in other words, to problems of orientation in the social world as one particular variety of the problems of social existence in general.

The problems of social existence in general are manifold. In Chapter 4 (pp. 137-143), I have discussed Elias's distinction into three types of dependence and control. This is indeed such a broad distinction that it may cover all problems of social existence. Its main function, however, is not to classify these problems into neat categories but rather to point to their complexity. According to another scheme to which I have referred, we may generally distinguish problems of physical protection, of material production, of orientation, and of affection and affect control. This second scheme obviously overlaps with the first one. For those who insist on systematic closure, this may seem an inadmissible anomaly. Neither list, however, is designed as an analytic instrument with which specific problems may be isolated as separate elements of any figuration. On the contrary, both schemes serve as reminders that the various problems and their solutions enter into one another and can only be understood in terms of the composite constellations they form together.

In this respect the present approach differs from the attempts by some structural-functionalists to draw up catalogues of 'system requisites' for any social system. As an example, take Marion Levy's list of universal 'aspects of social structure':

> Five aspects are distinguished: (1) role differentiation, (2) solidarity, (3) economic allocation, (4) political allocation, and (5) integration and expression. Briefly, role differentiation refers to the aspect of 'who does what when'. Solidarity refers to the aspect of 'who sticks with whom' under varying circumstances, in what way, and how strongly. Economic allocation refers to the allocation of goods and services. Political allocation refers to the allocation of power and responsibility. The categories integration and expression are catch-all categories. I find them unsatisfactory, but I have not been able to improve upon them; they cover such aspects as those having to do with education, religion, recreation, artistic expression, emotional reactions, etc. [Levy, 1966, p. 25].

Levy's classification has the virtues, first of being manifestly untidy, and second of being stated in rather plain language. However, instead of the singular 'who does what when', a plural is to be preferred. This may sound somewhat awkward; but it reminds us of the fundamental fact that human beings are interdependent. A second objection to be made against Levy's list is that the categories 'economic' and 'political' are derived from, and can only be fruitfully applied to, societies in which functional differentiation has proceeded as far, and in the same direction, as in contemporary Europe and America. Although Levy is aware of this fact, he intends his conceptual scheme to provide analytic categories which are mutually exclusive and ahistoric.

It is precisely this last ambition, however, that makes the whole enterprise dubious. Surely there is something to be said for a general inventory of 'aspects of social structure'. It can have useful heuristic functions. Thus, partly paraphrasing Levy, we may distinguish problems of solidarity ('who belong together with whom?'), problems of hierarchy ('who are superior to whom?'), problems of division of labour ('who are to do what, and for whom?'), and problems of property ('who own what?'). By defining each of these problems so as to make them perfectly distinguishable under all circumstances, however, we would obscure in advance the manifold ways in which they may actually interpenetrate. The main purpose of listing them is, on the contrary, to keep us from conceiving any single one of them as isolated and independent.

Thus we are again reminded of the importance of scope as an ideal for sociological research. This ideal does not imply that all sociologists should turn to the study of so-called 'macro'-problems. On the contrary, it is very possible to take a clearly-delimited 'micro'-problem—such as the conflict between two individuals—and deal with it in a manner that lends a perhaps unexpectedly large scope to the research. All that is required is to see the problem at hand not in isolation, but in the larger context of changing figurations. A single case-study conducted from within this perspective can be of far-reaching significance (cf. Elias, forthcoming).

This is not to deny that emphasis on scope—or on any other aim of sociological knowledge—can engender tensions. Again and again spokesmen for one specific aim of sociology have made themselves heard, pleading, if only by implication, against the other aims. Their arguments have followed the lines, by now familiar, of the rhetoric of precision ('observe carefully'), of systematics ('define your concepts'), of scope ('look at the wider context'), of relevance ('what is the use of it?').

Out of the controversies we may reconstruct, for example, an ascending series of arguments according to which precision is the foundation on which sociology is to be built. Precise information, so the argument goes, is the empirical basis without which any sociological theory hangs in the air. Systematic formal reasoning is a second precondition for arriving at conclusions of large scope. If these steps are not carefully made in proper sequential order, no knowledge can be acquired—let alone knowledge that is in any way 'relevant'.

It is not difficult to reverse the whole argument. We may begin by stating that a necessary precondition for knowledge is the urge to know, the need for orientation. The main criterion for assessing knowledge is the extent to which it meets this vital need; in other words, its relevance. In order to be capable of orientating ourselves at all, we need general categories supplying us with a means for sorting out our experiences. This puts scope on the second level of importance. In order to make the general perspective more orderly and more specific we need, finally, a measure of systematic consistency and empirical precision.

Thus two arguments can be put forward which are plausible, but mutually contradictory. This short-circuit occurs because both arguments are couched in fictional, static terms, as if in sociology one had the choice of starting from scratch—building a science either on 'observed facts' or on 'vital needs'. Obviously, no such alternative has ever existed. Sociology is a process; it has no definite beginning, and, one hopes, no end. During the nineteenth century, scope and relevance were rated higher, on the whole, than in the period between 1900 and 1975, when priority was given to precision and systematics. The student movement of the 1960s has helped to revitalize the goal of relevance. At the present juncture, a plea for scope is most timely.

This necessarily implies a critique of those sociologists who over-emphasize either the importance of other aims, or the extent to which those other aims can be realized regardless of scope. The importance of factual precision is over-rated by those who, in Mills's well-chosen phrase, suffer from 'methodological inhibition'. The actual accomplishments of fact-finders are over-rated by those who allow themselves such statements as 'The level of alienation can be empirically measured' (Etzioni, 1968, p. 618).

Similar attitudes prevail with regard to systematics. Some

critics deny sociology any claim to scientific status because its concepts fail to meet strict logical requirements (cf. Lachenmeyer, 1971; 1973). Others, however, assure us that such concepts are indeed available (cf. Zetterberg, 1965b). Against both parties, a more moderate stance is called for. Philosophical support for such a stance, if needed, can be found in the writings of Wittgenstein, among others. As Anton Blok (1975) suggests, Wittgenstein's theory of family likenesses in language may help to release sociologists from their obsession with formal logic. Wittgenstein's famous analysis of the word 'play' demonstrates that it may be impossible to give an adequate definition of a word, even though its meaning is perfectly clear. Therefore, it is not a defect if we cannot define a term. 'To think it is [a defect] would be like saying that the light of my reading lamp is no real light at all because it has no sharp boundary' (Wittgenstein, 1958, p. 27).

As with precision and systematics, there are again today some writers who put primary emphasis on the relevance of sociology. I do not know of anyone who has expressed himself as confidently about sociology's recent accomplishments on this score as Etzioni on precision, or Zetterberg on systematics. There is, however, no dearth of critics who denounce sociology—if not social science in general—for its lack of relevance. Words to the same effect as those uttered by Henry Sidgwick a century ago can still be heard on many occasions. As Noam Chomsky puts it:

Obviously, one must learn from social and behavioural science whatever one can; obviously, these fields should be pursued in as serious a way as is possible. But it will be quite unfortunate, and highly dangerous, if they are not accepted and judged on their merits and according to their actual, not pretended, accomplishments. In particular, if there is a body of theory, well tested and verified, that applies to the conduct of foreign affairs or the resolution of domestic or international conflict, its existence has been kept a well-guarded secret . . . To anyone who has any familiarity with the social and behavioural sciences (or the 'policy sciences') the claim that there are certain considera-

tions and principles too deep for the outsider to comprehend is simply an absurdity, unworthy of comment [1969,
p. 271].

This criticism has, to my knowledge, never been refuted
publicly by any social scientist. However, as Chomsky
himself indicates, the need for adequate oritentation in the
social world is great. Many of his own writings are intended
as contributions to meet this need. But it can also be seen
from these writings that the most difficult task today is
synthesis. There is no generally accepted overall perspective
into which the overwhelming multitude of available data can
be integrated, and which transcends the parochial views that
dominate social theory today.

Although none of the struggling parties in the contemporary world is likely to welcome such a perspective as
immediately relevant to its own purposes, one hopes this will
not discourage sociologists from working toward it. They are
sometimes accused of joining too readily the 'technocratic'
forces at work in modern society. As Chomsky reminds us,
their effectiveness in this capacity is probably small. Yet it is
more than just a play on words if we contrast the
'technocratic' model with the 'socratic'. For sociologists, the
socratic imperative implies a quest for understanding ourselves as social individuals, as interdependent human beings.

Bibliography

Abel, Theodor
1948 'The Operation Called *Verstehen*', *American Journal of Sociology*, LV, pp. 211-18.
Abrams, Philip
1968 *The Origins of British Sociology*, Chicago: University of Chicago Press.
Adorno, T.W.; Else Frenkel-Brunswik; Daniel J. Levinson, and R. Nevitt Sanford
1950 *The Authoritarian Personality*, New York: Harper and Row.
Adorno, T.W., and Max Horkheimer
1956 *Soziologische Exkurse*, Frankfurt a.M.: Europaeische Verlagsanstalt.
Agassi, Joseph
1960 'Methodological Individualism', *British Journal of Sociology*, XI, pp. 244-70.
Amalrik, Andrei Alekseevič
1970 *Will the Soviet Union Survive Until 1984?* Translated by Henry Kamm and Sidney Monas, London: Allen Lane.
Andreski, Stanislaw
1974 *The Essential Comte*, London: Croom Helm.
Apter, David E. (ed.)
1964 *Ideology and Discontent*, New York: Free Press.
Aron, Raymond
1965 *Main Currents in Sociological Thought*. Translated by Richard Howard and Helen Weaver, London: Weidenfeld and Nicolson. Quotation from Pelican edition, Harmondsworth 1968.
Austin, J.L.
1962 *How To Do Things With Words*, London: Oxford University Press.

205

Avineri, Shlomo
1968 *The Social and Political Thought of Karl Marx*, London: Cambridge University Press.

Baldamus, W.
1971 'Types of Trivialisation, *University of Birmingham Discussion Papers*, Series E, no. 15.

Baritz, Loren
1960 *The Servants of Power*, Middletown, Conn.: Wesleyan University Press.

Bauer, Raymond A. (ed.)
1966 *Social Indicators*, Cambridge, Mass.: M.I.T. Press.

Becker, Ernest
1968 *The Structure of Evil*, New York: Braziller.

Becker, Howard S.
1963 *Outsiders,* New York: Free Press
1967 'Whose Side Are We On?' *Social Problems*, XIV, pp. 239-47.

Becker, Howard S.; Blanche Geer; Everett C. Hughes, and Anselm L. Strauss
1961 *Boys in White*, Chicago: University of Chicago Press.

Bendix, Reinhard, and Guenther Roth
1971 *Scholarship and Partisanship*, Berkeley: University of California Press.

Berger, John
1972 *Selected Essays and Articles*, Harmondsworth: Penguin Books.

Berger, Peter L.
1963 *Invitation to Sociology*, Garden City, N.Y.: Doubleday Anchor.

Berger, Peter L., and Thomas Luckmann
1966 *The Social Construction of Reality*, Garden City, N.Y.: Doubleday Anchor.

Bierstedt, Robert A.
1969 'A Summary View', in Robert A. Bierstedt (ed.), *A Design for Sociology: Scope, Objectives, and Methods*, Philadelphia: The Academy of Political and Social Science, pp. 137-52.

Birnbaum, Norman
1971 *Toward a Critical Sociology*, New York: Oxford University Press.

Black, Max (ed.)
1961 *The Social Theories of Talcott Parsons*, Englewood Cliffs, N.J.: Prentice-Hall.

Blau, Peter M.
1955 *The Dynamics of Bureaucracy*, Chicago: University of Chicago Press.
1964 *Exchange and Power in Social Life*, New York: Wiley.

Blau, Peter M. and O.D. Duncan
1967 *The American Occupational Structure,* New York: Wiley.
Bloch, Marc
1949 *The Historian's Craft.* Translated by Peter Putnam, New York: Random House, 1953.
Blok, Anton
1974 *The Mafia of a Sicilian Village, 1860-1960,* Oxford: Basil Blackwell.
1975 *Wittgenstein en Elias,* Assen: Van Gorcum.
Blumberg, Paul
1968 *Industrial Democracy,* London: Constable.
Blumer, Herbert
1939 *An Appraisal of Thomas and Znaniecki's 'The Polish Peasant in Europe and America',* New York: Social Science Research Council.
1969 *Symbolic Interactionism. Perspective and Method,* Englewood Cliffs, N.J.: Prentice-Hall.
Booth, Charles
1902-03 *Life and Labour of the People in London,* 17 volumes, London: Macmillan.
Bouglé, C.
1935 *Bilan de la sociologie française contemporaine,* Paris: Félix Alcan.
Branford, Victor
1905 'On the Origin and Use of the Word Sociology', *Sociological Papers,* I, pp. 1-24.
Brown, George W.
1973 'Some Thoughts on Grounded Theory', *Sociology,* VII, pp. 1-16.
Buckley, Walter
1967 *Sociology and Modern Systems Theory,* Englewood Cliffs, N.J.: Prentice-Hall.
Burgess, Ernest W., and Donald J. Bogue (eds.)
1964 *Contributions to Urban Sociology,* Chicago: University of Chicago Press.
Burke, Edmund
(1790) *Reflections on the Revolution in France.* Edited by Connor Cruise O'Brien, Harmondsworth: Penguin Books, 1968.
Burke, Kenneth
1954 *Permanence and Change,* Indianapolis: Bobbs-Merrill.

Carey, Alex
1967 'The Hawthorne Studies: A Radical Criticism', *American Sociological Review,* XXXII, pp. 403-17.

Child, John, and Roger Mansfield
1972 'Technology, Size, and Organization Structure', *Sociology*, VI, pp. 369-93.
Chomsky, Noam
1959 'A Review of B.F. Skinner's *Verbal Behavior*', *Language*, XXXV, pp. 26-58.
1969 *American Power and the New Mandarins*, New York: Pantheon Books. Quotation from Pelican edition, Harmondsworth 1971.
Cicourel, Aaron V.
1968 *The Social Organization of Juvenile Justice*, New York: Wiley.
Clark, G.N.
(1948) 'Social Science in the Age of Newton', in: Oberschal (ed.), *The Establishment of Empirical Sociology*, 1974, pp. 15-30.
Cohen, Albert K.
1955 *Delinquent Boys*, New York: Free Press.
Cohen, Percy S.
1968 *Modern Social Theory*, London: Heinemann.
Coles, Robert
1970 *Erik H. Erikson. The Growth of his Work*, Boston: Little, Brown and Co.
Colfax, J. David, and Jack L. Roach (eds.)
1971 *Radical Sociology*, New York: Basic Books.
Comte, Auguste
(1838) *Cours de philosophie positive*, volume 4, Paris: Baillière. Quotations from Andreski, *The Essential Comte*, 1974.
Conquest, Robert
1971 *The Great Terror*, 2nd ed., Harmondsworth: Penguin Books.
Coser, Lewis A.
1956 *The Functions of Social Conflict*, New York: Free Press.
1971 *Masters of Sociological Thought*, New York: Harcourt Brace Jovanovich.
Crosland, Maurice P.
1962 *Historical Studies in the Language of Chemistry*, London: Heinemann.

Dahrendorf, Ralf
1958 'Out of Utopia: Toward a Re-orientation of Sociological Analysis', *American Journal of Sociology*, LXIV, pp. 115-27.
1967 *Pfade aus Utopia*, München: Piper.
Dalton, Melville
1961 *Men Who Manage*, New York: Wiley.
Davis, Kingsley
1959 'The Myth of Functional Analysis as a Special Method in Socio-

logy and Anthropology', *American Sociological Review*, XXIV, pp. 757-72.

Davis, Kingsley, and Wilbert E. Moore
1945 'Some Principles of Stratification', *American Sociological Review*, X, pp. 242-9.

De Moor, R.A.
1961 *De verklaring van het conflict*, Assen: Van Gorcum.

Deutscher, Irving
1968 'On Social Science and the Sociology of Knowledge', *American Sociologist*, III, pp. 291-2.
1973 *What We Say–What We Do*, Glenview, Ill.: Scott, Foresman and Co.

De Valk, J.M.M.
1960 *De evolutie van het wetsbegrip in de sociologie*, Assen: Van Gorcum.

Devereux, Edward C., Jr.
1961 'Parsons' Sociological Theory', in: Black (ed.), *The Social Theories of Talcott Parsons*, pp. 1-63.

Douglas, Jack D.
1967 *The Social Meanings of Suicide*, Princeton, N.J.: Princeton University Press.

Douglas, Jack D. (ed.)
1970a *The Impact of Sociology*, New York: Appleton-Century-Crofts.
1970b *The Relevance of Sociology*, New York: Appleton-Century-Crofts.

Durkheim, Emile
(1895) *The Rules of Sociological Method*. Translated by Sarah A. Solovay and John H. Mueller, Chicago: University of Chicago Press, 1938.
(1897) *Suicide: A Study in Sociology*. Translated by John A. Spaulding and George Simpson, New York: Free Press, 1951.
(1902-06) *Moral Education*. Translated by Everett K. Wilson and Herman Schnurer, New York: Free Press, 1961.
(1912) *The Elementary Forms of Religious Life*. Translated by J.W. Swain, London: Allen and Unwin, 1915.

Durkheim, Emile, and Marcel Mauss
(1903) *Primitive Classification*. Translated by Rodney Needham, Chicago: University of Chicago Press, 1963.

Elias, Norbert
1950 'Studies in the Genesis of the Naval Profession. Part One', *British Journal of Sociology*, I, pp. 291-309.

1956 'Problems of Involvement and Detachment', *British Journal of Sociology*, VII, pp. 226-52.
1969a *Ueber den Prozess der Zivilisation*, 2nd ed., Bern-München: Francke Verlag.
1969b *Die hoefische Gesselschaft*, Neuwied–Berlin: Luchterhand.
1969c 'Sociology and Psychiatry', in J.H. Foulkes (ed.), *Psychiatry in a Changing Society*, London: Tavistock.
1970 *Was ist Soziologie?*, München: Juventa Verlag.
1971 'Sociology of Knowledge: New Perspectives', *Sociology* V, pp. 149-68 and 355-70.
1974 'Een essay over tijd. Deel één', *De Gids* CXXXVII, pp. 600-8.
(Forthcoming) 'Drake and Doughty. A Paradigmatic Case Study'.
Elias, Norbert, and John L. Scotson
1965 *The Established and the Outsiders*, London: Cass.
Ellis, Desmond P.
1971 'The Hobbesian Problem of Order', *American Sociological Review*, XXXVI, pp. 692-703.
Engels, Friedrich
1845 'Die Lage der arbeitenden Klasse in England', in *Karl Marx Friedrich Engels Werke*, volume 2, Berlin: Dietz, pp. 225-506.
Erikson, Erik H.
1962 *Young Man Luther*, New York: Norton.
Etzioni, Amitai
1968 *The Active Society*, New York: Free Press.

Febvre, Lucien
1925 *A Geographical Introduction to History*. Translated by E.G. Mountford and J.H. Paxton, New York: Knopf.
Ferguson, Adam
(1767) *An Essay on the History of Civil Society*. Quotation from Schneider (ed.), *The Scottish Moralists*, 1967.
Filmer, Paul; Michael Phillipson; David Silverman, and David Walsh
1972 *New Directions in Sociological Theory*, London: Collier-MacMillan.
Finley, M.I.
1967 *The World of Odysseus*, revised edition, Harmondsworth: Penguin Books.
Fitzhugh, George
(1854) 'Sociology for the South', in: Wish, *Ante Bellum*, pp. 41-95.
Fletcher, Ronald
1974 *The Crisis of Industrial Civilisation: The Early Essays of Auguste Comte*, London: Heinemann.

Flew, Antony (ed.)
1951 *Logic and Language*, first series, Oxford: Basil Blackwell.
Frankfort, Henri; H.A. Frankfort; John A. Wilson, and Thorkild Jacobsen
1949 *Before Philosophy*, Harmondsworth: Penguin Books.
Freud, Sigmund
(1927) 'Die Zukunft einer Illusion', *Gesammelte Werke*, volume 14, London: Imago, 1948, pp. 323-80.
(1933) 'Neue Folge der Vorlesungen zur Einfuehrung in die Psychoanalyse', *Gesammelte Werke*, volume 15, London: Imago, 1944.
Friedrichs, Robert
1970 *A Sociology of Sociology*, New York: Free Press.

Garfinkel, Harold
1967 *Studies in Ethnomethodology*, Englewood Cliffs, N.J.: Prentice-Hall.
Garfinkel, Harold, and Harvey Sacks
1970 'On Formal Structures of Practical Action', in McKinney and Tiryakian, *Theoretical Sociology*, pp. 337-436.
Gay, Peter
1969 *The Enlightenment: An Interpretation*, volume 2, New York: Knopf.
Geertz, Clifford
1964 'Ideology as a Cultural System', in Apter (ed.), *Ideology and Discontent*, pp. 47-76.
Geiger, Theodor
1953 *Ideologie und Wahrheit*, Stuttgart-Wien: Humboldt.
Gerth, Hans, and C. Wright Mills
1953 *Character and Social Structure.* New York: Harcourt, Brace and World.
Glaser, Barney G., and Anselm L. Strauss
1967 *The Discovery of Grounded Theory*, Chicago: Aldine.
Glass, D.U.
1973 *Numbering the People: The Eighteenth Century Population Controversy and the Development of Census and Vital Statistics in Britain*, Farnborough: Saxon House.
Glucksmann, Miriam
1974 *Structuralist Analysis in Contemporary Social Thought*, London: Routledge and Kegan Paul.
Goffman, Erving
1959 *The Presentation of Self in Everyday Life*, Garden City, N.Y.: Doubleday Anchor.

Goldthorpe, John H.; David Lockwood; Frank Beckhofer, and Jennifer Platt
1968 *The Affluent Worker: Industrial Attitudes and Behaviour*, London: Cambridge University Press.
Gouldner, Alvin W.
1959 'Reciprocity and Autonomy in Functional Theory', in: Gross, *Symposium on Sociological Theory*, pp. 241-70.
1968 'The Sociologist as Partisan', *American Sociologist*, III, pp. 103-16.
1970 *The Coming Crisis of Western Sociology*, New York: Basic Books.
Gurvitch, Georges, and Wilbert E. Moore (eds.)
1945 *Twentieth Century Sociology*, New York: Philosophical Library.

Habermas, Jürgen
1971 *Theorie und Praxis*, Frankfurt a.M.: Suhrkamp.
Hannerz, Ulf
1969 *Soulside*, New York: Columbia University Press.
Hayek, F.A.
1952 *The Counter-Revolution of Science*, New York: Free Press.
Heilbroner, Robert
1974 *An Inquiry into the Human Prospect*, New York: Norton.
Hempel, Carl G.
1965 *Aspects of Scientific Explanation and Other Essays in the Philosophy of Science*, New York: Free Press.
Henry, Jules
1963 *Culture Against Man*, New York: Random House.
1972 *Pathways to Madness*, New York: Random House.
Hindess, Barry
1973 *The Use of Official Statistics in Sociology*, London: Macmillan.
Homans, George C.
1950 *The Human Group*, New York: Harcourt-Brace.
1961 *Social Behavior: Its Elementary Forms*, New York: Harcourt, Brace and World.
1971 'Commentary', in: Turk and Simpson (eds.), *Institutions and Social Exchange*, pp. 363-79.
Horkheimer, Max (ed.)
1936 *Studien ueber Autoritaet und Familie*, Paris: Alcan.
Horton, John
1966 'Order and Conflict Theories of Social Problems as Competing Ideologies', *American Journal of Sociology*, LXXI, pp. 701-13.
Hudgins, C.V.
1933 'Conditioning and the Voluntary Control of the Pupillary Light Reflex', *Journal of General Psychology*, VIII, pp. 3-51.

Hughes, Everett, C.
1958 *Men and Their Work*, New York: Free Press.
Hughes, Henry
(1854) *Treatise on Sociology, Theoretical and Practical.* Reprint, New
York: Negro University Press, 1968.
Hughes, H. Stuart
1958 *Consciousness and Society*, New York: Knopf.
Hurd, Geoffrey
1973 *Human Societies: An Introduction to Sociology*, London:
Routledge and Kegan Paul.

Inkeles, Alex
1964 *What Is Sociology?*, Englewood Cliffs, N.J.: Prentice-Hall.

Jackson, Elton F. and Richard F. Curtis
1972 'Effects of Vertical Mobility on Status Inconsistency', *American
Sociological Review*, XXXVII, pp. 701-13.
Jay, Martin
1973 *The Dialectical Imagination*, Boston: Beacon Press.
Johnson, Harry M.
1960 *Sociology: A Systematic Introduction*, New York: Harcourt,
Brace and Company.
Jones, D. Caradog
1948 *Social Surveys*, London: Hutchinson.
Joravsky, David
1970 *The Lysenko Affair*, Cambridge, Mass.: Harvard University Press.

Kirscht, John P., and R.C. Dillehay
1967 *Dimensions of Authoritarianism*, Lexington, Ky.: University of
Kentucky Press.
Koenig, René
1949 *Soziologie heute*, Zuerich: Regio Verlag.
Kroeber, Theodora
1961 *Ishi in Two Worlds*, Berkeley: University of California Press.
Kruijt, C.S.
1975 *Social Stress in the Affluent Society: Suicide as Indicator*, The
Hague: Ministry of Housing and Physical Planning.
Kuhn, Thomas S.
1970 *The Structure of Scientific Revolutions*, 2nd ed., Chicago:
University of Chicago Press.

Lachenmeyer, Charles W.
1971 *The Language of Sociology*, New York: Columbia University
Press.

1973 *The Essence of Social Research*, New York: Free Press.
Landau, David, and Paul F. Lazarsfeld
1968 'Adolphe Quetelet', *International Encyclopedia of the Social Sciences*, volume 13, pp. 247-57.
Landsberger, Henry A.
1958 *Hawthorne Revisited*, Ithaca: Cornell University Press.
LaPiere, Richard T.
1934 'Attitudes Versus Actions', *Social Forces*, XIII, pp. 230-37.
Laslett, Peter
1965 *The World We Have Lost*, London: Methuen.
Laurents, Arthur; Leonard Bernstein, and Stephen Sondheim
(1958) *West Side Story*. Reprint, London: Ace Books, 1961.
Lazarsfeld, Paul F.
1949 *'The American Soldier*: An Expository Review', *Public Opinion Quarterly*, XIII, pp. 377-404.
1970 *Main Trends in Sociology*, Paris: Mouton-Unesco.
Lazarsfeld, Paul F., and Morris Rosenberg (eds.)
1955 *The Language of Social Research*, New York: Free Press.
Leff, Gordon
1969 *The Tyranny of Concepts*, 2nd ed., London: Merlin.
Leiss, William
1972 *The Domination of Nature*, New York: Braziller.
Lenski, Gerhard
1970 *Human Societies*, New York: McGraw-Hill.
LePlay, Frédéric
1855 *Les ouvriers Européens*, Paris: Imprimerie Impériale.
Letwin, William
(1963) *The Origins of Scientific Economics*, London: Methuen. Quotation from Doubleday Anchor edition, Garden City, N.Y., 1965.
Levy, Marion J., Jr.
1966 *Modernization and the Structure of Societies*, Princeton: Princeton University Press.
Lewis, Oscar
1951 *Life in a Mexican Village: Tepoztlán Restudied*, Urbana: University of Illinois Press.
Lichtheim, George
1964 *Marxism*, London: Routledge and Kegan Paul.
Liebow, Elliot
1967 *Tally's Corner, Washington D.C.*, New York: Little, Brown and Company.
Linschoten, J.
1964 *Idolen van de psycholoog*, Utrecht: Bijleveld 1964.

Lipset, Seymour Martin, and Neil J. Smelser (eds.)
1961 *Sociology: The Progress of a Decade*, Englewood Cliffs, N.J.: Prentice-Hall.
Locke, John
(1690) *Two Treatises of Government*. Edited by Peter Laslett, London: Cambridge University Press, 1960.
Lukes, Steven
1973 *Emile Durkheim: His Life and Work*, London: Allen Lane.
Lundberg, George A.
1939 *Foundations of Sociology*, New York: MacMillan.
Lynd, Robert S.
1939 *Knowledge For What?*, Princeton: Princeton University Press.
Lynd, Robert J., and Helen M. Lynd
1929 *Middletown*, New York: Harcourt, Brace and World.
1937 *Middletown in Transition*, New York: Harcourt, Brace and World.

Macpherson, C.B.
1962 *The Political Doctrine of Possessive Individualism*, Oxford: Clarendon.
Madge, John
1962 *The Origins of Scientific Sociology*, New York: Free Press.
Malthus, Thomas Robert
(1798) *An Essay on the Principle of Population*. Edited by Antony Flew, Harmondsworth: Penguin Books, 1970.
Mannheim, Karl
1927 'Conservative Thought', in: *Essays in Sociology and Social Psychology*. Edited by Paul Kekcskemeti, London: Routledge and Kegan Paul, pp. 74-164.
1936 *Ideology and Utopia*. Translated by Louis Wirth and Edward Shils, London: Routledge and Kegan Paul.
Manuel, Frank E.
1962 *The Prophets of Paris*, Cambridge, Mass.: Harvard University Press.
Marcuse, Herbert
1955 *Reason and Revolution*, 2nd ed., Boston: Beacon Press.
1968 *Negations: Essays in Critical Theory*, Boston: Beacon Press.
Martindale, Don
1960 *The Nature and Types of Sociological Theory*, Boston: Houghton Mifflin.
Marx, Karl
(1852) 'Der 18. Brumaire des Napoleon Bonaparte', in: *Karl Marx Friedrich Engels Werke*, volume 8, Berlin: Dietz Verlag, 1972, pp. 111-207.

(1859) 'Zur Kritik der Politischen Oekonomie', in: *Karl Marx Friedrich Engels Werke*, volume 13, Berlin: Dietz Verlag, 1972, pp. 3-160.

(1867) 'Das Kapital', volume 1, in: *Karl Marx Friedrich Engels Werke*, volume 23, Berlin: Dietz Verlag, 1972.

(1894) 'Das Kapital', volume 3, in: *Karl Marx Friedrich Engels Werke*, volume 25, Berlin: Dietz Verlag, 1972.

Marx, Karl, and Friedrich Engels

(1847) 'Die deutsche Ideologie', in: *Karl Marx Friedrich Engels Werke*, volume 3, Berlin: Dietz Verlag, 1969.

(1848) 'Manifest der Kommunistischen Partei', in: *Karl Marx Friedrich Engels Werke*, volume 4, Berlin: Dietz Verlag, 1972, pp. 459-93.

Mayo, Elton

1945 *The Social Problems of an Industrial Civilization*, Cambridge, Mass.: Graduate School of Business Administration, Harvard University.

McKinney, John C., and Edward A. Tiryakian (eds.)

1970 *Theoretical Sociology: Perspectives and Developments*, New York: Appleton-Century-Crofts.

Medick, Hans

1973 *Naturzustand und Naturgeschichte der buergerlichen Gesselschaft*, Goettingen: Vandenhoeck und Ruprecht.

Merton, Robert K.

1957 *Social Theory and Social Structure*, 2nd ed., New York: Free Press.

1967 *On Theoretical Sociology*, New York: Free Press.

Mickiewicz, Ellen

1973 *Handbook of Social Science Data*, New York: Free Press.

Mill, John Stuart

(1865) *Auguste Comte and Positivism.* Reprint, Ann Arbor: University of Michigan Press 1961.

Mills, C. Wright

1959 *The Sociological Imagination*, New York: Oxford University Press.

1963 *Power, Politics and People*, New York, Oxford University Press.

Montesquieu

(1748) *De l'esprit des lois.* Edited by Gonzague Truc, volume 1, Paris: Garnier, 1956.

Moore, Barrington, Jr.

1958 *Political Power and Social Theory*, Cambridge, Mass.: Harvard University Press.

1966 *The Social Origins of Dictatorship and Democracy*, Boston: Beacon Press.

Mullins, Nicholas C.
1973 *Theories and Theory Groups in Contemporary American Sociology*, New York: Harper and Row.

Nietzsche, Friedrich
(1887) 'Zur Genealogie der Moral', in: *Werke in drei Bänder*, edited by Karl Schlechta, volume 2, München: Hanser, 1955, pp. 761-900.
(1889) 'Götzen-Dämmerung', in: *Werke in drei Bänder*, edited by Karl Schlechta, volume 2, München: Hanser, 1955, pp. 939-1033.
Nisbet, Robert A.
1966 *The Sociological Tradition*, New York: Basic Books.
1969 *Social Change and History*, New York: Oxford University Press.
1970a 'Developmentalism: A Critical Analysis', in: McKinney and Tiryakian, *Theoretical Sociology*, pp. 167-204.
1970b *The Social Bond*, New York: Knopf.

Oberschal, Anthony (ed.)
1972 *The Establishment of Empirical Sociology*, New York: Harper and Row.
O'Connor, James
1974 *The Corporations and the State*, New York: Harper.
Ollman, Bertell
1971 *Alienation. Marx's Conception of Man in Capitalist Society*, Cambridge: Cambridge University Press.
Ong, Walter J.
1958 *Ramus. Method and the Decay of Dialogue*, Cambridge, Mass.: Harvard University Press.
Orwell, George
1936 'Shooting and Elephant', in: *The Collected Essays, Journalism and Letters of George Orwell*, volume 1, Harmondsworth: Penguin Books, 1970, pp. 265-73.
1937 *The Road to Wigan Pier*, London: Victor Gollancz.
Ossowski, Stanislaw
1963 *Class Structure in the Social Consciousness*. Translated by Sheila Patterson, London: Routledge and Kegan Paul.

Pareto, Vilfredo
1917 *Traité de sociologie générale*, volume 1, Lausanne-Paris: Payot.
Park, Robert E., and Ernest W. Burgess
1921 *Introduction to the Science of Sociology*, Chicago: University of Chicago Press.

Parsons, Talcott

1937 *The Structure of Social Action*, Boston: McGraw-Hill.

1951 *The Social System*, New York: Free Press.

1954 *Essays in Sociological Theory*, New York: Free Press.

1961 'The Point of View of the Author', in: Black (ed.), *The Theories of Talcott Parsons*, pp. 311-63.

1966 *Societies: Evolutionary and Comparative Perspectives*, Englewood Cliffs, N.J.: Prentice-Hall.

1970 'Some Problems of General Theory in Sociology', in: McKinney and Tiryakian, *Theoretical Sociology*, pp. 27-68.

1971 *The System of Modern Societies*, Englewood Cliffs, N.J.: Prentice-Hall.

Parsons, Talcott; Edward Shils; Kaspar D. Naegete, and Jesse R. Pitts (eds.)

1961 *Theories of Society*, New York: Free Press.

Phillips, Derek L.

1971 *Knowledge From What?*, Chicago: Rand McNally.

1973 *Abandoning Method*, San Francisco: Jossey-Bass.

Pitt, David C.

1972 *Using Historical Sources in Anthropology and Sociology*, New York: Holt, Rinehart and Winston.

Popper, Karl R.

1945 *The Open Society and its Enemies*, 2 vols., London: Routledge and Kegan Paul.

1957 *The Poverty of Historicism*, London: Routledge and Kegan Paul.

1959 *The Logic of Scientific Discovery*, London: Hutchinson.

1963 *Conjectures and Refutations*, London: Routledge and Kegan Paul.

Radnitzky, Gerard

1973 *Contemporary Schools of Metascience*, 2nd ed., Chicago: Henry Regnery.

Raison, Timothy (ed.)

1969 *The Founding Fathers of Social Science*, Harmondsworth: Penguin Books.

Redfield, Robert

1930 *Tepoztlán: A Mexican Village*, Chicago: University of Chicago Press.

Ritzer, George

1975 *Sociology. A Multiple Paradigm Science*, Boston: Allyn and Bacon.

Roethlisberger, F.J., and William J. Dickson

1939 *Management and the Worker*, Cambridge, Mass.: Harvard University Press.

Ruestow, Alexander
1950 *Ortsbestimmung der Gegenwart*, volume 1, Erlenback-Zürich: Eugen Rentsch.
Ryle, Gilbert
1951 'Systematically Misleading Expressions', in Antony Flew (ed.), *Logic and Language*, pp. 11-36.

Sabine, George H.
1951 *A History of Political Theory*, 3rd ed., London: Harrap.
Salomon, Albert
1945 'German Sociology', in: Gurvitch and Moore (eds.), *Twentieth Century Sociology*, pp. 586-614.
1955 *The Tiranny of Progress*, New York: Noonday.
Schneider, Joseph W., and Sally L. Hacker
1973 'Sex Role Imagery and Use of the Generic "Man" in Introductory Texts', *American Sociologist*, VIII, pp. 12-18.
Schneider, Louis (ed.)
1967 *The Scottish Moralists on Human Nature and Society*, Chicago: University of Chicago Press.
Schulz, Gerhard
1969 *Das Zeitalter der Gessellschaft*, München: Piper.
Schutz, Alfred
1962 *Collected Papers*, volume 1, The Hague: Nijhoff.
1964 *Collected Papers*, volume 2, The Hague: Nijhoff.
Sennett, Richard, and Jonathan Cobb
1972 *The Hidden Injuries of Class*, New York: Knopf.
Shanin, Teodor
1972 'Units of Sociological Analysis', *Sociology*, VI, pp. 351-67.
Shils, Edward A.
1970 'Tradition, Ecology and Institution in the History of Sociology', *Daedalus*, IC, pp. 760-825.

Simmel, Georg
(1917) 'Fundamental Problems of Sociology', in Kurt H. Wolff (ed.), *The Sociology of Georg Simmel*, New York: Free Press, 1950, pp. 1-86.
Skinner, B.F.
1957 *Verbal Behavior*, New York: Appleton-Century-Crofts.
Smith, Adam
(1776) *An Inquiry into the Nature and Causes of the Wealth of Nations*. Edited by Edwin Cannon, London: Methuen, 1904.
Sorokin, Pitirim
1928 *Contemporary Sociological Theories*, New York: Harper and Row.

1956 *Fads and Foibles in Modern Sociology and Related Sciences*, Chicago: Regnery.
1966 *Sociological Theories of Today*, New York: Harper and Row.
Spaemann, R.
1959 *Der Ursprung der Soziologie aus dem Geist der Restauration*, Munchen: Kösel Verlag.
Spencer, Herbert
(1850) *Social Statics: The Conditions Essential to Human Happiness Specified, and the First of Them Developed*. Reprint, New York: Kelley, 1969.
(1854-59) *Education: Intellectual, Moral, and Physical*. Reprint, Paterson, N.J.: Littlefield, 1963.
Stein, Maurice
1960 *The Eclipse of Community*, Princeton: Princeton University Press.
Steinmetz, J.R.
1927 'Naar aanleiding van den Duitschen sociologendag in Weenen', *Mensch en Maatschappij*, I, pp. 1-8.
Stinchcombe, Arthur L.
1963 'Some Empirical Consequences of the Davis-Moore Theory of Stratification', *American Sociological Review*, XXVIII, pp. 805-08.
Stouffer, Samuel A.
1962 *Social Research to Test Ideas*, New York: Free Press.
Stouffer, Samuel A., and others
1949-50 *Studies in Social Psychology in World War II*, 4 volumes, Princeton, N.J.: Princeton University Press.
Sumner, William Graham
1883 *What Social Classes Owe to Each Other*, New York: Harper.

Thomas, William I., and Florian Znaniecki
1918-20 *The Polish Peasant in Europe and America*, 5 volumes, Chicago: University of Chicago Press.
Tiger, Lionel
1969 *Men in Groups*, London: Nelson.
Tiger, Lionel, and Robin Fox
1971 *The Imperial Animal*, New York: Holt, Rinehart and Winston.
Toqueville, Alexis de
1835-40 *Democracy in America*, 2 volumes. Translated by Henry Reeve, edited by Phillips Bradley, New York: Knopf 1945.
Tumin, Melvin M.
1953 'Some Principles of Stratification', *American Sociological Review*, XVIII, pp. 387-93.
Turk, Herman, and Richard L. Simpson (eds.)
1971 *Institutions and Social Exchange. The Sociologies of Talcott*

Parsons and George C. Homans, Indianapolis: Bobbs-Merrill.
Turner, Ralph H.
1953 'The Quest for Universals in Sociological Research', *American Sociological Review*. XVIII, pp. 604-11.
Tylor, Edward Burnett
1871 *Primitive Culture*, London: John Murray.

Van den Berghe, Pierre L.
1974 'Bringing Beasts Back In', *American Sociological Review*, XXXIX, pp. 777-88.
1975 *Man in Society*, Amsterdam: Elsevier.
Van Doorn, J.A.A., and C.J. Lammers
1959 *Moderne Sociologie: Systematiek en Analyse*, Utrecht: Spectrum.
Vansina, Jan
1965 *Oral Tradition. A Study in Historical Methodology*. Translated by H.M. Wright, London: Routledge and Kegan Paul.
Vidich, Arthur J., and Joseph Bensman
1968 *Small Town in Mass Society*, 2nd ed., Princeton: Princeton University Press.

Wagner, Helmut
1963 'Types of Sociological Theory: Toward a System of Classification', *American Sociological Review*, XXVIII, pp. 735-42.
Wallace, Walter L.
1971 *The Logic of Science in Sociology*, Chicago: Aldine.
Wallerstein, Immanuel
1974 *The Modern World System*, New York: Academic Press.
Warner, W. Lloyd, and Paul S. Lunt
1941 *The Social Life of a Modern Community*, New Haven: Yale University Press.
Wax, Rosalie H.
1971 *Doing Fieldwork*, Chicago: University of Chicago Press.
Weber, Max
(1904-05) *The Protestant Ethic and the Spirit of Capitalism*. Translated by Talcott Parsons, 2nd ed., New York: Scribner, 1930.
(1922) *Economy and Society*. Translated by Guenther Roth and Claus Wittich, New York: Bedminster Press, 1968.
White, Robert W.
1966 *Lives in Progress*, 2nd ed., New York: Holt, Rinehart and Winston.
Whyte, William Foote
1955 *Street Corner Society*, Chicago: University of Chicago Press.

Wippler, R.
1968 *Sociale determinanten van vrijetijdsgedrag*, Assen: Van Gorcum.
Wish, Harvey (ed.)
1960 *Ante Bellum. Writings of George Fitzhugh and Hinton Rowan Helper on Slavery*, New York: Capricorn Books, 1960.
Witt, P., Charles C. Gordon, and John R. Hofley
1972 'Religion, Economic Development and Lethal Aggression', *American Sociological Review*, XXXVII, pp. 193-201.
Wittgenstein, Ludwig
1953 *Philosophische Untersuchungen–Philosophical Investigations*, Oxford: Basil Blackwell.
1958 *The Blue and Brown Books*, Oxford: Basil Blackwell.
Wrigley, E.A. (ed.)
1972 *Nineteenth Century Society: Essays in the Use of Quantitative Methods for the Study of Social Data*, Cambridge: Cambridge University Press.

Young, Michael, and Peter Willmott
1962 *Family and Kinship in East London*, 2nd ed., Harmondsworth: Penguin Books.

Zeitlin, Irving M.
1968 *Ideology and the Development of Sociological Theory*, Englewood Cliffs, N.J.: Prentice-Hall.
Zetterberg, Hans
1965a *On Theory and Verification in Sociology*, 3rd ed., New York: Bedminster Press.
1965b *Social Theory and Social Practice*, New York: Bedminster Press.
Zorbaugh, Harvey W.
1929 *The Gold Coast and the Slum*, Chicago: University of Chicago Press.

Index of names

223

Index of subjects